LAW MAN

LAW MAN

MEMOIR OF A JAILHOUSE LAWYER

SHON HOPWOOD

Shon Hopwood
ISBN: 978-0-9994444-0-5

Published by PrisonProfessors
1629 K Street, Northwest
Suite 300
Washington DC 20006-1631

Contact
Prison Professors, LLC
Shon@PrisonProfessors.com

I dedicate this book to my father,
MARK ROBERT HOPWOOD.

...

Only now do I understand what
I put you and Mom through.

Young man, young man,
your arm's too short to box with God.
—JAMES WELDON JOHNSON

AUTHOR'S NOTE

I have modified some names to protect people's privacy and safety. The situations and conversations are otherwise my best recollections.

It has been twenty years since I robbed my first bank and another eight years since I was released from federal prison. For obvious reasons, looking back and reflecting has always been more challenging for me than gazing into the uncertainty of the future while carrying a felony conviction.

Life is so different now. This fall of 2017, I will celebrate eight years of marriage as my children go off to first and second grade. And I will begin the next phase of my career as an Associate Professor of Law at Georgetown University Law Center, where I will teach criminal law and civil rights classes to aspiring lawyers at one of the most prestigious law schools in the country.

Whenever anyone says, "Professor," I look around me to see if they're really talking to me.

The story you will read here is improbable. Believe me, I've lived it and it seems just as unlikely to me as it will you. There are many days where I question the blessings I've received. Why me and not others who've come out of prison?

My family, friends, and colleagues have poured out an abundance of grace in my life. And their support, their ability to look past my past, and their recognition that I was deserving of a second chance—well, that is the real story of *Law Man*. It is also the reason why I successfully navigated reentry into society in ways that other prisoners have not.

For policymakers, that last sentence should both encourage and frustrate you. It should encourage because I'm not an anomaly. There are many people residing in our state and federal prisons that have the capacity to change, find redemption, and emerge as a law-abiding and contributing members of society. But it should also frustrate you to know that successful reentry from prison is often due to circumstances outside a prisoner's control. And if most prisoners received just a fraction of the grace I've received, I believe most could be successful.

We all need to do better at welcoming and supporting our returning citizens. Me included.

In this new version of *Law Man*, you will see endnotes. The endnotes are for those interested in how to end the worst civil rights struggle of our time: mass incarceration.

There is a fundamental mismatch between what we believe about America and what has happened on our watch. We cannot claim that America is the land of liberty on the one hand and on the other acknowledge that our country incarcerates its citizens at a greater rate than almost every other on the planet.[1]

The endnotes explain the policies behind the story. I struggled with how to incorporate the policy implications of my story without it getting in the way of the story. The endnotes are my compromise. And I encourage everyone to take the time to read them.

For those who read *Law Man* and wonder how they could get involved in criminal justice reform, I've also provided some resources to connect with non-profits like Families Against Mandatory Minimums.[2] I've worked with these non-profits and believe your time, money, or efforts with them will not be in vain. Please support them!

Thank you for reading my book.

—SHON HOPWOOD

1
LIKE TRASH BLOWING IN

"Take a look at those clouds!" someone behind me said. I strained hard against my chains, leaning over a guy to see out the plane's window. A wild storm was building over Oklahoma City, our final destination. Lord, please just let this plane crash was my silent prayer. The storm seemed like an opportunity for an easy exit from life. I was through with it.

Growing up in Nebraska I had seen enough poached green clouds to know the most beautiful sky is the one about to kill you. As a kid, I had often heard the town's tornado siren and scampered to the top of the roof to see for myself, watching horned monsters form in the clouds until Mom shouted me down. My brothers and sisters and I would huddle with her under the splintered stairway of our basement, safe in her embrace. My mother, I think, liked the drama of those moments.

Over the years, I'd given her plenty of that.

Under the stairs was probably the only time she felt in control of her three headstrong boys; my two sisters were well behaved.

Dad's red rusted toolbox was down there. I saw it in my mind when I thought of that basement. On one of my bank jobs I had borrowed it just to drop it a few feet to the shiny floor tiles. The bang was loud enough to draw everyone's attention.

That's how the first bank robbery began, a year and a half earlier—already a lifetime ago.

In the plane, downdrafts were rattling our chains and bucking us around like a two-dollar state fair ride. I was nervous enough just to be going where I was going—federal prison.

If Marty Barnhart still wanted to pray for me, this would have been a good time, I thought. Marty was the pastor of our church, and when my downward slide had first started, my parents had asked him to come visit me in county jail, where I was staying after buying beer for my barely underage brother. Marty came because he had been asked to, but also—I could see it in his face—because he sensed I was on the brink of something a lot worse.

Marty held my hands through the bars and prayed for me. Little did he know I had already robbed one bank and would rob four more. I liked him, but I figured I was too far gone for his medicine.

My hometown of David City is an hour and a half due west of Omaha, or forty-five minutes northwest of Lincoln, the home of the Cornhuskers football team—football being the state's second religion.

The land is mostly flat. Modest hills of corn, grass, and soybeans rise just enough to spoil your view of the Empire State Building and the Golden Gate Bridge. Those hills play havoc with the crop pivots, which are quarter-mile-long steel sprinklers that look like shiny backbones left over from some science fiction war. They come alive once or twice a week, spitting water and chemicals as they roll slowly in great circles. They save work, allowing sons and daughters who once toiled with irrigation pipes the time to get into trouble.

I certainly am not blaming the sprinklers for what my best friend, Tom, and I did.

For us, David City was about fifteen hundred miles from anywhere fast enough and slammed up enough to be worthwhile, meaning L.A. or New York. The very tranquility of the town irritated us. We felt landlocked and depressed. So we lived from weekend to weekend, party to party, inventing half-assed rowdiness after the football games and speeding off to drinking parties out under the stars with girls.

That would pass for happiness for a while. Tom and I were both sports stars in high school. I had worked for that brief stardom. Back before I was old enough to start driving, I would dribble a basketball with my weak hand all the way to school each day, and all the way home each evening. At home, I practiced endlessly under the old hoop in our driveway, even when it was dark and so cold that the ball was hard as a rock and full of bounce. The purpose of life was tracked on score-boards in those years. I had always been determined to have an interesting life. Not a superstar life necessarily. But, you know, at least something—not the wasted life of a wage slave shoveling cow manure—my last real job before the banks.

Now I was on my way to spending a decade or more in federal prison, which wasn't exactly like heading off to summer camp. It would be heavy weather no matter how you looked at it. And if I didn't make it, well, I had always figured I would die young anyway.

The plane banked sharply and I saw the suburban fringe of Oklahoma City close below—clean little cars on clean little streets in shopping center parking lots, and the green and brown athletic fields of perfect high schools.

Regular life can seem small and too well ordered, but seeing it, I longed for all that suddenly, to be small and well-ordered and free. All those people down there were doing whatever they wanted today—or at least choosing who would tell them what to do.

The airline flying us through this storm was JPATS. Trust me when I say you don't want frequent-flyer miles on this one.

The initials stand for the Justice Prisoner and Alien Transportation System. It is operated by the U.S. Marshal's Service, and it moves a few hundred thousand federal prisoners around the country each year. Inmates call it Con Air. The planes are like commercial jets, though a bit worn inside from years of handcuffs, belly chains, ankle shackles, and sociopaths.

The seat belt sign always stays on, though mine had a little broken blink to it. The bathrooms are for the marshals. The conversations with seatmates differ from other airlines— they're mostly about robberies, drug deals gone bad, snitches, and news about who is now in which prison.

We banked hard again, and I took another look at the town below, now a worried brown. The hardworking people down there were no doubt looking up fearfully, but not at us—we were the lesser danger that day.

You have probably looked up and seen, without knowing, these prisoner planes flying over like white and mostly unmarked Pandora seeds blowing in the wind.

The marshals, mostly in their thirties, were more professional than the guards back in the county jails. The county guards looked like people who had fallen into those jobs, not by choice, and while they had grown a bit mean, you could at least picture having a drink with them someday. Not these federal marshals. They resembled mercenaries who had come back to the States after working in tough places, doing tough things. I was sure that if they suddenly received an order to march us out the back door without parachutes, they would not hesitate to do so.

Shortly before landing, to my surprise, they handed out apples, bone-dry crackers, and tiny boxes of juice. "Eat up fast, we're almost there," they repeated as they tossed the food from the aisle to a chained wave of big tan hands that shot up like rattling tambourines.

My seatmate, a black kid a few years younger than I was, watched as I struggled to place the drinking straw into the juice box and into my mouth.

"Why you got special handcuffs?" he asked.

He seemed too young to be going to a federal prison.

"Bad luck," I answered. "They think I'm a flight risk."

He looked confused. "Like this flight?"

"No, like flight in general, as in run away."

He still didn't get it.

"It's just some bull." He accepted that with a nod. I guess his ears were plugged, or maybe he was just slow or had an undiagnosed hearing problem. Maybe something like that had screwed him up in school, and here he was. When you come from poverty and a bad neighborhood, you're always walking the tightrope, and any wrong move or bad luck can knock you into a free fall. This kid should have been flying to meet his iron-willed grandmother instead of meeting armed guards and years of steel doors. But in my ten months in county jails, I had learned to toughen my feelings about the many young lives you see wasted by bad drugs and bad drug laws. Most of them seemed so beaten down. The smarter and nicer ones—those qualities usually go together—really stood out. Some would even return a smile.

My special handcuffs had a rigid plastic piece between them that kept my hands stiffly apart like a stockade. Called a black box, inmate lore says it was designed by a former convict. The rigid piece connects to a belly chain. My leg shackles ensured that I could take only baby steps, but we all had those.

I had been flagged as a flight risk because back in the St. Louis county jail where I had been warehoused for two weeks an albino meth addict with two teeth had gotten angry at me and Craig, one of my codefendants, for changing the channel on a television. He told the guards we were planning to escape, and they believed him. We were all on the eighth floor of a high-security jail, a place where the elevators didn't move unless you had a key and a security badge.

Only Houdini would have tried it from up there. But whenever I was transported after that I received the special restraints otherwise reserved for murderers and terrorists. At least they made me look dangerous; I would take anything that might help protect me.

My travels that morning had begun with a St. Louis guard pushing my face into a wall and calling me white-boy, emphasizing the boy part. He was yelling in my ear that he would take care of me if I tried to escape, as if my even thinking about it was akin to challenging his manhood.

He had me by the hair and could have cracked my skull like a coconut against the bricks. Even so, I mouthed off. I said he must be incredibly stupid to believe a meth-head and think I was trying to escape. Or that I'd announce it to the world. That basically did it. I could feel it coming. But another guard intervened and held the guard's arm. They compromised on a kidney punch that sent me to my knees.

The first thing you realize once you're in custody is that any sense of fairness and justice have no place there. You could be beaten for no other reason than the guard was having a bad day.

A dozen of us were taken by bus to an airport on the other side of the river from St. Louis and there we were met by fifty or so men with rifles and shotguns. They thanked us for our visit and showed us the way to the plane. We flew to Terre Haute to pick up more prisoners, then Detroit, Chicago, then Rochester, Minnesota, then somewhere in South Dakota, then finally to the back of the Oklahoma City airport, where there is a large holding facility for federal prisoners. It was like a garbage run: we were coming into the Oklahoma City transfer station, on our way to a landfill somewhere.

Assuming we didn't crash, of course. I knew there was a tornado or two in the storm. On final approach, my seatmate began mumbling.

"I never done this before," he finally blurted out.

"You mean going to prison or flying?"

"Both I guess. They always jump around like this?"

"It's not unusual." I lied.

There was in fact a tornado coming, and more than one. The Oklahoma tornadoes that day were among the most powerful ever recorded. The main one was a hair under a category six—almost unheard of. In those four days of tornadoes, in the first week of May 1999, sixty-six twisters would kill forty-eight people around Oklahoma City.

We touched down and tipped slightly to the right as the pilot fought to keep us on the runway. He throttled the engines louder and then back, and we settled in. As we taxied, marshals rushed through the cabin to unfasten our seatbelts. "Get ready to move fast when we give the word," they yelled a dozen times. "We're racing a twister, so move when we say move."

Everyone contorted to look out the windows. I could see a black funnel cloud approaching, maybe two miles from the airport. All the guys on my side of the plane could see it.

There were a lot of comments, all beginning with the word "holy."

The plane rolled past the civilian terminal to the federal facility. Extending from that large fortress were two Jetway ramps like a mother's impatient arms. The pilot was making fast turns and hitting the brakes at odd times. He stopped at the gate with a sudden deep dip like a teenager in driver's ed, sending the marshals into an aisle dance that drew some laughs.

"Move it, boys, up, up, up!" the marshals shouted.

We clanked our way through the aisle and shuffled as fast as we could into the tin corridor outside.

"Faster, men, go, go, go!" The federal guards in the Jetway seemed anxious for their own survival as they shoved and shouted us along. There were about seventy-five of us, each with ankle chains, belly chains, and wrist shackles, all running in baby step rhythm now: chink chink chink—go go go! Running in ankle chains is like running with skinny jeans around your ankles.

We fast-stepped it as the apocalypse roared louder overhead.

Near the front of the line a man tripped, and down went fifteen behind him. They were pulled to their feet by guards and each other, and the line again started jerking ahead, with the men in the back yelling to hurry up and the men in the middle, including me, trying not to trip. My basketball years helped me move better than most. The metal corridor was rocking. The kid in front of me, my seatmate, glanced back for moral support. I gave him a smile like this is always the way we do it.

I was actually okay with all of it. I was hoping the funnel cloud would take us away to Kansas or home to Nebraska or wherever it had in mind—right into the next life would have been fine. Had the whole chain gang swirled up into the cloud, most of the dots would have been black; I would have been one of the few white charms in the necklace.

I was twenty-three.

2
HEAVY METAL

We made it into the safety of the building. The guards marched us to a crowded common cell with a stinking, unscreened toilet in the middle.

If the storm happened to take off the roof, I was hoping it would please take away the toilet. But the twister skipped over, sparing us at the expense of innocents several miles away. For six hours, still in cuffs, we waited around the stinky halo of that toilet like homeless men around a fire—except that someone occasionally sat on it. There was a collection of stink, from vinegary body odor to sweaty socks to the frequent testimonials of the bean-heavy menus of a dozen county jails.

I escaped into a daydream about driving my dirty white Ford Thunderbird around David City. There was a pretty girl in town, Ann Marie Metzner, who was always out running.

She had been a cheerleader at the Catholic high school—I went to the public one—but I knew her well enough to include her in my daydreams. Her running landed her in the women's edition of *Sports Illustrated*, so she was a town star on several levels, and way above me. Still, she smiled at me when she ran through my daydreams. Then I would go deeper, almost into a trance, rewinding my life back to some fork-in-the-road moment, like, say, my first week of college. I would take the other path, let the story play out the way it should have: me with a career and my parents proud, no banks robbed, no people scared, possibly a family, a respectable position in the community.

The smell of regurgitated cheese crackers broke the spell—a guy next to me burping.

One at a time we were taken from the cell, fingerprinted, strip-searched, asked to raise our genitals and spread our cheeks, allowed a one-minute shower, and tossed into smaller cells. The shuffling and separating of prisoners into compartments reminded me of the way Dad and I used to separate the sick cattle from the healthy when I was a kid.

That night passed, and the next and the next.

After two weeks, some of us were herded onto a JPATS flight to Chicago O'Hare. The first time I flew to O'Hare had been a few years earlier, before the bank jobs, when I was heading to Navy boot camp after ditching college. By coincidence my uncle Dan was the pilot on that flight. He spotted me and took me into the cockpit until it was time to take off. I wondered what he must be thinking about me now.

In the Midwest you define yourself early in life, and that's who you are forevermore in your town. You are the guy who got a nickname like "Gumby" based on your wrestling skills, only to find that it came to represent your goofy demeanor. You are the girl who disappeared for a weekend right when that teacher disappeared for the same weekend. You and your brother are the entrepreneurial twins who ran a lawn mower service and now build houses. I was the guy who had robbed five banks. I wouldn't live that one down. Not ever. I was not going to be invited into any more cockpits by proud uncles, nor driven around in the town parade. I would forever be the bruise on the town apple.

We landed on the back strip of O'Hare; they weren't foolish enough to march us wolf-whistling through the terminal.

That was just as well for me, as I wouldn't enjoy being taunted by things I couldn't have—with the aroma of coffee and food I couldn't taste, with glimpses of well-dressed travelers I couldn't talk to.

From a back ramp we were stuffed into a bus and driven to the Federal Correctional Institution at Pekin, Illinois, just outside Peoria. That was as close as the sentencing judge's recommendation could get me to my family—about an eight-hour drive from David City. I was thankful to be even that close, as it would mean the possibility of visitors.[4] As we neared the prison, I saw its razor-wire fences, towers, and lights. Otherwise the low modern buildings looked more like a business park than a federal prison. Green land surrounded it. Our bus pulled up to the gate. We again faced a reception line of guards with shotguns and automatic assault rifles. Some of the prisoners relished the attention.

"Look at this. We some killers," a fat Hispanic guy with a long goatee said, admiring the firepower.

The twenty of us marched in, handcuffed and shackled.

You'd think this would be the worst day of your life.

But after being herded around between county jails for ten months, the idea of staying in the same place for a while, the ability to go outdoors and exercise, and the luxury of having a bunk to call your own was a relief.

I could now move on with my life. I knew I had to make something of this strange period. Here I would have enough time to design a new life of some sort. Unlike a lot of the men around me, who had been beaten down longer and harder than me and were not blessed with good families, good hometowns, and decent friends, I still believed that I wasn't a lost cause. I had made a mistake—a gigantic mistake times five. I had hurt and traumatized people. Yet I was certain that, if I survived, I would graduate from this place a better person. I had to believe that. The other possibility was too depressing to think about.

Mostly I wanted my hard time to begin so it would start to end.

And, honestly, there was a certain excitement to the idea of a federal pen. I looked over the place with Jimmy Cagney eyes. Although I was scared, I wanted to see the place and know that I could handle it—that I could survive. I knew my courage would be challenged. It was inevitable.

The doors closed behind us. We were taken to small holding cells where we slept on concrete slabs and waited until guards pulled us out one by one for cursory medical exams and fingerprinting. We were each issued a hunter orange jumpsuit and a pillowcase containing a toothbrush, toothpaste, and bar of three-cent soap that, according to a couple of guys with me, would dry out your skin and leave you scratching for a week.

We were given a handbook of rules and etiquette. It began with an assurance that Pekin inmates "are housed in a facility which best meets their security needs . . . " I wished it was honest enough to say we were housed in a facility that best met society's security needs, but the deceptions and fantasies of American culture take an extreme form in prison.

After two hours of processing, a young guard finally walked me across the large yard—a grass acreage surrounded by buildings and webbed by sidewalks in the manner of a shopworn campus. He escorted me to my housing unit, Illinois One. He was pimply faced and looked like maybe you could trick him into opening the front gate and away you'd go. He pointed out the buildings: the mess hall, the other housing units, my housing unit up ahead, the athletic fields, the gym. The cell-blocks, he explained, include four houses named after the states of Illinois, Missouri, Iowa, and Indiana, with two units in each.

"I think I've seen enough of this place," I said. "I'd prefer something closer to town."

He smiled and sighed, and we kept walking. I think he was picturing himself in my shoes. Some people can empathize and some people can't. I think he could. I was still working on it.

As I walked closer to what would be my home for a decade, the reality of my situation flooded in. I had done a lot of harm to a lot of people, including my family. I wasn't one of those guys who was cool with all that.

I had poisoned my life and future, not to mention the lives of a few others, and I was being escorted to a little cage in a zoo, where the days and nights would extend as though forever. I did not cry, but if there had been a secret place under a bush where I could have curled up like a kid and let it out, I might have.

I knew this was all a big storm coming and I wanted to be under the basement stairs with Mom and my brothers and sisters. "You're a good boy, Shon, and God will protect you. Remember that," she had whispered in the courtroom after I was sentenced.

I shook off the emotion. I was on a different planet now.

Sure, a strong will is what landed me here, but it was also the only thing that might help me make it out.

The young guard turned some keys and led me into Illinois One. Like each of the housing units, it has two levels of cells arranged in a U around a sky-lit dayroom and a guard's office. I scanned the space quickly. Except for the cigarette smoke and urine yellow lighting, it was clean and modern. We walked through the dayroom past tables of men playing cards and dominoes, and watching half a dozen TV sets mounted on balcony railings above them. They had earphones tuned to whichever shows they were watching: a couple of ball games, a soap, a Spanish-language soap, and a Golden Girls rerun. Most of the men were black, and they showed no interest as I walked by them.

I was marched to the guard's office, a converted cell with its door open to the dayroom. The guard on duty continued filling out a report as I stood there waiting.

An inmate who had been watching TV spotted me and popped up to meet me. He smiled but offered no handshake.

He was taller than I, thin, about my age, with thick dark hair and chalky white skin. He looked like a cheerful castaway hermit who thought I might have a pocketful of cheese for him.

"Milan's my name. It's spelled like the city in Italy, but you say it like, you know, this land is your land, this land is Milan—that's how you can remember." The headphones parked around his neck were blaring canned Golden Girls laughter timed to his lines.

I nodded but was wary of making the wrong first friend.

I told him my name. We waited for the guard to finish his report.

"I will tell you something," Milan said. "New guys go into the three-man cells. You get transferred to a two-man cell when one becomes available. Three-man cells are a little crowded. Did you know that?"

I shrugged.

"Where you from, Shon?"

"Nebraska," I replied.

"I'm from Chicago," he said, "the best state, if you ask me." On the bus ride to Pekin I had already experienced the sentiment that Chicago is a state. A lot of Chicago guys seem to believe that.

"My guy, Bee Dog, has a two-man cell. His celly was transferred out a few weeks ago, so maybe you could get that bed. Bee Dog is good people. He's about the same age as you and me. So tell the cop here you want cell 304."

You don't want the first thing you do on your first day to be some sucker move. I thought this might be a gay thing or a setup. Maybe the white guys were trying to keep the cell white. I had no idea. And why didn't he just ask to be moved in with "his guy" himself?

The guard was named Vaughn. On top of his wrinkled and stained shirt sat an anvil-shaped head.

"Hey, Vaughn, why don't you put him in with Bee Dog. He don't have no celly now, and they would get along."

Vaughn glanced at the cell assignment board.

"Bee Dog has been saying he don't like it, not having a celly," Milan rattled on.

I liked the idea that things were maybe negotiable, as I considered myself fairly competent at persuasion.

Vaughn hadn't looked me in the eye yet. He was still shuffling and signing papers—his big head bouncing side to side as he signed.

"That's a two-man cell, Milan," he finally said.

"Right, but who cares? It's been open for two weeks."

The guard finally glanced up at me to see if I looked worthy of this early and unearned bonus. I put my hands up and raised my shoulders, as if to say "why not?"

"What the hell. If the counselor don't like it, they can move you out."

Vaughn took me to a supply closet and handed me a two-inch thin, dark green plastic mattress. I hoped it had been steam cleaned. Milan tagged along. When we got to the cell, Bee Dog was reading a girlie magazine, discreetly tucked inside a biker magazine with an equally lurid cover.

Nudy books, as they were called, would be banned a

couple of months later, courtesy of a congressman from Florida.

"Bee Dog, this here is Shon, your new celly," said Milan.

The guard went away, having said nothing, really. He pointed to my upper bunk and I slid the mattress up there. The cell doors were wide open, which is the way it is most of the day in a medium- to high-security pen like Pekin. The building's doors are locked, of course.

Bee Dog mumbled, "What's up?" then tried to return to his reading.

"So you owe me one. You said you don't like having no celly. I guess I got you one, so don't forget." Bee Dog looked up from his magazine. I worried that maybe I was a peace offering from a guy Bee Dog didn't much like or respect.

"Well, I'll leave you two guys alone," Milan said. "Let's all go out for a drink later."

I was still new enough to incarceration that I thought for half a second that he had a good idea and that we would do that. The habit of freedom dies hard.

Bee Dog chuckled at Milan's joke, so I figured they were friends after all, and I was in a stable situation—assuming I hadn't cut in front of some killer waiting in a crowded three-man cell for Bee Dog's spare bunk. Maybe that was it.

Bee Dog was pale white and short and knuckly with a few faded prison tattoos. He was a Piru Blood gang member from Tacoma, serving six years for illegal possession of a firearm—illegal because he was a felon. He was about my age, early twenties, and was built like he had lifted some iron when he was in high school or juvy.

He asked questions and I gave the answers: Nebraska, five bank robberies, twelve years and three months.

A new cellmate always wants to know what you did so he knows what kind of animal he is bunking with. The last thing anyone wants for a celly is some chester— short for child molester—or someone who snitched on his codefendant.

Chesters are the lepers of prison who hang out only with each other and are regularly chided, cheated, and sometimes brutalized. Snitches are pariahs, too, though the War on Drugs has turned nearly everyone toward plea deals to avoid mandatory minimum sentences and three-strikes provisions.

Now only 5 percent of federal defendants take their cases to trial; the rest either plead guilty or cooperate in some way. So you accept some of that cooperation, whether or not you want to call it snitching. But you don't talk about it or admit to it.

Bee Dog seemed okay with the bank robbery thing, even somewhat pleased. I laughed when he asked if I was a snitch.

He took that as a no.

"But how'd you get only a dozen years for five banks?"

He was suspicious. Gangbangers especially do not tolerate any form of snitching—loyalty is their primary belief system. Life imprisonment would be preferable.

"Criminal history category one," I said. Federal sentencing was guided in part by your number of priors. Never having been in real trouble before, I was in category one.

Bee Dog continued to squint at me, so I added some information. I never fired a gun during the robberies, nobody was hurt, good lawyer, great judge. He nodded, processing it.

He massaged the little bit of stubble on his chin and made a De Niro frown as his head kept nodding. "Okay," he said. It was feasible.

"So another bank robb-air." He French-accented it, as if bank robbery was a silly Pink Panther crime.

"How many?" I asked.

"There's a lot, actually. Milan, for one. He's been in for about two years and has four or so to go. Had a good lawyer I guess, like you, though I think he just robbed one bank."

"Where?"

"Chicago or north of there. I don't ask him about that stuff much. He doesn't talk about his past. And, hey, when you see him in the shower, you'll see those big whip scars across his back. Don't ask. He doesn't like to talk about it.

He had a tough daddy. His folks were from Yugoslavia or somewhere, and they raised him old school, which didn't do him much good."

"He seems like a good guy."

"He is a great guy, always looking for some way to help—and very loyal. You can probably take lessons from a guy like that."

I didn't know if he was trying to imply something.

He went back to the magazine.

There is no best way to settle into a prison cell. I didn't have IKEA furniture to assemble or paintings to hang. Someone takes you to your cell and pretty much says to wait here for a dozen years. It's awkward.

And it's lonely, even when you do have a celly. You look around, not knowing what to do in the first few minutes.

"Take a nap," Bee Dog said. "They'll start your orientation in a day or two, and you'll have a job soon after that. So take a nap while you can. Later I'll tell you what you need to know about this place, and you can tell me how to get caught robbing banks. Right now, I want to finish this important article, so take a snooze. When you get up, I'll give you the news."

It was the first rhymed rap line I had heard at Pekin, but I knew there would be lots to come. There are more metered rhymes in any jail or prison than in all of Shakespeare.

I climbed up to my bunk and closed my eyes. Everywhere was the deep sound of metal and machinery: the clank of metal doors, rattling keys on chains, the starting and stopping of air-conditioning that just moves musty cigarette smoke and the smells of crowded humans from cell to cell.

It was a metallic world that, except for the grace of one window, might have been in a submarine.

This was the middle of May 1999. The Kosovo War was under way. George Bush was governor of Texas. The Twin Towers were still standing. The Backstreet Boys released their Millennium album. That crappy Star Wars movie, The Phantom Menace came out; so did Windows 98, second edition. Google was getting its first major financing and Mark Zuckerberg turned sixteen. A lot of things would freeze at this time. I would barely touch a computer again for ten years.

It is beyond strange to be in such a place and feel your life freezing over, like a sci-fi story where you lie down in your rocket, not to return until everyone you know is old.

I stretched out and decided the first thing to do the next day would be to find out how to send letters. I would write to my family and then to Tom, who was settling down in a Minnesota prison.

Tom and I had been friends since grade school. The first bank was his idea, but it only happened, really, because I pushed it. We were in a bar and in a bad mood and it was just crazy talk while drinking, until I said yes. I was living in my folks' basement in David City at the time, after an honorable discharge from the Navy.

I had first taken an apartment in Lincoln, but other than partying and college girls there wasn't anything for me there—not that I looked too hard.

I'd hung out with a guy named Kirk who'd introduced me to a guy named Tyler, a medium-level drug dealer and part-time college student. We hadn't done one another any good.

Tyler didn't look like the Midwest; he was short with a fade haircut. He wore a baseball cap and baggy pants, and he had a vacant face. He sold drugs and could provide whatever a bad guy needed: guns, stolen cars, whatever. Had he started life in slightly different circumstances, he would have been fine. But somewhere along the way he broke bad.

I needed out of Lincoln, out of the orbit of these guys. My parents helped me settle some debts, and I moved into their basement in David City. Dad found me a job working for a gruff old farmer he knew, but it didn't help. I was depressed and broke and literally shoveling crap seventy hours a week. Usually when I was down Tom would pick me up, or vice versa, and we could keep each other going. But when we were both way down, things could get out of control in a hurry.

On the Saturday when Tom and I went scouting for a good bank to rob, Tom was driving a blue Ford Tempo. Its trunk and bumper had recently been repaired after I had crashed into Tom in a snowstorm a few weeks earlier.

That snowstorm had come in April, which was late, but all the snow had melted, and the green buds were winning out over the brown and white of winter. We drove around the countryside scoping out banks. I was in a pleasant mood.

Even my folks had noticed it, and they had seen it as a sign of good things to come. I had a notebook on my lap, a pen in my mouth, and a map spread across the dash.

The small-town banks were quaint; I hadn't really noticed that before. Some had front pillars, some had a single drive-in or walk-up window, some a sign announcing simply bank, like one you might find in the toy town of a train set.

We were headed north because Tom's father owned a small farm property around Norfolk, Nebraska. The cornfield was the ideal place to conceal Tom's car after the bank robbery until things cooled off—assuming we could find a decent bank in that area. We would need to be hidden away while the cops combed the highways looking for two bad guys.

We had a standard for selecting a bank. The town

had to be big enough for the bank to contain more money than an ATM, yet small enough not to have a local police station. It couldn't be a county seat or it would have a sheriff's office.

And we needed to see the FDIC decal on the door, because we had no clue that all banks are insured. We wanted to know that we were robbing the government, not the farmers, who are robbed enough. Besides, we would rather have cops coming after us with pistols than farmers with shotguns and rifles.

We drove through every little village in northeastern Nebraska. That's what bank robbers had to do before Google Earth and all that—you had to do it analog.

After a long day we reached the town of Petersburg. The bank met our specs. It was on the main downtown street but only two blocks from the highway, our escape route.

Although it was a town of only a few thousand people, it looked quite prosperous.

We should have stopped there while still in the planning stage. We felt bad about it already, and we hadn't done anything yet. But somehow, together, the sum of our combined resolve pushed us forward, contrary to our common sense and moral upbringing. As Homer said, "There is a strength in the union even of very sorry men." There is strength especially in the union of sorry men.

CHAPTER 3
STEALING RESPECT

I heard Bee Dog stirring. I heard the stream of urine landing in the toilet and the trickle of water in the sink. He brushed his teeth, gurgled a time or two, washed his face, and left the cell. When it's early in the morning and your cell is only a few feet by a few feet, you can hear everything, from a yawn to the sound of cracking ankle bones taking the day's first steps.

A controlled move was under way—when you're allowed to go outside the housing unit to get some air or head to an activity or to your prison job. I went to see the outdoor recreation area, where rusted free weights were stacked. Just inside the indoor recreation area were a few dilapidated stationary bikes and a pullup bar. I jumped on an exercise bike, and it felt great. A black guy was executing pull-up after pull-up. We exchanged nods.

It felt exhilarating to be in motion, since I had been living in matchboxes for ten months. My leg muscles began to warm and ache but in a good way. I breathed deeply and closed my eyes and cranked my legs faster. I could be riding anywhere, going wherever I wanted.

Two black men stepped into the building and ripped the guy from the pull-up bar. I kept cycling.

They punched him until he hit the ground, then kicked and stomped him with their steel-toe boots.

The prison factory that employs several hundred in Pekin is a metal fabrication plant. That means most cons wear steel toe safety boots and smuggle a variety of metal pieces out from the factory to their cells. The metal is fashioned into various weapons.

For large, imminent problems, two-foot sword like knives are made. For smaller worries, easily concealed shivs are tucked up shirtsleeves.

I don't claim to be a genius, but a metal fabrication factory seemed like a poor choice for a prison industry; only a gun or explosives factory would have topped it.

Pieces of the poor guy's scalp were starting to come loose; I watched pink chunks of hairy flesh splatter and stick against the wall as they kicked him. The wall was becoming more saturated with blood with every kick. I kept cycling, watching it like I saw that sort of thing twice a day. When they were about done, one of the guys gave him a good-bye stomp, bringing his boot straight down on the man's head.

"Don't ever do that again, homie."

The downed man mumbled, "My bad." In the blood around him were pieces of broken teeth.

"You got that right."

After they left I helped him to his knees. He asked me to find a guard to help take him to medical, which I did.

That evening Bee Dog listened to the story of my first day.

"Crips," he said. "I heard about it in the unit. Probably the guy stiffed them in a drug deal, or he told a guard too much." He then began a prison life primer. He was in a sort of lotus position on his bunk, with his arms moving around as he spoke—an urban Buddha.

He told me how each day is a game of red light, green light, using his hands to flash the imaginary traffic lights overhead. I was in my upper bunk, but I could watch his animated shadow cast from his reading light.

There are set times throughout the day, he explained, when you can make your move from one activity to the other.

You have ten minutes. The controlled moves are announced on the PA system like class changes in high school.

"Then, bam, red light. You gotta be where you're going."

I had already learned much of that, but he gave me the finer points of what you can and cannot get away with.

There are set times for counts, he explained, when they come through to make sure you haven't gone home without saying good-bye. The counts are at midnight, 3 a.m., 5 a.m., 4 p.m., which is a stand-up count so they can see you and not some dummy in bed, and 10 p.m., which is lights-out. More guards come through late at night and usually just look in your cell.

"But the sadistic ones, like that punk Israel, will bang on the window with their flashlights until you wake up," he said.

"Why do they do that?"

"Because they can."

I learned that you wash your own clothes, and you

buy overpriced soap for that. Beds must be made and wrinkle free by 7:30 a.m.

You are to keep yourself clean and your shirt tucked in and your hair decent. That I knew.

"Things are looser on the weekends," he said.

I annotated the inmate handbook in my mind. I wanted to know about etiquette in the chow line, in the workout room, and how to avoid an ambush in the shower. He said it was all about friends and alliances.

"In the morning you don't just sit down in the chow hall anywhere you want. You sit where you're invited. Maybe your Nebraska homeboys will invite you; there's a group of them.

Or maybe I will invite you to our table, but maybe not, depending on whether the other guys think you look like a douche. Otherwise just ask first before you sit down somewhere.

Doing this wrong is the first big mistake you can make—"

"But, won't everyone think—" I was worried that I would look weak.

"There are no buts," he said. "Respect is the only thing these guys got left to steal, and the place where you give it up to these dummies is mainly in the chow hall."

"What about when I'm working out?"

"I'll get to that. When you get to the yard, you ask before you pick up weights, and you ask if this machine is okay for you to use. People will tell you if it's reserved for someone else or for some other group. So you ask if you don't know. You shouldn't have problems unless you go looking for problems.

Don't ask like you're scared; ask like you don't want to touch it if it's someone else's."

"Anything else?"

"Always watch where you're going and don't bump into nobody or step on their feet. Stick close with your friends until you have a chance to prove you're not to be messed with. It's like animal training in the circus. The animals got to know you are not to be messed with."

He held up an imaginary whip and chair; I saw it in shadows because he was on the bunk below me.

I thought about Bee Dog after things got quiet. I could imagine him headed back to the West Coast after all this, finding a good woman he had probably known before, taking care of her and being taken care of. He would drink Coronas and eat fish tacos with his old gang friends, all mellowed and nearly harmless now. Maybe he would work a job as a mechanic in a motorcycle shop or work behind the counter at a biker bar. Maybe he would have a daughter from somewhere who would come back into his life, and they would become great friends. He surely had a streak of kindness in him, I could see that.

At breakfast he invited me to sit at his table as his guest.

He introduced me to some other Nebraska guys as they passed. Everyone I met was white, though most at Pekin are black.

There is just no way around the fact that if you're white in prison most of your friends will be white. If you're black or Hispanic, you are going to be in those groups. Outside prison I had black friends, but inside those towered fences everything had an edge to it. The worst characteristics of every racial group, including whites, become exaggerated—almost like a parody skit, but with weapons.

That evening I had more questions for Bee Dog.

"So how many guys are carrying knives in here? Do I need something?"

"Hold on." He left the cell and came back a moment later.

"Like this?" He pulled from his sleeve a long steel rod with a wooden handle. The rod was needle-sharp. He had borrowed it from next door like a cup of sugar.

"You don't see knives so much as pokers like these," he said. "These are better than knives because you can run it straight through a man's liver. But what's better than one of these is a lot of friends. Don't get in trouble right off. If, later on, you need to take somebody down, you can get something like this easy enough, like I just did. Really, man, you can kill someone with a toothbrush if you sharpen the end and stick it in his jugular."

Bee was making stabbing motions with a crazy Heath Ledger, Joker-type grin, and I was hoping I'd never see the day when I'd seriously need a weapon.

"My best advice is just don't take insults from anybody. Don't let things fester. Somebody messes with you, you go postal right then before anybody has any big weapons. If you get a reputation for allowing people to call you a punk, soon they're calling you something else. And next they're stealing from you or worse. It's best to take your lumps, even against someone twice your size."

This was all very good advice. I could sense that.

"In any prison, man, no matter how bad, you don't go poking people unless you are told to." He said that as he wagged the sharp rod. "And if that happens, man, you'll be given the weapon you need. Otherwise the peace is kept by deterrence, by mutually assured destruction, like the Cold War. Having friends in prison is the surest way to stay safe.

And if everybody knows you will do what it takes, they will do the same for you, and nobody is going to mess with you because you got a big force shield around you." He was still standing up with the poker and made a sci-fi buzzing sound as he waved it over me and my bunk. "Nobody keel you 'cause we here to shee-ld you."

That was maybe rap number twenty already. Bee Dog was always rapping and rhyming. He was going to be a rap star someday. Too many guys in prison have that as a business plan.

4
NEWS FROM EARTH

Every afternoon during the weekdays, a few minutes after the stand-up inspection at 4 p.m., a guard lugs a big
plastic crate of mail into the dayroom and starts calling
names. Most of the men hover around him, hoping and
sometimes silently praying—their lips move—to hear
their names called. Some hang out on the balcony, and
some stay in their unlocked cells so they don't look stupid
if their names aren't called. Some never get mail. Some
subscribe to magazines and catalog mailing lists so they
won't always walk back to their cells empty-handed.

There was nothing for me at first, but then I received
a letter from an elderly doctor in David City. Dr. Jack
Kaufmanwas a friend of the family, a friend of most
families there.

It was just a few scribbled lines to say that I was
missed intown and that he was praying for me. It seemed
strange that someone would take the time and trouble to
do that—write or pray—for someone he barely knew.

Growing up, I had seen him walking all over town
making his rounds. He walked with some difficulty, his
head slightly more bowed as the years passed. I didn't
know him well, so his note was unexpected. I looked
at it as if it were some artifact from a distant world I

once knew. I appreciated the kindness. When his second letter arrived, I realized he was set on becoming a part of my prison experience; he understood that prison, over many years, wears away a big part of you, and whether it wears away the good part or the bad part is the question.

There were competing truths battling within me. The first was "You are from a good family, from a good town, and though you screwed up royally, you will recover, make things as right as you can, and have a good life." The second truth was "You're a thug who robbed banks and will always be a thug. You'll probably spend your life shuffling between prison terms and crappy jobs." The letters from the doctor and others helped to keep the brighter possibility alive.

I was not a religious man, but it did strike me that, if there were some real Christians in the world, meaning people who actually acted a bit like Jesus might, then the good doctor was surely one of them.

I saved the letters from him and from my family, and some evenings, to feel not so alone, I reread them, sequentially, under my breath, one right after another in the same way a monk repeats a mantra. It was as close as I could come to praying.

Mom wrote often, usually including a reminder that God was at work in our lives, and I had better think about that.

More than once she told me my plight was small potatoes compared to the burdens of others, such as Job in the Old Testament, who kept his faith despite everything thrown at him. Her letters were full of love for me, and full of newsabout the family and her new job at KV Vet Supply, the company at the edge of town owned by Raymond Metzner, Ann Marie's father. I thought about the fact that Mom saw Ann Marie there.

Ann Marie was the girl who was always running. In high school, she was a cheerleader for the Catholic school, and when our school was playing against their team during the holiday basketball tournament, the sight of her would make me lose concentration.

After high school, she ran cross-country at Creighton and in the Boston Marathon. I would see her out running, and I would wonder what it would be like to talk to her. The few times I did talk to her back in high school she seemed kind of shy.

In a town of pretty girls, she was, without a doubt, the prettiest. Especially when she ran by in a T-shirt and shorts. She had emerald green eyes, long dark hair, and a beautiful smile that would creep out from under her ball cap. She was not sort of, or kind of, she was, in fact, my fantasy, and it seemed odd that my mother was seeing her in an office, just doing the kind of work that regular mortals do.

Dad would sometimes write his own letter or add a note to Mom's. He would mostly tell me about things happening at Grass Valley, the farm where he worked and where I basically grew up. My arrest had taken a toll on him, and I was not his only big problem, since my brother Brett was serving time, too, thanks to me. I hadn't wanted Brett anywhere near the bank jobs, but he knew what I was doing because there are no secrets between brothers.

Brett witnessed me living the fast and easy life and

said he would rob a bank with his friends if I didn't let him in on a job. I finally gave in, kind of. I told him there was no way he could come inside a bank or touch a gun, but if he would provide a getaway car, I would give him a taste of the loot.

I thought that would be enough to provide a thrill; then I could chase him away. But that was the bank job where it all came down, and he was an accomplice. Of my many sins, this was the worst, and the hardest for me to forgive myself for. If I ever have.

Brett received a short sentence, being a juvenile. But it's hard for me to know how deeply my father must have hated that I did that.

On the road into David City from the state highway, a billboard promotes our town. One evening in June 1999, as Brett and I were settling into different prisons, someone spray-painted over it. My brother Brook told me about it when I called home that Friday.

"What's it say?"

"You don't want to know," he said.

"Yes, I do."

"It says, right under the 'Welcome to David City' line, something like 'Home of the Hopwood crime family.' "

"Did Mom and Dad see it?"

"I think everyone has seen it."

We were both quiet on the phone.

After the call, I sprinted up to my cell where I slept all day long and most of the next day and the next. I emerged only for a week of obsessive exercise.

Someone in David City had mercy and replaced the billboard.

My younger sisters, Samantha and Kristin, were

taking abuse, too. The kids at school would taunt them until they cried. Nobody in school wants to be different in a bad way.

They never complained to me; they just took it, mainly because Mom kept them focused on their own lives, not mine.

She had to be brave for the girls, for Brook, for Dad, and for herself. That was a lot. She worried mostly about Dad, whose health seemed off.

After those days of horror, Dad carried a few more wrinkles and a little less enthusiasm for life. He was a dedicated worker, the only way he knew to be, but he may have been on automatic pilot. He was not one of those fat, rosy-cheeked farmers, poured into their overalls each morning; he resembled Wyatt Earp with his mustache and Levi denims—except for maybe the John Deere cap he liked to wear.

His father was tough, too—strong-willed with a temper.

Dad must have fought against him all the way. As a young man and a young father, Dad had drunk and gambled too much. When my brother Brook and I were toddlers, before the other kids were born, our family moved farther west to Kearney, Nebraska, so he and Mom could start over.

I was the only kid old enough to remember when Miller Lite beer cans and empty bags of Red Man chew littered my dad's pickup. But living out there on the horizon, he was transformed. One day he just believed in God and became a Christian. I don't know if it was Mom's patience and love or God's that got him there, but something did. From then on, he was a responsible father and husband.

We moved back to the circle of family in David City, and Dad became well respected around town. He organized the community basketball program for elementary and junior high kids, just because he enjoyed coaching them. "I like yelling at other people's kids" is the way he put it. By the time we boys had moved out of the house, he had become an assistant coach for the high school team, I think because he missed the camaraderie of his own boys.

He was a good father, my activities notwithstanding. My problems were simply not his doing; he was strict and caring and a good moral example. But it is a fact that the men of our family surely bristle against authority when they are young, and I was no exception.

Dad knew I could change, because I wasn't that different from him. He didn't say it word for word, but I knew that was what he meant in short notes when he said, "I love you, Son," or "I'll take you to a ball game when you come home."

I knew the history. I could feel his despair at how my path had strayed, but he hadn't given up on me yet because the show wasn't over. In the same way that a great success sometimes comes before a great fall, sometimes it works the other way around, and he was holding out for that. He believed in the medicine of rock bottom and the tonic of God's grace because those were the things that had changed him.

When he got mad at me, maybe it was like getting mad at his old self. More than once during my high school years he had tossed a suitcase with a change of my clothes onto the back step because I had broken his curfew rule again. Mom would soften him, but then it would happen again. Whatever he told me to do, I would do the opposite. I was his son and his father's grandson, and, like I said, I guess we don't like being told what to do. Although Mom's calming voice always worked a little.

I rolled Dad's pickup in a ditch, and he was furious. Then my grandparents, Dale and Sandra, sold me their used Thunderbird, and I drove it way too fast and didn't take care of it, and that irked him, too. I would break a rule again, and he would place my bag on the steps again. We were like the wrong ends of two magnets, pushing away from each other no matter how hard Mom tried to make us stick.

Growing up, the thing I disliked most about my father was that he could outshoot me in basketball. He would take hook shots over me, even after I was taller than he was. The shots would bank off our floppy plywood backboard, caroming right down through the net. With each shot he would say stuff like "I guess the old man is the real ballplayer in this house," or "This is the difference between men and boys."

I practiced every day after school and sometimes at night, right through the dead of winter. I practiced so I could beat him someday, and I did. It happened at home out on the driveway one evening, and he hung his head and went inside as I proclaimed myself king of the court. When I went in he was sitting at the kitchen table smiling at me.

Few things in life have felt that good to me—not the smile, really, but beating him at his own game. And maybe some from the smile.

He had married the prettiest girl in town, and her father owned the John Deere dealership. He could have slipped into that business, of course, but he wanted to make a life of his own.

He would get on the line when I called home, and we would talk about sports and the farm. But it was enough that I could tell when things had started to warm back up a little.

During one of those calls home, Mom said Ann Marie Metzner would sometimes stop by her desk to talk. I told her to say hello from me, but I didn't really mean it. I knew I was probably an embarrassment—that spray-painted billboard was within view of their office at KV, and Mom probably shouldn't go around mentioning me to the owner's daughter.

Dad and I rarely talked about religion; that was mostly Mom. When her Christian books arrived in my mail, I always had better things to read, so I set them aside. But I would eventually pick them up, like it was my penance owed to her. Otherwise religion failed to interest me. If there was any truth to any of it, I was probably going to hell anyway, so why bother?

"Your mama trying to save your soul again?" Bee Dog once said when he saw another book arrive. "You don't wanna read it 'cause you know you really need it," he rapped.

"It's all yours, Bee—you read it for me," I said, tossing it over to his bunk. "I'll see if you sprout a halo."

"I already got a halo!" he said. "It's so bright, it's my reading light!" he rapped, holding out a nudy book so I could see it from my perch.

The guy had grown on me a little. He was good company.

5
LITTLE MIRACLES UNSEEN

Men define themselves through their stories. Prison is a great pile of stories, told from bunk to bunk to lay down the background hum of prison life. You wake up and fall asleep to the murmur of biographies and bull being told in a hundred cells for the hundredth time. Stories are cultivated and honed for compactness, for rhythm and effect.

The subject matter is hardly spiritual: which brother was the biggest baller, which Latin gangster had the nicest ride, which whiteboy could cook the baddest meth.

One night toward lights-out, Bee Dog put his feet up, folded his arms behind his head, and said, "Okay, Shon, I have been telling you everything you want to know. Now I want to know about robbing banks. Tell me a story, man."

I was at the window but I looked at him. I really wasn't in the mood, but he wanted a story.

"What made you decide to rob banks?" he asked. "Were you trying to impress your mama? You come from a long line of bank robbers, Shon? Your daddy take you into the family business and you screwed it up by getting everybody busted?"

I told him that no one in my family, as far back as

anyone knew, had ever been in jail before, much less prison.

I told him that my family didn't take money; they gave it away, mostly to churches and charities. I didn't represent them very well.

"Well, tell me about the town where you grew up, and I'll figure you out for myself." Most prison biographies generate spontaneously from the mud of bad places; if you know the place, you know the story.

So I stood and looked out through the bars at the outside world at sunset and started describing David City, Nebraska, a sprawling metropolis of a little under three thousand people. I described my family's old two-story brown and white house; I imagined it among piles of leaves. It sits on the western edge of town— the last line of houses before Nebraska resumes its flat, corn-furrowed infinity.

"Your pop's a farmer?"

"He manages cattle—not enough money to have his own farm."

Farmland costs too much money for most people. If there had been another land rush offering free homestead farms, Dad would have put us all in the station wagon and had us at the starting line.

Every morning he would climb into his Ford F-150 pickup and dissolve into Grass Valley Farms.

I tried to give Bee Dog a picture of it. I described my old bedroom window, under the long brow of a roofline, with a view left to the farmland Dad managed, and right, through leafy front yards, toward town. As a kid, I often escaped from my window at night, climbing up and over the steep summit, then down through the branches of a big tree—off into the dark to some fresh adventure with Tom.

I described the square, downtown. It's a wide street that spreads out from a row of historic brick buildings that hold the latest generation of bars and farm insurance offices.

The reddish cobblestone street is so wide that cars park in the middle of it. Street dances are held there, and people wander around with a beer in hand or just stand and visit. In my mind the people were all out there and most were smiling at me, despite how I had shocked and embarrassed them. It is, in fact, a forgiving town.

Bee Dog still didn't see how all that computed into my taking up robbing banks. He said something along those lines, and he fell asleep. I kept wandering around town. I imagined Mom hanging the wash and calling us to dinner, my brothers chasing each other with the garden hose. I saw the basketball hoop bolted to the plywood backboard on the telephone pole.

You think about little things like that in prison, like the backboard, the sound of it wobbling when the ball hit it. I knew that sound. I could probably pick it out from a thousand recordings of other floppy plywood backboards. Men go crazy doing this, falling into their stories, but a measure of it is a drug you need.

I shadowed Bee Dog for those first few months, trying to analyze the people and understand the place. Because inmates often react violently to imagined slights, I tried to create a narrative of myself as a quiet but fearless guy who would welcome a good fight, yet was otherwise decent when treated decently. I tried to show everyone respect, and so far, so good. Maybe it helped that people knew I had robbed five banks and wasn't in for something less physical, like embezzlement or tax evasion. In their eyes, bank robbery, unlike child molesting or domestic abuse, was the all-American crime, complete with a populist tradition and a cultural hall of fame. Or maybe it was my demeanor. Who knows? Still, I knew I would have to prove myself physically sometime.

Even the biggest, meanest guys must prove themselves.

"Don't think about it when it happens," Bee Dog advised.

"Think about it now instead, so you know just what you'll do. It'll be something stupid that someone says. You might just want to laugh it off, but that would be a big mistake if it's not coming from a friend."

I was vigilant, almost looking for the fight.

My first assigned job wasn't the best. You must have a job in prison; it's not supposed to be a vacation after all. You need it to kill time and stay productive; you need it to earn enough money to survive, and you need it because, well, that's the rule. I signed up for a job in the prison's metal factory because I had riveted and welded at a truck company for a time after high school. But I was told my name would be added to the years-long waiting list. Being at the bottom of the food chain as a newbie, my first job was in the kitchen—cleaning pots, pans, steam trays, food trays, the floors, and tables.

The kitchen is a sauna of clanging aluminum pans and greasy equipment. It is also the place where people are most likely to be beaten, because there are too many unwatched corners and because someone might want to make an example of you in front of the munching masses.

In the kitchen, you are forced to listen to the dumbest imaginable conversations, everything from why Hitler was a great man to screaming matches over which rapper makes the most money.

One day a guy was using a long stick to retrieve a hidden plastic bag of homemade wine from a shelf near the kitchen ceiling, where it had been fermenting in the heat. The bag caught on a jagged piece of metal. He jerked it, piercing the bag, and the hooch poured over him and flooded the kitchen floor.

"What I spoda do?" he said, almost in tears, to the kitchen guard. He spent a few weeks in the hole. "What I spoda do?" became a favorite bit of racist slang for months. And this is the environment where prisoners are expected to rehabilitate!

In those work environments, you have to look like you're cool with everything stupid that's happening. When you are back to the relative sanity of your friends in the dayroom, you vent. I was watching a game on television, and I had been complaining about my job to a guy named Ryan, a white guy in his mid-thirties. Ryan had a six-postage-stamp bet on the game we were watching, to make it interesting. Stamps are the ready currency of prison.

After a while he looked away from a commercial and responded.

"Shon, you should work in the law library with me. I

know Burress real well, the guy who runs it. It's a good job, man. You've been to college, so maybe you could get in."

I knew Ryan was supposed to be some type of jail-house lawyer. Guys would pay him in stamps and other things for his help in preparing legal filings. He was sharp but slippery.

"I was in college for about ten minutes," I replied. We were trying to hear ourselves over some awful singing. There was a new music video on MTV, which you could only hear through earphones, but guys were singing along. It was like listening to a room full of the people kicked off American Idol in the first round.

"Yeah, but you act smart, and all you really got to know is how to read and write so you can find books and check them out. If I talk to Burress, I could get you the job. Maybe you could do some work for me. I would teach you."

It couldn't be worse than the kitchen. Boring, probably, but maybe I could read novels in there. Even better, it would be a fresh break in the pattern of my days. The passage of time in prison is felt only through changes like that; my kitchen era would be over, the clock would have ticked.

Some guys will cause trouble just to feel the passage of time. There is otherwise a lead-heavy sameness to prison days. Clocks and calendars cut too slowly through the big mountain of a prison sentence; freedom seems to come faster through sudden movements: a new man arrives, a man is transferred out, a new guard is hired, a guard leaves, they serve something new in the chow hall, someone is clubbed with a can of Goya beans stuffed inside a sock.

Watching the game, I kept glancing at Ryan and wondering if I really wanted to be working with him closely every day. He was a schemer, always concocting some way to score dope, or wine, or both. His breath was always a horrid mix of rotten orange juice and cheap tobacco—he rolled his own.

If that wasn't enough, he had a slick grin that belonged in a slasher film.

But it was an opportunity. I might otherwise be stuck in the kitchen for years if I turned it down. So I went for it. I was hired after my minimum ninety-day stint in the kitchen.

I didn't know, and Ryan didn't bother to mention, that the Crips were using the law library for other reasons altogether.

6
WHITEOUT

The big fight I was expecting kept not happening. I had been following the rules: respect everyone, ask first, stay close to your friends. I was lifting weights, doing pull-ups, and running every other day, thinking I needed to be in top shape—first because it was a morale booster, and second because every day in prison made me a day older than the teenagers arriving and looking for trouble.[5]

My last real fist fight had been a couple of years earlier, and I hadn't exactly won. It had been with my friend Tom in the spring of 1997. I was working at a farm and living day to day, camped in my parents' basement. My small paycheck would be overspent by the time the next one came around. I had returned from two years in the Navy the previous summer.

I was twenty-one and clueless.

After plowing fields for twelve straight hours one day, I was heading home in an old truck when I saw Ann Marie out running. She was coming toward me on the farm road that runs west of town. I was surprised because I thought she was away at Creighton, the Jesuit university just north of downtown Omaha. What I didn't know was that she often came home on the weekends to run in the wide-open spaces.

There had been some snow that April afternoon, late in the season for snow, but not so much that you couldn't run if you were a fanatic about it. It was coming down lightly as she ran. She looked a little too thin but otherwise just beautiful.

She smiled as I passed her.

I should have stopped and said hello, but that would have seemed pathetic. Besides, I was embarrassed to be working on a farm back in David City, while she was finishing up her degree in the city.

A real blizzard moved in that evening. By midnight I was drinking in a David City bar with Tom. The joint smelled like it had been mopped with stale ale, and cigarette smoke hung in layers. The tattoos on the new bartender's arms made it clear he had been a Marine in Vietnam. He was our parents' age.

"Must bother you that you went and put your butt on the line for your country, and you end up serving beer in this dump," Tom said. It was odd for him to be overtly rude and hostile like that—by Midwest standards, that was rude and hostile. He usually wasn't that way.

The bartender shrugged it off at first. But after a few more of Tom's sharp remarks, he was becoming angry and ready to do something. That would have been a mistake, as Tom would have thumped him.

I slammed two shots and settled into a draft of beer.

"Just leave the guy alone," I said.

"You his protector?" Tom said.

"What's your problem tonight?"

"Maybe you're my problem. Maybe you're the bartender's friend and not mine," he said.

"Whatever," I said. "Is it because he made it into the Marines and you didn't?"

"Oh, yeah, you two are the real men here!"

When I joined the Navy and left Nebraska, Tom decided he wanted to be a Marine. He had a meltdown somewhere along the recruitment path, so it hadn't worked out.

"You're crazy," I said.

"Really? All of a sudden you want to protect this guy and challenge my mental health? Maybe you forgot about who's your pal and who isn't," he said. He was beginning to slur.

Tom had been moving from college to college, dropping out, drifting between jobs, never finding the right thing. He had ultimately returned to school, but I could tell he wasn't happy about it.

He finished another beer, downed a last shot of Jack, and walked out into the blizzard. He sped west out of town in his Ford Tempo. I headed after him in a Grass Valley pickup that my Dad drove; I didn't have a car. I was soon speeding along about ten feet behind him through the zero-visibility blizzard. We were doing eighty or ninety down farm roads, drunk.

Four miles out of town, Tom jammed on his brakes for no apparent reason. I skidded into him; the trunk of his Tempo folded upward as I hit. I stumbled out and checked the truck I had borrowed from Dad—not a scratch. It had a cattle catcher that shielded the bumper and front end.

I can't remember who threw the first punch. My guess is he did, considering I had smashed his car. His face was red with the cold but mostly with anger. This should have concerned me, as he was the stronger by far, the result of pumping weights for football since freshman year in high school.

His bulk and his blue eyes and olive skin stood in contrast to skinny, pale, green-eyed me. We didn't look like brothers, but we did look like pals, and you wouldn't pick a fight with either of us without getting both.

My hand and face stung, so I knew I had hit him hard and that something had hit me.

We had fought each other a few times growing up but this was something different. When he regained his footing, all I could see were the whites of his rolled-back eyes—no pupils. His fist moved too fast for my drunk brain to process.

He caught me in the cheek, knocking me back against the wrecked quarter panel of the Tempo.

In the surreal seconds just standing there waiting for another punch to land on my face, I looked down at the spinning road. The snow was blowing through the beams of our headlights. I looked to see if Ann Marie was running. It was well after midnight in a blizzard, and I was drunk, in a fist fight, but that was my thought because this was the road where I had last seen her.

I bucked around and buried my head into Tom's stomach.

We worked along between the vehicles, punching away, slipping and then falling into the snow-banked ditch beside the road. Tom was getting the better of me. We struggled in the snow, swiping and falling and sometimes disappearing into the white.

"You're an idiot," he said. Somewhere above my eye I was bleeding. He was right, I was an idiot. Always joking, never serious about anything except basketball. It was always Tom who brought me back to where choices meet consequences.

Hey, you going to actually take a book home? was the kind of thing he'd say in high school when I almost flunked out.

We were a good match. I needed his dose of reality, and he needed somebody who could deal with his depressions. That was the contract of our friendship.

I aimed for his chin but my punch landed behind his ear.

Tom came from a good family. His dad, like many in David City, was a strict Catholic and a good lawyer. His mom was a teacher and attended the nondenominational church that my parents helped start. Because of that, Tom and I grew up almost like brothers, chasing and pounding each other when we were kids. Tom had the brains to do anything he wanted.

"You know what? You've screwed up everything you've touched," he said, sitting deep in the snow. He was right, dead so. His face was bleeding and so was mine.

"It's cold," I said. Blood was freezing on my face. We had become a couple of losers despite everything we had going for us—good families, good schools, great hometown.

"Well, maybe you're my bad luck charm," Tom said.

"Like it was my fault you flunked out of college?"

Now that you mention it, I was thinking. Yeah, he

should have followed me to college to make sure I did my course work. So he had abandoned me long before I abandoned him.

I had attended a small college in Nebraska called Midland University on a basketball scholarship but was kicked out a few weeks into the spring term. A coach named Rich McGill had taken a recruiting chance on me, and I returned the favor by attending every practice but cutting nearly every class. It must have been some form of academic suicide. I could see I wasn't going to be the star of the team—I was just average—and that was a big surprise. Average was unacceptable.

In my first and last visit to the head office, the dean called me a jerk-off, and I returned the compliment. I think it was something similar to clinical depression— another smalltown sports star forced to see he wasn't so hot in the bigger world. It's a common problem, but I didn't digest it and move on like most do. I kept falling deeper into a self-pity that became the seed of self-destructiveness to come.

I called Tom, and he collected me and my stuff from the dorm and drove me back to David City. He was always the one I called, and he was always the one I listened to, because I knew he was smarter than I was. Instead of breaking the news to Mom and Dad, I went drinking with Tom, who toasted me with "It could be worse, brother."

Yes, it could.

I had a good family, same as Tom, so nobody could understand what my problem was, including me.

Tom didn't want me to leave town for the Navy, but

I had joined up out of necessity. I had been working as a riveter in a truck trailer factory, living in an apartment furnished with a cruddy couch, a wobbly kitchen table, a rusty stove, and a single bed. I ran out of money and Dad bailed me out, but insisted I sign up for military service. Since joining the Navy meant leaving David City, the idea seemed decent.

After boot camp and then Stinger missile school, I was sent to Manamah, Bahrain, an island just east of Saudi Arabia in the Persian Gulf.

Within three months I was promoted to a position of authority. I helped administer a group of men who protected U.S. warships in the Gulf with shoulder-mounted Stinger missiles. When my commander was away I was given some authority and handled it well. I was good at my job and was succeeding at something. But for some reason I needed to find a whole new way to fail. It's funny, really, that I had spent all my growing up years rebelling against authority, and here I was deep inside the most powerful organization in the world, the U.S. military. I guess I had to rebel against my own self.

Most days ended with me consuming over a dozen beers and half a bottle of Jose Cuervo, one shot at a time, with my buddies.

All of the guys in my Stinger detachment lived in the same apartment complex. It was like a frat house. There was a guy named Ryan who was a lot like me. He came from a devout Christian family and was now enjoying his newfound freedom halfway around the world from them. Another guy, I partied with daily was Jude. His parents were hippies; they had named him after the Beatles song "Hey Jude." He spent most of his time in Bahrain drinking, to pay them back for the name. And there was another kid from somewhere in the hills of Kentucky who could drink whole bottles of liquor at a time and reminded me of the inbreeds from the movie *Deliverance*.

We were all under twenty-one and in a country where it was legal for us to drink, so we did. It almost killed me.

"Acute pancreatitis" is what they called it. For three days it felt like I had swallowed hot coals.

On the third night, I collapsed buck naked in front of my roommates and the girls they had invited over. They loaded me into a cab that dropped me off at a Bahraini hospital. The hospital hooked me up to three IVs, a catheter, and a stomach tube.

I wasn't that concerned until I learned that the hospital was not allowing my boss, the chief petty officer, to come visit me. Instead, the base chaplain came and started asking me about God. That made me nervous.

My family was advised by the Navy that I might not live, but after a week I started to recover. When I was well enough, the Navy sent me to Bethesda to finish out the remaining months of my two-year enlistment. While in D.C. I quit drinking but ran with Navy guys who introduced me to rave clubs and party drugs.

I should have re-enlisted, but the idea of being aboard a ship with no girls and no beer seemed like prison to me, which, as it turned out, was ironic. So I went home to Nebraska.

I lived with high school friends in Lincoln but ended

up falling apart. Like I said before, I moved into my parents' basement. I was arrested and charged with writing bad checks. Sometimes it was a result of poor bookkeeping; other times it was the result of desperation because I was out of money. Anyway, Dad bailed me out, but there was to be a trial down the road. I suddenly figured I should re-enlist in the Navy and earn a degree in something, or make a career in the military. That would move me out of the basement and out of the shadow of Dad's anger. I would just start over. I drove to Omaha to re-enlist. Good idea.

Unfortunately, my pending charges were not what the Navy was looking for. They turned me down.

Right after that Tom and I fought in the snow. We fought slower and slower and the snow flocked us white as snowmen in the ditch as we got up and fell down. We should have died from hypothermia.

Tom's frosted face looked beaten up, so I knew mine must be worse.

"I have been a better friend to you than you've been to me," I said. This was the meanest thing I could think of to say; our friendship was the only solid thing either of us really cared about.

"That's bull." For a second I thought he would throw another punch, but we were finished. And he was right: it was bull. We always had our differences, and we'd had a few fist fights, but he had been my best friend always. "It ain't easy havin' pals," was a line we sometimes repeated from Young Guns, the movie about Billy the Kid and his friend Charley Bowdre.

We finally dragged ourselves out of the snow and

drove back to town, his trunk flapping up and down like the jaws.

We didn't talk for a week. When our bruises had turned from purple to a greenish yellow, he called, wanting to meet at Don's Bar on the town square, down the street from the bar with the Vietnam vet bartender. He said he had an idea.

It was a chilly night, but spring was settling back in. Tom was already at the bar when I arrived. There were a few other customers sprinkled around, including an old man nursing a single shot of something at the far end. I bought a beer and took a swig. Tom clinked my bottle.

"Sorry about all that," he said.

"Me too."

"We're not doing too good," he continued.

"No, we're not." We sat and drank in silence.

I was working at the time for a farmer who had a blueberry muffin gut that fluffed over his belt. He was an acquaintance of Dad's, but he treated me like the cow dung he made me scoop. One day he said I was a moron—actually he said something way worse— for not knowing how to run a machine he hadn't yet shown me how to operate. I walked away instead of punching him.

Dad was after me to find my own place, because he saw me going into a dark spiral and was worried I would drag my two younger brothers down with me. I couldn't disagree.

Tom did have an idea. I could always tell when he was about to throw an idea on the table. He turned his beer bottle around in its sweat puddle as he built up steam to say it.

He cleared his throat and glanced around behind us.

"So what do you think about us robbing a bank?" he said.

Most people would have laughed that off. But to me, the world was newly framed in that instant. Everything once bleak was now interesting and new. The beauty of the idea was that we would either go down like Butch and Sundance or we would have the money to really live. Either way, it would be a big improvement. Over the next few beers we began to make our plan. We decided we would drive north on a Saturday to look for a proper bank.

For the first time in a long time, we were excited about the future.

7
THE DEEPEST LEVEL OF HELL

Joining gangs and other mutual protection societies in prison isn't like joining a fraternity. Some guys arrive having been in prison a time or two before, possibly with longtime gang affiliations from the joint or from their old neighborhoods. For others, there is a gradual process of assimilation into different circles. But not all circles are gangs.

Some, like me, eventually find maybe half a dozen friends who seem human—people who share something in the way of goals or attitude. Maybe they are the guys who can actually imagine getting out someday and not coming back, and who are trying to prepare themselves for that day. Maybe they can imagine each other having successful lives when released.[6]

They will be construction contractors or ministers or auto mechanics—not meth cooks or dealers. Years later, on the outside, they will recognize each other, even if they've never met, thanks to tattoos, a kind of respectful straight talk, and a sort of unflappable manner that comes from living in danger long enough that nothing really bothers you.

Some guys will cluster in prison because they share interests—something as general as music or as specific as a favorite sports team. Their little affinity group is called a "car." A car can be any activity, and not necessarily related to gangs. For example, some men turn to religion and spend their free time studying and praying together; there are many monasteries, churches, synagogues, ashrams, and mosques in our prisons. Other men simply exercise together.

The more gang-oriented men usually want to make some money in prison, usually by selling drugs so they can gamble on the televised games or so they can buy drugs and alcohol for themselves. Or maybe they are still running things on the outside. Gangs are accustomed to having some of their executives on involuntary loan to the state or federal government.

And some guys are just thugs and don't know how to be around anyone but thugs. But, contrary to popular belief, this group of guys is small minority.

You might belong to several cars for your several interests. Some cars might be mixed race, but that's rare, except among the church guys.

My first car was the "iron pile." Most guys in prison work out, but some of us took weight training very seriously, working out in sub-zero temperatures through the winter. Early on, Ryan invited me to join his workout car at 6:30 each morning. These guys were my first ring of protection.

There were also some other men who took me into their circle. These were men of reasonable, even friendly attitude, intelligent but unassuming—the type who weren't looking to make trouble, guys you could absolutely trust. I usually ate with them. And there were the 047s. The last three digits of your prisoner number indicate your home state. The Nebraska boys were the 047s. It should have been 037, as Nebraska was the thirty-seventh state, but whatever. Together with some guys from the neighboring states of Iowa, Indiana, and Illinois, we generally watched out for each other.

Your car might be plugged in to a gang, or maybe not.

If you're plugged in, you're part of Gangster Disciples, Latin Disciples, Latin Kings, Vice Lords, Bloods, Serenos, Dirty White Boys, Mafia, Aryan Brotherhood, or one of several others. Black guys from California might be Crips or Bloods.

If they were in a California prison, the Crips and Bloods would be trying to kill each other, but exiled in faraway Pekin, Illinois, they hung together and didn't fight—just as black ants and red ants floating on the same twig will be more interested in the water than in each other. The Chicago gangs also worked to keep the peace between all the gangs, but for a different reason: their families were close by, and any war between the gangs would result in either a transfer far from their people or lockdowns that would cost them visiting time.

If none of your cars are plugged in, you are unaffiliated. Whether your car is affiliated or not, the other guys in your car are the people who will have your back. When people know that you have representation, they are less likely to rob, steal, or sucker you. But membership also comes with a price: if your group has one idiot, one guy who runs his mouth, that guy can cause a train wreck for everyone. It happens a lot.

But if there is going to be any protection for anybody, you have to seem very comfortable with the idea of fighting to protect a guy for the dumbest of reasons.

You can try to serve your time outside a circle of protection, but chances are you will be stolen from, beat on, and generally abused. You may survive on your own for a time, but eventually something will happen. Maybe your locker will be emptied while you're on the yard. So you don't really have a choice.

Some guys are just so far out of it that they can't find comrades. Maybe they're too angry or bizarre to deal with, or maybe they are chesters or snitches who live in constant fear. Maybe they are very introverted or have an actual antisocial disorder. Prisons are chock full of people with undiagnosed and untreated mental illness.[7] Over time these loners become magnets for everyone's anger and darker instincts.

I saw them walking alone and knew it might someday be me. Not one person in Pekin knew that my codefendants and I had cooperated with the government. At any moment someone could transfer into Pekin who knew it, and I would be viewed much differently. So I looked at each new guy coming in, just to see if he was someone who would know and who would tell. I knew it was bound to happen.

Tyler, off in another prison, was my main concern. He was the guy who had sold us dope and guns and stolen cars. Even though he had never robbed a bank himself, the feds had him as an accessory. Between the people who had already cooperated with the feds at the time of my arrest and some physical evidence they had gathered, there was more than enough proof establishing Tyler's guilt.

I figured he would sign a plea agreement like Tom, Craig, and I had signed—Craig was my partner in robberies two, three, and four. But Tyler decided—maybe based on poor advice from his attorney or maybe just from stubbornness—that he should plead innocent and go to trial.

The three of us who signed were bound by our plea agreement, compelling us to testify to everything we knew.

We hadn't imagined anyone would be outside the plea, as the chances of serving a very long sentence or even life if you were found guilty were too high. With my plea, I would serve twelve to fifteen years; without it, eighty-five to ninety-five. I had discussed the situation with my parents, and I knew the longer sentence—effectively a life sentence—would be as crushing to them as it would be to me. There was no reason to back away from my plea deal, because there was no way it would do Tyler any good.

Three days before his trial I talked to Tyler through a wall at the county jail and begged him to accept the deal.

The day before trial I called his attorney and asked him to reconsider. He was playing Russian roulette, but with all the chambers loaded. It didn't make sense.

Tyler walked past the holding cell with vengeance in his eyes. After my testimony, he changed his mind, or his attorney changed it for him, and he pled guilty and received a ten-year sentence. That was probably three years longer than it could have been.

He was somewhere in the federal prison system now, and it isn't that big a world. I knew something would happen. Even though the majority of federal inmates have cooperated at some level, they won't talk about it, and they'll abuse anyone known to have cooperated. They talk endlessly about how the blankety-blank snitches should die. It's hypocritical, but that's the way it is.

I didn't consider myself a snitch, given my circumstances.

Nevertheless, my paranoia grew more intense the longer I was at Pekin. I felt something coming, my luck running out, or as if I was in a nightmare where you don't have any clothes on, but no one has noticed yet.

I still thought Bee suspected. He sometimes talked about what they did to snitches in his old gang. He gave me a speech about snitches once, about why they were such a big issue.

"Shon, you know about Dante's Inferno? Do you know what Dante said was the lowest circle of hell? The deepest region of hell, level nine, is reserved for the sin of betrayal.

I mean, like, killing someone is only seven. Dishonesty is eight. But betrayal, in this world and the next, that's the pit, bud. That's it." He would look at me like he knew everything about me.

What's strange is that later when I learned more about the law, I realized that a person who had committed the crime he had, with his lengthy criminal history, could not possibly have received such a lenient sentence without some sort of additional help from the prosecution. Either that or his mama knew the judge.

...

Bobbie, who arrived from Champaign, Illinois, when I had been at Pekin about six months, quickly became a good friend, thanks to basketball and a shared temperament. Bobbie looked the inmate part. He walked with an attitude that said "Don't even try it." On his arm was a tattoo memorializing a friend who had been killed, and years later, another tattoo would be added, remembering his mother, who died of brain cancer a few years before he got out. He had a big square head, which I ridiculed daily, just to push his buttons.

It wasn't really that big or that square, but you look for things to employ as petty taunts.

Bobbie was a freak like me: a white kid who could actually play basketball. We played ball and lifted weights daily.

Bobbie was one of the few white guys I had ever heard of being sentenced for selling crack cocaine. He had grown up in the black area of town, and while he was comfortable around black guys and chummy with everyone at Pekin, he rarely let anyone get too close to him. He was the champion of throwing the mean-mug look. He'd puff his chest out, cock his head, squint, and pull his eyebrows down. It didn't scare me, though; I laughed at it.

"Don't start mean-mugging me. I know you're a coward."

"If we weren't friends, Shon, I would honest to God kill you. Seriously."

"You're not my friend, you wrecked my headphones. And your name is spelled like a girl," I said.

I had saved enough money to buy my first set of decent headphones, and he borrowed them the first day I had them.

When guards rushed our unit due to a fight between gang members, Bobbie gave a lieutenant the mean mug. The lieutenant took three guards to Bobbie's cell and they roughed him up and cuffed him. Then they dragged him down the steps. In the process, my brand-new headphones were trampled by the boots of the officers.

They charged him with disobeying a direct order to return to his cell. In other words, he lost good time and had to spend extra days in prison for looking at someone the wrong way. That's prison.

We had a few good-natured fights, but nothing too serious.

He was stronger than I was, but I could sometimes get the better of him and toss him on his back. I once did that, sending him into the corner edge of a locker. They had to put a staple in his head. After that I called him staple whenever he got under my skin.

Bobbie would often join Ryan and me for a smoke in Ryan's cell. I had no secrets from Bobbie, except the one. The longer I kept it from him, the worse I felt about it. But I just couldn't risk it, because you never know if your friend today is going to be your friend tomorrow. Unlike in the outside world, an inmate doesn't go away when he stops being your friend.

8
SHOOTING FOR RESPECT

Prison is danger in a box, but it is also, at bottom, a grinding routine of boredom. You wouldn't think those two things go together, but they do. The most dangerous moments often come because someone is so bored they finally start trouble just to break the torture of monotony. I was feeling that boredom, and I needed some challenge, some competition, something to push back against. And for my own safety, I also needed a long-haul way to establish respect. So I had an idea.

...

The black, white, and brown inmates mingle across color lines except at the dining tables and on the sports teams. The lower-ranked teams were often racially mixed, but the top leagues were all black. There were three basketball leagues: the A League was four teams with the best players from the four main housing units; the B League had the lesser players; the C League consisted of men over forty-five and a few of their younger friends playing by invitation. I was told that no white boy had ever played on the A-League at Pekin.

That struck me as a worthy challenge. I decided I wanted to force my way in.

"I would not recommend that," Bee Dog warned. "You could ask them if they'll let you play, but I don't think that's going to come out good for you. If you play bad, they will be talking smack to you every day. If you play good, then someone will get pissed. I mean, to get beat at basketball by a whiteboy would be hard to live down, know what I'm saying? And they'll take it out on you when they can."

I understood. I saw the downside, but I couldn't resist the opportunity to play. Basketball had been my first love when I was a kid.

Some people remember the first girl they kissed in junior high, or the first teacher they had a crush on. I remember what it felt like after I scored eighteen points in a freshman basketball game.

In junior high I was short, so I played point and shooting guard. But between the end of basketball season in eighth grade and the start of my freshman year of high school, I grew six inches and became one of the taller players on our team, but with the skills of a guard.

Jump shots were great, but my talent was driving to the basket. While I wasn't fast, I had a quick first step. There was nothing better than making older players look bad in practice and having the coach yell at them. They, of course, hated me for it, and some days I would cool it just so they wouldn't want to beat me up after practice.

By junior year I was a starter on the varsity team. I had worked all summer practicing against guys older than me. I would see Ann Marie at our games because she was dating a classmate of mine. So I met her a few times back then. That's why she knew to wave at me when I passed her on the roads, though she was the kind of girl who would have waved a few fingers and smiled anyway. The first time I really noticed her seriously was at a holiday tournament when our team, David City High, was playing Aquinas, the Catholic high school Ann Marie attended.

During the pre-game I was supposed to be warming up, practicing my shot for the game.

"Wake up, Shon," the coach said to me, knocking me several times in the arm. Annie was dressed in her black and gold cheerleader outfit and was doing a cheer: A.W.E.—S.O.M.E . . . Awe-some! Awe-some! Awesome are we! I was distracted all night. We lost.

We did make it to state that year—the first time in a long time that my school had played in the state basketball tournament.

But I couldn't tell Pekin's A League players that they should let me play on account of how my junior-year team had made state—in Nebraska no less. So while they were watching a game on TV, I told them I had played college ball on scholarship.

"Was it Duke?" Coop said, to everyone's laughter.[8]

"Not exactly."

"Well then, we watching a game, here. Come back when you been to Duke."

They didn't look away from the screen. After a few plays Coop said, "I seen you shoot. You can shoot. But what you saying? You saying you want to play with us, whiteboy?"

Everyone chuckled again.

"So when are we playing next?" I said.

"Oh, it's like that, huh? You just decided we letting you play?"

"I could be your token."

"Token, what?" Coop asked.

"Token whiteboy, aren't you equal opportunity?"

They were laughing.

Later their coach, an inmate called Old Man George, invited me to practice.

I told Bee Dog about the practice. It didn't change his opinion of what would happen down the road. He changed the subject.

"Why'd you drop out of college, man? You could be in the NBA by now if you're all that good."

I wasn't, but at least I could have graduated by that time. Every year since high school had been wasted. Parts of the Navy years had been good because I was confronted with lots of challenges and life-and-death responsibilities. And if I hadn't started drinking or if I had re-enlisted before I came home, that might have all worked out. The only thing I took from any of it was the certain knowledge that for me to be engaged in life in a healthy way, I needed big challenges.

I showed up at A Team practice and held my own. I could take anyone off the dribble, but I encountered a lot of, shall we say, resistance at the hoop. I was knocked to the ground nearly every time, but I bounced back up and never called my own foul.

That night Bee Dog wouldn't say a word. He did, however, point generously to his own well-ordered locker when he saw me searching and cursing through mine for my small box of bandages.

I practiced with the team for a week before they reluctantly agreed to let me play in a real game. I did all right. I made an impressive layup with my left hand through traffic, even though I'm a righty.

I was soon playing every game. It seemed like everyone was on a mission to knock me to the ground. I started finding my old shooting range, and I kept driving to the hole, knowing the punishment waiting there. Finally they became used to me as a fact of life. "The whiteboy can play" was something I started to hear, though it came off as a half joke.

The fact that I cared more about the game than about getting hurt earned me some respect around the yard, which was the long-term point of it—along with the instant gratification of dominating big guys on the court.

Doing something well was, for me, the next best thing to freedom. Basketball was my first love, but it had been my downfall, too, making me think I was more special than I was. I didn't feel that old glow around me at Pekin, and there sure were no cheerleaders and pompoms at prison games—unless you count the several inmates who tied their shirts into bows and took female names like Ashley and Pocahontas.

...

I was now working in the law library, checking in books, shelving books, checking them out again. Guys coming in would recognize me from the games. The white guys wanted to know if I was crazy for playing in a black league. Some of the black guys in the library said I had game, which I appreciated.

The library wasn't as boring as I had expected. I was finding my way around the thousands of books packed in numerical order on the shelves. The books were big, thick and intimidating, but I became adept at searching for the correct rules and cases when guys asked. Sometimes I didn't know exactly how I knew, I just did.

Members of the Crips gang, most of them from California, would come around and call Ryan out to talk.

"If one of them goes into those back shelves, don't bother them," Ryan told me. "They like to do their research in private." He winked. I didn't know what all that meant, but I stayed clear.

I did get curious, so one day when nobody else was around I asked Ryan to spell it out. He told me that large plastic bags full of weed were taped underneath the rolling bookshelves.

"Keep your mouth shut about it. The weed that I smoke and share with you guys is what they give me as a storage fee."

In his cell on a regular basis, Ryan would roll a joint as fat as a Swisher Sweet Cigarillo. You don't see that in prison.

You see weed smoked in joints you might mistake for toothpicks.

That's because weed costs a fortune in there, and because you want to finish the thing in a few hits before a guard comes around. Even so, guys get the small escape they are seeking from that little bit, so Ryan's fat joints looked as obscene as a Rolls-Royce at a homeless shelter.

An ounce of weed is worth a pound of cash in prison— about a thousand dollars. Most of what Ryan had was going up in smoke, but he must have been selling some, too. You don't sell things for cash in prison. Arrangements are made by your friends on the outside: they send money to an inmate's prison account. For the small stuff, you use postage stamps as cash.

Postage stamps were sold at the commissary for thirty-two cents. Once they left the commissary their value was reduced to twenty-five cents for trading convenience; few could count in increments of thirty-two.

If you're lucky, you have people on the outside sending a little money each month into your account. You have your job inside, which pays money into that account, too. A good job at the prison metal factory might pay a few dollars an hour. Otherwise, menial jobs pay from twelve to forty cents an hour. I was getting about thirty cents an hour at the law library. That money, plus any money sent from the outside, would go into my account, and I would use it for my once-a-week visit to the overpriced commissary, where a tiny box of laundry soap, for example, cost six bucks.

I would buy a few snacks, ramen noodles in various flavors; pens, paper, and envelopes for correspondence; an occasional can of pop; and stamps for mailing letters and for use as cash. I might throw a few extra stamps on a televised football game and buy snacks from guys who set up little stores in their lockers. They restocked weekly when it was their commissary turn.

If you made a profit from gambling or selling drugs, that profit would usually be in the form of stamps, and you needed to spend them somewhere. So the inmate stores did all right.

Whenever the commissary or U.S. Post Office raises prices, it throws the prison economy into uncertainty, like the Fed had just raised the interest rate by a whole point. Inmates who run stores must raise prices or accept reduced profits, and the guys who run the gambling tickets must decide when old stamps can no longer be used. When rates went up, as they did six times while I was at Pekin, subtle adjustments had to be made.

Prison cafeteria food is predictable. The staff must have a committee of misinformation that devises different names for the same thing. It was always a slightly different sauce on the same shriveled-up piece of chicken. As a result, a lot of cooking is performed in the units. I made a home-cooked meal myself now and then, just to invigorate my taste buds. I could cook a fine pot of spaghetti or heat up my cup of coffee using a home-made heating coil plugged into a socket. The devices were called stingers, and they were surreptitiously made in the metal factory. Yes, you could use the microwave oven in the dayroom most of the time, but sometimes your cell was locked, and sometimes you just didn't want to be around anyone. Pasta and sauces could be purchased from the commissary, or from guys who worked kitchen jobs and had big pockets.

A few Chicago Italians managed to prepare real pasta meals, complete with vegetables and cheese stolen from the kitchen. I made a point of having Italian friends. Friday night nachos were the most popular meal. Here's the recipe: Buy tortilla chips at the commissary. Place them in a cardboard box top lined with a plastic trash bag. Purchase a can or two of refried beans; slices of summer sausage; canned chicken; a tub of nacho cheese; and freshly stolen bell peppers and onions from the kitchen. Place the vegetables on the chips, along with the summer sausage and chicken. Heat the cheese and refried beans separately in the dayroom microwave, then pour them over the entire concoction.

Eat immediately, usually during a long-anticipated TV movie or game.

On Friday nights, the prison ran a system-wide movie. For some strange reason I never did understand, they played mostly romantic comedies—like we needed to be teased with that.

If some of the cooking was against the rules, the wiser cops understood that people need to live. When the aromas snaked down the corridors, the better guards generally looked the other way, just as they did when homemade incense and cigar smoke were used to cover the perfume of a little weed. Even so, the right times for doing certain things were selected according to the personal temperaments of the guards on duty.

Every Friday night Ryan bought a large, expensive box of nachos with everything. And he was smoking weed with everyone, me included. I wondered what sort of game he was up to—living large like that.

...

The months passed and it was summer. I was settling deeper into the law library and into basketball, too. It was time for the big summer league games, and I had trained into shape with long daily runs around the track and lifting. The summer league games were unlike winter league. You picked your own teams. A few white guys I knew wanted to form a team. In retrospect, it was not one of my wisest moves, as the summer games were played on concrete instead of on the indoor court, and because these games were pitting black versus white.

My teammates were better than I expected. We had Pistol Pete, whose real name was Chris. He was from Nap Town—Indianapolis—sported some gold teeth, and could shoot set-shot threes from almost anywhere. On the other side of the court was Bobbie. He also could shoot threes. Together they opened up the court for me to drive whenever and wherever I wanted.

On the inside we had Joe, a six foot four slender Latin Disciple who was half crazy. One wrong move and Joe would go ballistic. Then he would apologize profusely the next day for losing his temper. Actually, that describes about 80 percent of the guys in the joint. Our other post players were Milan and an Iowa boy named Shane.

We also had a black guy named Myron. He played with us because he was good friends with Bobbie and me, and because he was a lockdown defender—one of those guys who pesters good offensive players into frustration. I am sure Myron received his fair share of ribbing over his decision to play with the "whiteboys."

The worst thing that could happen to a black team, of course, would be to lose to a team of whiteboys. The several black teams that we beat early on were the subjects of general derision that stopped only when we had beaten another team.

We made it into the playoffs, but no one believed we would win after that. The referees, the scorekeepers, and the league commissioner were all black, and it was widely assumed, even amongst the black guys, that they would not let us win the league title. It was all fairly moot, as the team we were selected to play next had a six foot six player named Ford who was a remarkable athlete.

Things were not going well in the first quarter. Ford shoved everyone around and scored basically when he chose to. But we erased a large deficit, mainly because Pistol and Bobbie started heating up from three-point range.

I drove to the basket a few times and gave Ford a series of head fakes to keep him off balance. I had scored fifteen points when early in the fourth Ford decided I had played enough. I figured he would be looking for the head fake, so I went straight at him in the air. He never tried to block the shot. Instead his arm went straight out like a tollgate—more like a steel girder. It's called clotheslining for a reason. My head hit that steel girder and my body flipped back like a bike rider meeting a low branch. I landed flat on my back, and my head slammed on the concrete. I got to my feet with the help of teammates and continued playing but was off my game. My guess is I had a concussion. We lost.

Ford came up to me in the kitchen about a week after the game. His big mitt landed on my shoulder and he said he was sorry about that. How was my back? My back would, in fact, never be quite the same, but I told him it was not a big deal.

He said that was good, because he might need my help in the law library with something. I said I'd be happy to help him.

That much was true. I had started to enjoy the challenge of helping guys figure out how to research their cases. I even fantasized that maybe, when I got out, if I ever did, I could work in a library somewhere or even become a paralegal in some clinic that would be desperate enough not to check my past. It could happen.

"I want to talk to my lawyer," Ford said when he came into the library a few days later. I was way back in the stacks, but I recognized his voice. I enjoyed his company, and having a few black friends made me feel more normal, like the times back in the Navy and in the happy days of bank jobs. It also set me apart as someone a little different in prison, and I think I wanted that. It was sometimes risky to walk that line, but that was where I always liked to walk.

He would be about the last guy I helped before a bolt of lightning came down from the Supreme Court and caused nearly everyone in Pekin to almost wet their pants with excitement.

9
LIKE A TUNNEL OUT

The bank of phones was at one end of the dayroom. You could hang out on the balcony rail next to them and overhear entertaining conversations if you were that bored, which was a given.

"No, baby, that's not what . . . You know I . . . No, baby, I'm just . . . You know I got to . . . " and on and on in long blues ballads. Most calls were made in the evening after chow. "She don't mean nothing, baby. I don't know why she come to visit; you know I love you best, baby."

The charges for the calls came off your account. The cost was three dollars for a 15-minute call. Somewhere, someone is becoming rich off the families of prisoners.[9] For me it was worth the ten hours of work it took to hear fifteen minutes from home. Those voices were a reminder that there was a life outside the walls. I would have called every night if I had the money.

The law library in Pekin was a sleepy place. A few regulars would amble in, check out one book each, and hand me their ID. I would make a note on the book register. When they came back, I reversed the process and shelved the book. There was an abundance of time to read between tasks. Although the U.S. Supreme Court hands down decisions that affect large numbers of people, rarely does the Court issue a ruling that brings about a system-wide change in the criminal justice system. But that happened on June 26, 2000. In a case argued by Solicitor General Seth Waxman, the Court issued a decision declaring that the famous *Miranda* warnings are part of our constitutional heritage.

Somewhat unnoticed was the other case announced that day, the decision that would more immediately rock the prison world: *Apprendi v. New Jersey*.

Ryan and I conducted some preliminary research and requested that the library staff make extra copies of the case

for prisoners to check out. Ryan and a black jailhouse lawyer named Stix held an impromptu meeting of the other dozen or so jailhouse lawyers. We huddled with yellow legal pads and pens at a wooden table for a briefing. Ryan took the lead.

"You know how guys take a plea deal to a lesser crime, thinking they will avoid doing time for the worse crime, only to see the judge sentence them to the bigger crime's penalty anyway?" he said.

Yeah, we all knew that one. It had arguably happened to me.

"Or when a guy is convicted of distributing fifty grams of cocaine, but then the judge sentences him based on five pounds?" I said.

That was a common occurrence in the federal system.

"Well, they can't do that no more," Ryan said. "So we're going to see everybody and his uncle coming in here trying to figure out if they can get their sentences reduced. It's going to be a freakin' zoo."

The decision indeed filled the law libraries of America's prisons with interested customers; we went from serving a small handful of men each day to serving forty or fifty. Guys were asking questions and almost fighting over the same few books and printouts of the decision. To accommodate the rush, we started opening on Sundays.

In *Apprendi* the Supreme Court ruled that judges were wrong to add harsher sentences based on facts not proven to a jury or confessed in court. In plea deals, prosecutors had been charging a person with lesser crimes to speed things along, but then after the conviction they were asking judges to sentence the person based on the suspected but unproven additional crimes—just as if that person had been convicted of the greater crime instead of taking the plea deal. Sometimes the facts of additional crimes were clear, but oftentimes they were hazy and based on the hearsay of drug addicts trying to obtain sentence reductions by implicating others.

To put it in a different context, imagine being convicted at trial of possessing one kilo of cocaine, only to have a judge, rather than the jury, find afterward that while you were dealing drugs you shot and killed someone. Then the judge sentences you to life for the murder. With such practices in place, juries were reduced to little more than gatekeepers, and sentences had but a slight correlation to the convictions.

The Supreme Court said that kind of sleight-of-hand

maneuver was now unacceptable, as should have been obvious.

The same reasoning also applied to plea deals. In my situation, bank robbery is a separate charge from armed bank robbery. My plea deal listed the crime as unarmed bank robbery.

The judge, however, knowing I possessed a gun during the robberies, sentenced me for armed bank robbery anyway.

Naturally, I believed the *Apprendi* decision applied to my situation.

I'm sure some would see this as a technicality, but the prosecution had not charged me with armed robbery, so I should have been sentenced based on the crime they had charged me with and what I had pled guilty to. It was that simple. At least, that was my analysis of how *Apprendi* applied to me. Not pursuing it would be like not taking a tax deduction to which you were technically entitled.

I began to research cases in piles of dusty books. Could I knock a couple of years off my sentence? I had no idea, but like the Tim Robbins character in The Shawshank Redemption, I suddenly felt like I was digging a tunnel to freedom.

My tunnel ran paragraph by paragraph through the law library. The more I dug, the more I believed a sentence reduction was almost certain.

I soaked up everything I could find about the history of our right to a jury trial and our rights more generally. The First Amendment acknowledges our natural right to free speech, to a free press, and to free religious practice. It is therefore considered the flagship American right. But the right to a jury trial is not far behind. It is the only right established both in the body of the Constitution and in the Bill of Rights.

In addition to the right to a jury trial, I studied the body of law known as habeas corpus, which is incorporated into our Constitution from an old English right, and is essentially the right to be heard by a court if you believe you are being held in violation of the law. Habeas corpus is a Latin phrase meaning "you have the body." Translated further: the prison warden has a real person in custody who must now be brought before a judge who will rule if there is legal justification for continued imprisonment.

Habeas law is widely regarded as impossibly difficult and has defeated many attorneys and countless jailhouse lawyers. But I was making sense of it. I was never one for Dungeons & Dragons, but I think it must be like habeas law: complex and full of trapdoors and instant death if you make a wrong turn.

In any case, I had nothing to lose and freedom to gain.

...

We had no computers in the law library, no access to the legal databases like Westlaw or LexisNexis that everybody in the free world was using. So I had to go from book to book, tracing cases back and forth, taking volumes of notes. A computer search would have given me a list of pertinent cases, but without that I had to read everything. That is harder by far, but you end up learning a lot more. I was forced to remember cases because making copies of everything was too expensive. Keeping cases in your head is good, too, because cases are like puzzle pieces floating around in your mind, and sometimes, in moments of creativity, they fall into place and form a picture. If they were words on a screen that you could pull up anytime you wished, that phenomenon wouldn't happen as easily.

Every guy in Pekin thought he had a case for resentencing, and the issue kept getting bigger; there were rumblings that the entire Federal Sentencing Guidelines were called into question by the *Apprendi* decision. The library remained hectic for several months. Similar claims for resentencing were constantly arising so, like a coach running plays from a well-worn playbook, I was churning out similar drafts for several people at a time. I had devised my own legal research methods and was becoming expert at finding relevant case law and seeing arguments where other people, including the inmates' real lawyers, sometimes hadn't. What had started as a solo mission to help myself had now brought me, really for the first time in my life, into a situation where I was helping others and enjoying it.

The *Apprendi* decision was a morale booster for everyone, as if we were all planning a big prison break.

The more advice I gave in the prison library, the more guys throughout Pekin became aware that I could help them.

Vic, a Chicago Italian, was the best of the prison gourmet chefs. He used his food to obtain what he wanted. He wanted legal work from me.

"Shon, good friend, how are you doing with my case? Listen, do you like a marinara better, or maybe an alfredo for your linguini with roasted peppers?" He came bearing a wooden spoon in his hand to make the food seem imminent—something to stir around in the air when he spoke, as Italian cooks like to do.

He answered for me. "Maybe the alfredo. The alfredo with nice peppers." Then he left. I hadn't responded at all, but when he was gone

I moved his file up to the top. Such is life.

Some of the motions were gaining traction, but my own was dead. The judge who sentenced me said that since my case had been long settled and closed, the *Apprendi* decision did not apply, and even if it did apply to my case, it didn't apply to the sentencing guidelines. I was devastated. No matter how much I wanted to stop myself, I had already started some preliminary calculations of a possible sentence reduction.

Thoughts of Christmas with my family in a couple of years, of eating steak again and smelling fresh Nebraska air, seemed realistic. The judge's denial meant I still had to serve eight more years—an eternity.

The judge, by the way, was partially right. *Apprendi* did not apply to my case because it had long been final. But he was wrong about the application of *Apprendi* to the guidelines, as the Supreme Court held a few years later.

The resentencing process was working best for guys who still had some kind of appeal in the works. I tried to forget my own disappointment by burying myself in the cases of people who had a higher probability of success.

I started guarding my private time in my cell, sending away visitors so I could work on cases. It made me unpopular.

Some thought I was becoming unfriendly because I didn't want to discuss the latest prison gossip anymore.

My new cellmate, Robby, was a few years older than I was by birth and fifteen years older by appearance. He had been ravaged by intravenous meth use. His teeth looked like he gargled espresso for mouthwash, and his hair was patchy—what remained of it hung in long strands. Although he had started his sentence with a few tattoos, he was soon sleeved out—meaning you couldn't fit one more tattoo on his arms.

But Robby was the classic case of why you shouldn't judge a crook by his cover. For the five years we were cellies, he was my loyal friend and bouncer, keeping visitors away when I was deep in legal books or writing briefs.

"Hey, look, ol' Shon there is pretty busy," he would say.

"Maybe we should let him have some quiet." He said that maybe a few thousand times, giving me his jack-o'-lantern smile after each visitor was dispatched. I would look up from my books to see it. It was, all things considered, a great smile.

I needed peace because, in addition to working on the appeals, I was enrolled in correspondence courses at Illinois Central College and Ohio University, and legal courses at Kaplan. I realized that if I wanted a career as a paralegal, a college degree was a necessity. For the first time in my life I applied myself academically. It turns out that school is not so difficult if you read the textbooks. Who knew?

It's not easy to take courses from prison. Even when I did it through correspondence, professors simply couldn't comprehend the logistics—some seemed to assume I had a large research library at my disposal. And the prison staff members are not exactly helpful. Fortunately for me, a lady at the education department, Angela, volunteered to proctor my exams. Without her it simply would not have worked.

My parents were pleased that I was taking college courses and that I was excited about something, anything. It was a time of change for them, too, as their nest was slowly emptying.

Something happened to my brother Brook in those years. He was on track to finish his undergraduate degree when he started behaving very oddly. First, he started isolating himself even from his best friend and girlfriend, and then he accused them of sleeping together and plotting against him. A few weeks later he had a nervous breakdown. The doctors diagnosed him with paranoid schizophrenia, and he was institutionalized in a state facility for a time.

It wasn't an easy time for Brett either. He finished his high school education and was a free man again, but it's difficult to break into any decent field without a college education and with a rough juvenile past. He moved around from telemarketer to telemarketer. He was good enough at selling things that he never stayed unemployed, but he longed for something better.

Mom was earning promotions at work, and she began spending more time with the boss's daughter, Ann Marie, who was now out of college and setting up a human nutrition product line for her father. She was also helping produce KV's big catalog.

In one of our weekly phone conversations, Mom told me that I should try to find a nice girl like Ann Marie someday.

Sure thing, I said. Sometimes I let Mom be in her dream-world.

But it was encouraging that she thought wonderful things were still possible for me.

10
THIS IS A ROBBERY

My work with the law provided a mental escape. But escape always comes with a price. I needed to remain grounded in who I was and where I was, because if you become disconnected from that, if you are off in a cloud somewhere thinking you are a young lawyer or a college student, and that the prison life is some inconvenience that doesn't really define who and where you are, you will become sloppy. You will let your guard down. You will forget the rules. And you will get hurt. Your friends will drift away, and they won't be there when you need them.

Fortunately, Robby and Bobbie kept bringing me back to who I was and where I was and who my friends were. Those two were as different as could be, but they were together in their enthusiastic friendship for me. You can't imagine how much that counts in such a place.

"Tell the truth, did you piss your pants during the first robbery?" Robby asked.

"Shut up," I said.

"Well, you may not have soaked your britches, but I bet you wet 'em just a bit," Robby said.

Bobbie thought that was funny.

"Seriously, tell us how you managed to pull off the first job," Robby said.

"We just went in and took the money."

"Really!" he said. He was sitting on the top bunk, his legs swinging. "I guess I was thinking it was a bit more complicated than that. Now I'm wondering why more people don't do it. I'm going to write my mother and tell her how she can get a little extra money every week. Just go in and take the money. I guess most people think you need a gun and a plan and a getaway car and all that."

"You really want the story?"

"Just tell us," Bobbie said, trying to gangster the conversation.

"What kind of gun, at least?"

"Rifle on the first one. A nine-millimeter Smith and Wesson on the others."

"Nice. Black?"

"Of course."

"You really can't go wrong with black," Robby said. "Was it just you? How much did you get?" So I described that first day when Tom and I went driving north to find a likely bank to rob. They inhaled every detail.

After Tom and I preselected the bank in Petersburg, we found an abandoned farm just outside town where we could stash a stolen car taken from another town. That car would be used only to drive the couple of miles to the bank and back to the abandoned farm, where we would stash a big grain truck. The truck would be borrowed from Tom's father's farm, which was not far away. The grain truck would be our second getaway vehicle, one that the police would never suspect. That would get us back to Tom's dad's farm, where our own car would be stashed for use when everything had cooled off. That was the plan. If it didn't end with us shot up and making our getaway, or if the abandoned farm didn't become some Butch and Sundance last scene, we would be okay.

We drove around until we knew just how we would do it. We even picked up some brochures from Wayne State so that if we were pulled over we could say we were just out looking for a college to attend.

After we scoped all that out, we went home to David City for a few weeks. Our next move was for Tom to go back alone. He walked into the bank and asked about opening an account and storing some insurance policies in a safety-deposit box.

They showed him the vault. On the way home, he pulled over and drew a rough sketch of the bank. We let time pass so they would forget about him.

As the planned robbery date approached, both of us were wondering if we would really go through with it. Sometimes we had doubts and sometimes we were sure we would do it.

Our minds, our realities, were on two tracks, and it wasn't clear which track would win out. Sometimes we didn't talk about it for a week, but neither of us liked to think that we were the kind of guys who were all talk and no action. So a kind of moronic shame set in, like, if we didn't rob a bank, it would be another reason to think we were losers.

I was still working for the fat farmer. Just as my dad had taught me, I would go through the cattle checking for sick ones, which you can tell because they have strings of saliva suspended from their mouths, glassy eyes, and general sluggishness.

I washed cow dung from the feeding troughs and

kept thinking that the barn stank like my life. I figured I needed some sort of flood to wash away the stink, and this part of my life.

My trial date on the bad checks had come and gone and I hadn't shown up. I didn't have the money for a lawyer, and I was too depressed to ask Dad for a loan or to show up in court by myself. My arrest was imminent.

Tom and I did have the plan, however. Next time I saw him at the bar I said it was time.

On a Sunday morning in August of 1997 I was waiting for Tom to pick me up at my parents' house. I had a small duffel bag of clothes and hygiene items. I had Dad's old toolbox stuffed with canvas totes for the cash.

Before Tom arrived, I asked my brother Brook to come down to the basement. I told him that I was going to do something that could possibly get me killed if things went badly. I might have to drop out of sight, maybe permanently.

When he asked what it was, I told him. I also told him that I wanted everyone in the family to know that I loved them. I trusted that he wouldn't go run to Dad and try to stop me, because once right after I had come back from the Navy and was still recovering from pancreatitis, I had opened a beer and Brook, thinking it might land me back in the emergency room, had run to tell Dad. We had had it out over that.

There was a honk at the curb. Brook gave me a hug.

"Don't get hurt," he said.

"I don't intend to."

Tom and I drove north. We had run through the plan so often that doing it seemed like being in a movie that we had seen too many times—if never quite to the end.

Listening to the story, Robby nodded.

"Man, that's a good feeling," he said. "I used to feel the same way when I was finally on the road to go cook a big batch. On the road about to make something happen, yes sir."

I told him happiness was not exactly the feeling. I had been happy shooting hoops with my father. I had been happy out hunting on the farm when I was in high school. I had been happy chasing girls around David City. That was a lively kind of happiness. This was something else—an anxious feeling twisted up right underneath my navel, but, yes, it was a relief to be in motion.

When we were a few towns away from the bank in Petersburg, we started to look for a car to steal. Neither of us knew how to hot-wire a car, so we needed to find one with the keys in it, which isn't too hard in a small town on a Sunday evening. We needed a car that was nondescript, so no one would recognize it. "Oh, here comes Dr. Smith's car with two punks in it."

We thought the parking lot of a church might be a good place, since everyone would be inside for a long time. That's what happened. Wearing a ball cap and work gloves, I walked along a sidewalk with Tom following a little ways behind in the car. I saw keys dangling in an ignition. It was a Chrysler New Yorker, a car that would not have any mechanical problems.

I nodded to Tom. I looked around and just did it.

I really felt like a jerk for doing it.

I was driving out of town, fast, but not too fast. Suddenly I couldn't figure which street would take me to the highway.

I pulled onto a wide street and nearly collided with Tom. I followed him out to the highway. I was a nervous wreck. I had never committed a felony.

There was a pocket radio scanner plugged into Tom's ear to monitor the cops. He was very professional about all this. He was exactly the kind of partner in crime you would want to have, except for his conscience, which was a bit too developed for this work. He stayed ahead of me, driving and listening. I had my eye constantly on the rearview mirror, sure we would see a cop blinking after us any second. You can see it in your mind: a guy rushes into the church, says, "Hey Bill, some kid just drove away in your car." They get on the phone to the sheriff, and it's off to the races. You see that in your mind and you feel stupid, like, how did I think we could get away with this?

Tom's turn signal was suddenly blinking. He turned onto a gravel road and I followed. I could see why. On the highway ahead were the flashing red and blue lights of a cop car. Was it a roadblock, or just somebody stopped for a ticket? We couldn't chance it. We took back roads to the abandoned farm. I kept listening for sirens behind us but they never came.

We stashed the stolen car in the barn and drove the Tempo farther down the highway to Norfolk, where we checked into a cheap hotel using Tom's name. That doesn't seem too bright, but we couldn't obtain any fake identification. Monday morning arrived. It's hard to pull yourself out of bed when you know your life is going to change that day or maybe end. I felt the cool of the pillow for a few seconds more. Then I sucked up the air and sat up to do it, to have a new life, short or long.

We drove to Tom's family farm property and stashed the Tempo. From there we drove the big grain truck to the abandoned farm above Petersburg, jumped in the stolen car, and drove down to the bank. In town we noticed a sheriff's patrol car parked about half a block from the bank. We rolled past the bank a second and third time, killed some time out of town, came back, and the sheriff's car was still parked there.

We went back to the abandoned farm to wait and think. We cruised around and found another abandoned farm, this one with an old chicken coop, leaning and almost collapsed. There wasn't anything else around. If the thing caught fire, it would probably be doing someone a favor. And it would likely make a plume of smoke so that the volunteer fire department, and any deputy in town, would go roaring out to see what was up.

We sat on a hill and watched the town. We looked over at the hill where a few generations of chicken feathers produced a greasy streak of smoke across the sky. The town remained still; no siren sounded or light blinked. No person moved on the street. The whole town had the look of one of those fake towns they built in the 1950s to test atom bombs.

"What do you think?" Tom asked.

"I think the whole town fell asleep," I said.

"They're probably looking out their windows and thinking, thank God somebody finally burned that ugly chicken coop," Tom said. "Maybe we should just take all this as a sign. Maybe we should just go home. We don't need to do this," he said.

"I need this, Tom. If I don't rob a bank, I'm going to jail for sure. If I do rob a bank, I'll have some money for a lawyer and maybe I won't go to jail. It's backward, I know, but it is what it is."

Tom stood glaring but didn't answer me.

"With or without you, I'm doing it," I said. "You don't have to. Give me the keys and you take the grain truck back to the Tempo and go home. I'll make do with the stolen car. Just let me have the keys."

He spun the key ring on his finger for maybe half a minute. I would not see a look that serious on a man again until prison.

"There's no way I'm letting you go down there alone," he said.

We suited up, gunned up, and headed for the Petersburg State Bank. The deputy's car was still there, but we figured we would ignore it and hope for the best.

People who say they don't get scared when committing crimes like robberies are either high on crack or liars or both. From the moment I walked into the bank, every part of my body wanted to walk back out. I was sweating profusely, my heart rate was elevated, and I had that eerie feeling of hypersensitivity, like I had some sort of super power of hearing, smell, and sight.

I walked in first, dressed as a construction worker with big boots, coveralls, a hardhat, and a mask covering everything but my eyes. As I stepped inside the double doors, I expected all eyes to be on me, but people were busy. A teller was handing a deposit slip to a customer, and a manager was talking with a farmer in an office to the side of me. I noticed a banner with the high school football schedule displayed.

There was a brief moment of calm before I dropped the metal toolbox to the floor. I almost didn't want to drop it, but I did.

When it landed, everyone jumped. I calmly unzipped my coveralls and pulled the rifle from the right leg—I had walked in stiff legged—and announced the day's revised agenda.

"This . . . is . . . a . . . robbery!" I shouted.

From the corner of my right eye I saw movement in the office as the manager and a farmer moved toward the glass vestibule through which I had just entered. I wasn't worried, because I knew Tom would soon enter, cutting them off from escape. He did.

People sort of smiled or looked confused, like Who put you up to this? A teller asked if it was a joke, with a stare that made me understand that such jokes were certainly not welcome. I had to yell again at everybody to get down.

They finally understood it was serious. People dropped, their bellies touching the polished floor. Tom grabbed the canvas bags from the toolbox and went to the tellers' tills. He emptied them.

He wanted me to keep a vigilant eye on the windows facing the street, to see if the sheriff's deputy was coming. We had a modified system of nicknames pulled from the movie Reservoir Dogs, like I was Mr. Red and he was Mr. Black, so we could use those names if we had to yell at each other. He suddenly wanted me to keep a better eye on the windows. He meant to yell, "Check the windows, Mr. Red." What he said was, "Check the windows, Hopwood!"

For a brief moment, I thought about pointing the gun barrel toward my own head and pulling the trigger, but I figured I could always do that later. I might as well play out the scene.

A lady entered the double glass doors, about to come inside the bank. Through the inner glass door she studied me—first the mask, then the rifle at my side. She smiled and entered anyway.

I ordered her to the floor. She was nervously shaking on the ground. But I tried not to think about it. I focused on the small tasks. Check the window. Survey the room. Check my watch. Check the window again. Yell at Tom—not by name—to hurry because we were already into our third minute.

Tom emptied the tills down to the change. He was living in an apartment with coin-operated laundry and had decided to take the quarters; his plan was that he would never need quarters for laundry again. He told me before the robbery that all the quarters would be his, and I almost thought that was half his reason for going ahead with the thing.

We locked everyone in the vault. Nobody cried. We said they would be out and safe in just a few minutes. It was, in fact, our intention to call the cops ourselves if we didn't hear on the scanner that the people were soon out.

The plan was for Tom to exit the bank first and jump

in the driver's side, since he would be driving. I would come out behind him with the bags of money.

But when we left the bank he walked to the passenger's side, opened the door, and plopped himself down on the seat. He looked up at me, and he could read my expression even through the mask I was wearing.

Tom was normally the calm one.

We sped at ninety down the highway for five miles before turning onto the gravel road. Once we arrived at the farm, we drove the car as far into the woods as we could. We switched from coveralls to farm boy attire. With my rifle, with the moneybags, and with the portable scanner— listening to the dispatch commotion through the earpiece—I sat on the bed of the grain truck.

As the truck rolled slowly away from Petersburg, the scanner lit up with cop chatter—it was pandemonium. The good news was that everyone was out of the vault. The bad news was they had provided excellent descriptions of us already.

The Norfolk police dispatcher that day was a girl we both knew. Trish had graduated from David City a year before us, and her husband, Scott, was a friend and classmate of ours.

He had been the football team quarterback and the basketball point guard—the guy who had thrown me a couple thousand bounce passes to start our motion offense.

The cops started yelling over the scanner. They said they had the vehicle spotted and were about to take it down. I clutched my rifle and waited for the grain truck to either pick up speed or stop. I couldn't communicate with Tom up front, but I figured he would soon see the blinking lights of the cop cars. There was nothing I could do. I guessed it was all over.

Then maybe two minutes later there was a shout on the scanner.

"We got 'em. They did not resist. We have them in custody. No sign of weapons or money."

Twin boys, eighteen years old, had been pulled over at gunpoint while we ambled into thin air. The twins were questioned and later released. We owe them an apology for sure.

We had successfully robbed our first bank. We split $50,000.

A week later we met at a bar in Lincoln. Tom felt terrible about what we had done. So did I. He thought we should give the money back. I didn't.

"We could just send it to them in a box, with a note of some kind."

"What kind of a note?"

He tried a few ideas for notes, but they didn't make much sense. Something about how they should tighten their security or stop robbing farmers blind, but I'm sure they weren't doing any such thing.

"Listen, man, we have the money and we are not giving it back," I said. "That's how bank robbery is done. You keep it. It's a risk and reward thing."

Tom decided to just go back to college and have a life and hope this thing never caught up with him. He would use the money for tuition.

He almost made it work. A year and a half later,

when he was finally arrested, and after I had held up four more banks without him, he was taken down and cuffed right as he was coming out from taking a test. He was a criminal justice major. There was a chance he would have applied to become an FBI agent. He would have been a good one. When you think about it, the world is full of people doing good work because they never got caught doing that very stupid something when they were younger and crazier. Of course, we were way over the top in that department.

The money didn't do me any good, by the way. I went to jail anyway a few weeks later for buying my underage brother beer. That's when Pastor Marty Barnhart came to see me, wanting to save me. But I was already planning the next bank job.

11
BEAUTIFUL LIGHTNING

Mail call. The big plastic tub was dragged in, scraping along the concrete floor. We waited on our perches, hoping to be called down. I would often receive encouraging letters, as I said, and by this time I was also receiving legal mail relating to the work I was doing for the other guys.

It was December of 2000, almost two years since my arrival at Pekin. Back home, except to my family, I was becoming a forgotten man.

"Hopwood!"

I walked down the steel stairs. It was a postcard. I looked at the return address. It was from Ann Marie Metzner. What the . . . ? I tried not to look excited, but there was a small bounce in my step on the way back up to my cell.

Mom had mentioned a few months earlier that Ann Marie had asked for my address, but I didn't believe she would actually write. I simply couldn't fathom the possibility.

For a minute I couldn't bring myself to read it. I stared at her neat printing, with tiny circles dotting her i's.

I read the card. I read it again as I paced the cell. Robby came in and I tossed the card down like it was a trivial piece of junk mail. After he left, I read it once, twice, maybe ten times. The card had a faint scent of perfume—surely the result of resting next to an envelope doused in perfume from some other woman sent to some other prisoner.

Ann Marie wrote to say hello and to ask if I needed anything. She had been following my situation through her visits with Mom at the office. She mentioned, in a few words, her engagement and about problems with an eating disorder. I knew from things Mom had said that Ann Marie had been fighting anorexia and that her health had been damaged by it. I knew she had turned her college studies to nutrition as a way of fighting back.

Prison life is made bearable by fantasies. I thought I already had a quality one with the imagined paralegal career.

Some guys imagine they will own a strip club and have gorgeous girls hanging on them. Or, like I said, they'll be rap stars. Some just want to get back to a farm or family. I had always tried to keep my fantasies within the realm of reality.

But with this card it was suddenly difficult not to imagine a friendship with Ann Marie. I could no doubt learn something from this woman. Maybe some of her kindness would rub off on me. And maybe I could give her strength through letters and an understanding of her situation.

Yeah, right, like she needed anything from a guy in the joint. I kept picking up the card and wondering exactly how real it was. It seemed real.

I wrote back immediately. I'm not one of those guys who needs days to process something. The reply ran too long at first, so I rewrote it. I wanted my handwriting to appear neat, but that was a task beyond me. I rewrote it again.

The first thing I asked was whether she had written out of sympathy, for either me or my mom. I didn't need that.

Friends, I needed—sympathy, not so much. I asked if that was why she was writing. Assuming she wasn't writing out of sympathy, I was also concerned that one wrong word might make her swim away from her little nibble, never to write again. So I wrote the initial letter over and over again, hoping to choose just the right words. In closing the letter, I asked her to please write again, and I asked if she might send some pictures, as I was curious to see what she looked like.

I figured it would take a day or two for her to receive the letter, a day for it to sit on her desk, a day for her reply, and then it would have to go through the mail, if she replied at all.

I had sent her a sufficiently inappropriate, too long, too personal reply, surely asking for more than she was willing to give. But prison dreams prosper in the thinnest of soils, so I kept standing at the rail for her reply.

Finally, there it was, handed to me like it might have been any piece of mail from just anybody.

"Here you go, bud."

It was not a card this time but a manila envelope, fat with a letter on stationery and several pictures, including a few professional glossies from her modeling days. It was like the fat acceptance letter you receive from the college admissions office instead of the thin rejection. I sat on my bunk and placed my headphones—the ones I had bought after Bobbie wrecked my first set—over my ears, not for music but to block out the prison chatter. I let some silence settle in before

I started reading.

The letter was an invitation deeper into her world—into her health problems, her fears about life. My letter to her had been a calculated manipulation to hook her into another letter, but after reading her thoughts and fears laid out so intimately, it was my heart that had the hook in it.

Dear Shon,

Okay, I want to be clear about one thing. I definitely did not write you out of sympathy. I wrote you because deep in my heart it was something I really wanted to do. I have thought about you often throughout the last few years and always wondered how you were. I have wanted to write you for a long time but didn't have the courage to until now. I was so afraid you would be upset by my contacting you or that you wouldn't even remember who I was. But I finally decided that was a chance I would have to take. So my intentions are pure—I am writing you simply because I want to. And I hope that we will continue to correspond.

I find it rather funny that you said you used to follow me a couple of blocks when you would see me out running. What is

*even funnier is that I remember getting an adrenaline rush every
time I saw you drive by when I was running. I might as well
admit to you that I had the hugest crush on you from the first
time I ever saw you. But I never thought in a million years that
I would catch your eye.*

Ann Marie Metzner had a crush on me in high
school? Right. For a second I thought someone was
playing a cruel joke on me. That someone had some girl
write this letter to mess with my head. Maybe someone
from back home who despised me?

The letter went on to fill in some of the gaps in
her story: how her NCAA Division I running days at
Creighton had been cut short by a serious bone frac-
ture caused by poor nutrition because of her anorexia;
how she had studied nutrition after that; and how she
was now helping her father to diversify KV from animal health supplies into human nutrition products.
She said she loved visiting with my mom at the office
and assured me that this was not my mom's idea. That
claim, of course, was met with some skepticism. I may
never know for sure.

I can tell you with confidence that the medium of the
handwritten word is the superior one—with physical
separation the walls of ego and security crumble. Also,
you have the luxury of pondering your words before
communicating.

If we'd been face-to-face the chance of my mouth
making a mistake would have been far greater.

After a few letters, I noticed she was struggling with
something, but I didn't know what it was. Then in
August of 2001:

Shon,

>*I just wanted to write you a quick note to let you know about a major decision I made this last week. As we have discussed a little, I have struggled quite a bit this last year with the anorexia. I haven't told you much about it yet, but I promise I will. Anyway, my health has begun to deteriorate rather rapidly in the last two weeks and my osteoporosis has worsened significantly, leaving me in daily excruciating pain from several small-scale fractures in my back, pelvis, hip, and leg. With each passing day it has been harder and harder to walk. This situation combined with many other signs I have received in the past two weeks has led me to make a tough decision. I will be leaving to go to a place called Mirasol in Tucson.*
>
>*It has become very clear that if I continue with my life here as I have been doing, I will die, and I do not want that. I want to live.*

I was concerned that before I had the chance to really know Ann Marie she would be gone. When she had settled into Mirasol, she sent me a note:

>*I have many moments of utter despair and hopelessness. And many moments where my entire body shakes as I cry from the pain, anger, sadness, and confusion I hold inside. It is very intense here at Mirasol and I am very disconnected from the world. I only get to use the phone twice a week for about 15 minutes and I do not have access to television, radio, newspaper, or magazines.*

I could relate. I later learned the reason that the clinic is so strict. Eating disorders are among the toughest mental health disorders to treat. And anorexics are notorious for ditching their food, sneaking in exercise, and doing whatever it takes not to gain weight. It takes round-the-clock supervision to force them to gain weight. Ann Marie, I would learn, had dropped to sixty-seven pounds and was on the brink of death.

> *They want us to just focus on our healing.*
> *Sometimes I feel so trapped here and trapped in my own mind with all the horrible thoughts and feelings that I cannot escape. They keep telling me that the worse I am feeling is progress and I just have to work through it. And I know that is true, but moments seem almost unbearable. I stepped outside the other night and was looking at the beautiful sky filled with stars. And I thought of you, said a little prayer and felt the connection we share.*
> *In that moment, I understood what it feels like for you to be in prison. Even though I am not physically in prison, I live in the prison of my own mind.*

Annie, which is what I now called her, was worried about my state of mind, even when she should have been focused on her own recovery. In every letter, she asked if there was something she could do to make my time pass more quickly, to make life easier.

> *Dear Shon,*
>
> *Thanks for sharing so much with me and for trusting me. I believe I was spiritually guided to write you. I believe that there is a special connection between us and that there is a lot we can learn from each other.*
> *Take care Shon!*
>
> *Love,*
> *Ann Marie*

Was the word "love" just the customary courtesy? Did she write it just to be nice? If it was love, what kind was it? The love of a good friend? Something more?

I knew I shouldn't, but it was happening anyway; I was falling for a woman I knew only from scrawled letters and high school fantasies, and who was now evaporating before I could ever touch her.

I had formed two delusional ideas. Maybe I could have a life with Annie. I had eight years left in prison, but it's possible she would wait for me. It's possible that she would one day love me despite my circumstances.

Although she said she was engaged, I shut that out. People get engaged. They also go to dentists and buy car insurance. It's just a routine thing between birth and death. It isn't final. People break off engagements all the time. There are Hallmark cards for it, something people from David City know because Mr. Hall of Hallmark fame was born there.

The second impossible idea was that it would be difficult to win her if I didn't think bigger than I had been thinking. My universe was expanding because of her. Maybe I could go to law school? Become a lawyer? Near impossible, but worth thinking about.

I was, after all, becoming a decent jailhouse lawyer. So good, in fact, that I was in trouble with Ryan and a few other jailhouse lawyers for taking some of their "clients" away from them. Clients were a good thing to have, as they tended to be very grateful if you could help cut some years off their sentences. Some Friday nights I was up to my gills in pasta.

And I was making friends across racial lines and even earning some respect from the guards.

The idea of being a real lawyer someday just sort of blended into my Annie fantasy. I thought about mentioning it in a letter. Or maybe I shouldn't.

I talked to Bobbie about it as we were working out. He understood that I was becoming fixated with these twin passions: Annie and the law.

He asked me about her. I guess he couldn't know what to advise me if he didn't have a sense of what she was like. I told him some of what I knew, but held back certain parts, like her struggles with anorexia. I didn't want Bobbie to judge her without knowing the entire story, because most people don't understand the disorder.

"Quit being such a chump," he finally said. "I think you really are interested in this law thing. You're just scared. I don't think you're fooling yourself. Man up with her about it. But at the same time, I mean, you don't have to oversell it."

"You don't think it's a bit of a stretch?"

"If it is, who gives a—"

"I do. I don't want to lie to her."

"Maybe that's what she needs. She might need someone who has cajones enough to chase after big dreams. Chicks dig that. Plus, maybe she needs that in her life, something big and inspirational."

We worked out in silence for a minute.

"The thing is, maybe it's not bull if you put it out there, even before you can say it's a sure thing."

"We both know it's nowhere close to a sure thing," I said.

"Then make it come true. I think you should go ahead and tell her that this is what you're doing so she can see who you are. She's a smart girl. I don't think she'll judge you based on whether it happens. But make sure you let her know she is your inspiration."

That was the truth.

Just the same, what I wrote her was that my dream was to become a paralegal at some law firm. I didn't want to sound like a delusional idiot.

Shon,

Ya know, you mentioned that you would like to get a job with a great law firm. Well, here is what I think about that. To heck with working for a firm, you are so intelligent and so good with legal work that I could see you getting a law degree and opening up your own darn firm! Whatever you decide your heart is calling you to do, I know you will always be very successful in your endeavors.

Love,
Annie

She was always two steps ahead. As I read her letter, I suddenly believed it to my core. Just knowing she saw it made it all real, and I could see myself doing it, being it. One way or the other, my life was going to change because of her. Her contacting me was like some intervention; it felt more like a religious experience to me than anything I had experienced before. This was new for me.

After that letter I had the nerve to ask Annie if I could call her.

The last time I had heard her voice was back in high school—a lifetime ago. I knew she had a very limited ability to take calls at Mirasol, but I asked anyway. She didn't reply.

I started standing on the balcony during mail call to be that much closer to the stairs and not miss my name. Every time they said "Hopwood," I shot down the stairs. Letters from family, from friends, always so welcome before, were now stained with disappointment because they were not from Annie.

My trip down the stairs slowed a little. I settled into the idea that we were writing friends and nothing more. I had blown it by trying to break through the wall of our platonic pen pal situation.

She was engaged after all. I was just her brother confessor—someone safe like a monk, locked away for private prayers and whispers. I was officially outcast from the world, so communication with me could be more intimate than if I had been, say, a young chamber of commerce type back in town. I was privacy itself, a fellow cave dweller. But the vision of someday having a life with her would not leave my consciousness.

A week later—it seemed like forever—she wrote to set up a time for me to call. I called. Her voice was innocent and gentle—the ideal elixir for my world of imprisonment.

The call was short but it made me even more anxious to win her. I could not afford one wrong move. I would be the friend, the old hermit with the long beard and kind eyes. I was stuck in time and could use that time to get to know her perfectly and maybe even make her fall in love with me. I was an optimistic fool.

My energy for everything in life increased. I

expanded my college classes. I continued reading legal opinions. I encouraged her to be healthy every way I could; she was still in great danger. I wanted to be a source of hope.

I suddenly was the only guy in Pekin with a big smile nearly all the time—other than those who smoked too much weed.

When new guys arrived at Illinois One, I became the welcome wagon. I collected snacks and laundry soap, decent shower soaps and shampoos, so that we could sit down with new arrivals and give them something, anything, to cheer them up and make them feel human. The men closest to me knew very well that it was Annie who was doing this to me.

I didn't want to make a big deal about Annie, not publicly, as it could all stop and I'd look stupid. So I soft-pedaled it. Besides, she was engaged. She was not my girl.

But when I taped her portrait up in my cell, guys accused me of cutting it out of a fashion magazine.

"Well, you look happy today. You must have got a letter from your girl?" Bobbie said plenty of mornings as we worked out.

I would joke it off with something stupid, like saying the only girls he knows are the ones who look back at him from the magazines.

Prison conversations are childish like that, but everyone expects their friends to make dumb remarks, which is the main entertainment for the continually bored. Nobody has good comedy writers to back them up. For that matter, there are no Morgan Freemans to offer up daily wisdom. Beyond the wisecracks of friends, the best entertainment in prison is guards tripping and falling, gossip, fights, and the endless Seinfeld reruns.

...

In July of 2001 Annie left Mirasol and headed home. In November she sent me a letter saying she wanted to come visit. We were all still in shock after 9/11, and there was a great emotional shift in the country. I was horrified that some inmates seemed to welcome the terrorist attack. They viewed an attack against the Twin Towers as an attack against the government that had locked them up. And yes, I know that most twelve-year-olds have higher reasoning capacity than that.

The comments alienated me from some of them and made me realize how out of place I was, or had become. I just wanted to hug Annie and then sign back up for active service. That was my big reaction to 9/11, besides the anger and nausea of those days. Every time you looked at the dayroom televisions, it was the towers falling and three thousand people dying until you just couldn't stand it.

The trip to Pekin from Omaha is about an eight-hour drive. There are papers you must fill out to visit, so I sent her everything and hoped she would go through with it.

The plan was for her to arrive the day after Thanksgiving, which was also the day my Cornhuskers were matched against Colorado for a shot at the national title. The first half was disastrous. The Buffaloes ran the ball at will and we could not stop them. The third quarter started better, and our Heisman quarterback, Eric Crouch, was leading a comeback. Just as the fourth quarter began my name was called. I had a visitor.

I backed away from the game screen, torn between two heavens. Annie won.

I had been thinking all week about how to approach her. I could walk over to her, hug her, and thank her for the visit. She would expect that. It would be the conventional thing. The other approach involved something different— something that might end with me getting slapped. But what was there to lose? I was already in prison. Don't get scared now.

She was seated in the visiting area when I walked in. She recognized me instantly, which was a relief— you do change after a few years. But she saw me and smiled.

"I'm glad you're here, Annie," I said. I took her face in my hands and I kissed her on her mouth.

It was the best five seconds I spent in prison.

I led her to a table, pulled out a chair for her, and we visited for hours. Her engagement ring featured a large diamond. It meant nothing, I assured myself. Women receive these things all the time, and they wear them for a while and then send them back.

She spent the night at a nearby hotel and came back to visit me the next day, Saturday.

The diamond ring was no longer on her finger.

The fresh little furrow in her finger was stark white and her finger looked happy to be free of the tiny shackle. She appeared more peaceful.

"You're not wearing your ring today?"

"I was supposed to be with him and his family yesterday."

"So why aren't you?"

"We have both been going through the motions. We have called off the engagement four or five times. Our relationship hasn't been the same for a while."

She was quiet, studying her finger. She looked up at me with those green eyes.

"I'm sorry," I said. I sort of meant it.

"It's not fair to anyone to keep pretending," she said.

"And I can't help the way I feel about you. I didn't plan this."

"This . . . yes, what is this?"

"It's . . . It's I don't know what," she said.

We were quiet but then began to visit like friends. We talked about the books we had read. Annie didn't own a TV, so books were her primary form of entertainment. I had been devouring novels, old and new, between law books.

She preferred spiritual "awakening" books. My latest reads were *Fight Club*, *Requiem for a Dream*, and *Blood Meridian*, books that young men in prison should probably avoid.

"What do you want to do in the next eight years?" I asked her.

"I want to get healthy, become a better person," she said.

She looked away and I could tell her struggle with anorexia was an embarrassment.

"What do you want to do?" she asked.

"Make these years disappear," I said.

She came back Sunday. Sometimes we just watched the room in silence, surrounded by armed guards, barbed wire, and baby mamas.

"I will make you a deal," I said.

"What kind of deal?"

I looked around the room. Many lies were being told around the visiting room tables. I would not do that.

"If you are healthy when I get out, I will come find you and marry you."

"Okay," she said.

I had thought of it the night before and though it was a spur of the moment decision, I knew it wasn't the kind of statement that people pass off as the truth. I meant it.

Her smile said she didn't believe me—maybe she didn't think she would be alive. Or maybe she thought that men, even ones who are locked up, just don't have an eight-year attention span.

After her visit, the word spread that for some strange reason a supermodel had come to visit the legal nerd, Shon.

"Why would that be strange?" I said to a guy on the yard. But inside I knew it was beyond strange.

After the visit, while we were in line at the chow hall, Bobbie asked me about Annie being in a Sports Illustrated story. Someone heard him talking to me and assumed that Annie was in the swimsuit edition. News spread quickly.

Without knowing it I was earning some juice; a visit from a beautiful woman earns you respect outside and in.

12
THE BIG SNAG

Each letter from Annie lifted me—each like a tiny pardon, a temporary reprieve from my day-to-day surroundings. She gave me confidence to push forward harder with my schoolwork and the law.

I took on a new batch of habeas cases that Ryan was intent on giving me grief about. "If you need to do that, take it to your cell tonight, Shon. Take all the stuff you want, but for now get back to shelving books and updating the records."

He was right that I was spending most of my time reading books like *Federal Habeas Corpus Practice and Procedure* instead of doing the grunt work. But he was primarily upset because people were asking me legal questions and not him. And he didn't like it that I was sometimes missing his weed sessions in his cell, which served as his office meetings.

He insisted that I come to his cell for the meeting that evening because something was up.

"So who do you think is snitching on us?" he asked. Several of us had been called for pee tests that always coincided with the days after we had smoked. But those drug tests could be evaded by drinking lots of water because it diluted the urine.

"I don't know who it is, but I would pay to find out!" Milan said.

Roger, a junkie from Minnesota, had already been busted twice—once for weed, once for heroin. His favorite form of entertainment was taunting known snitches.

"I'd love to catch the rat that got me," he said. "I would take off his face with a cup of good stuff." What he meant by "good stuff" was a prison concoction of baby oil and Magic Shave, the gel used by the black guys to remove stubble. The mixture was heated in a microwave and then thrown on someone's face, producing disfiguring burns. But Roger was only talking big; he never really did anything like that.

The meeting went downhill from there, reduced to rumors about who was scheming with whom. I split early; I just didn't have the time or the inclination to be stoned all the time. Not anymore.

Sometimes Bobbie would come over so we could go smoke with Ryan. After one of these meetings Ryan decided to hit us with it.

"We have a snag," Ryan announced. "The thing is . . . ," he stumbled. "The thing is, we kinda smoked up all the weed, and, you know, it kinda belonged to the Crips."

"Then ask them for some more," Bobbie said.

"You don't understand," Ryan continued. "We done smoked up my ounce, and we done smoked up all the weed the Crips had stashed in the library. We smoked it all up. They are going to be coming for their regular pickup in a day or two, and there ain't nothing left but some worthless stems and seeds."

The more Ryan talked, the more he used the pronoun "we." But it wasn't we who had deliberately smoked up all the Crips' weed. But the Crips knew we spent time smoking it in Ryan's cell, so he was right, we would all pay.

I had to convince Bobbie not to beat Ryan, even though I wanted to do just the same. Bobbie knew the drug business, knew the Crips, and knew this was serious. They would have to make an example of us. We would be hurt, and maybe one of us would be killed. Our vote, if we had one, would be for Ryan to be the guy.

Bobbie knew a lot of the drug dealers in Pekin, and I knew guys through the ball teams, but not many Crips; they weren't much on sports because they were too busy doing business. I could, of course, nod to them on the yard and they would nod back because they had seen me play, but they were not my friends.

If Bobbie and I took it to our car of friends, they would have our backs, because that's the deal. Of course, that would just start a war. I wasn't going to do that, nor was Bobbie. This had the potential to seriously hurt too many people if we made it a group-versus-group thing.

The Crips were different from other gangs. They were always the hungry sharks in the water, the kind who didn't mind conflict.

We kept everything to ourselves for a day, until Ryan had time to scheme. I knew I could count on his slippery mind—if he could slip it in gear soon enough.

That evening it seemed like some of the Crips were looking at me in the chow line. Maybe they always returned glances that way, but it seemed different, like they were wondering if it would be better to skewer my liver from the front or the back.

I am not prone to paranoia, but I thought we should move with whatever it was we were going to do in the way of a plan.

"We gotta be smarter, that's all," Bobbie told me as we were working out the next morning and nobody was nearby.

We tried thinking of a plan, but Ryan beat us to it. Ryan was chummy with the staff in the library, and he told one of the women guards that a gang was stashing contraband in the law library.

When I arrived at the library the door was blocked by two guards. The place was being ripped apart.

"You can't go in, Hopwood," one of the guards said.

"What's going on?"

"Seems your little Walgreens is going out of business."

"Where you going to get your Depends?" I replied. He didn't understand. I walked away.

They found a few empty bags of weed shake—mostly sticks and stems—plus some heroin, a dozen well-made shanks, and two new boxes of syringes that could only have come from the prison medical facility. The amount of drugs and the syringes suggested something the guards didn't want to think about: at least one of them was dirty.

If you went to the wrong staff person to snitch about the stash, it could all go wrong very quickly. Ryan was lucky, we were lucky. But we still had to worry about the Crips thinking we were to blame.

The guards were sneaky. They knew Ryan had dropped the dime, but to make it look good and to gather more information, they called everyone who worked in the law library to the lieutenant's office. They questioned all of us about where that stuff had come from. When I suggested that the boxes of syringes weren't made in the prison, the lieutenant nearly came unglued.

"What are you trying to say?" he said.

"Nothing, I am trying to say nothing about nothing," I said.

"Do you know if my staff is giving this stuff to prisoners?" he asked. We both already knew the answer.

"Nope, I was just saying that boxes of syringes aren't made here."

"That's all you know, smart mouth?"

"That's all I know, Lieutenant."

The fallout came without delay.

Ryan lost his job and was sent to the hole for two weeks. Little did the guards know that he had the remainder of the weed keistered up his behind, along with some matches. Anytime he needed a smoke in solitary, he just reached up, pulled the bag out, and rolled some "butt weed."

I lost my job, as did everyone else who worked in the law library, but we weren't sent to the hole.

I worried that without the law library my legal career would stall. It would be much harder to study law if I returned to work in the kitchen.

And I didn't know how the Crips were taking all this. The funny looks from them continued. My paranoia spiked. Maybe some staffer had found out from other staffers that there had been no weed in the haul and had found out that somebody had snitched, costing the Crips all the rest of their stuff. The Crips seemed to be still measuring me with cold stares.

I received a couple of brief respites from the Crips mess. The first was a letter from Tom, who was finishing out his four-year term in a low-security prison in Minnesota. It seemed like the kind of letter you might receive before dying, if God wanted to help wrap things up for you. I had always felt guilty for not laughing off Tom's bank idea. That's what a friend should have done.

Wood,

> *It's been a long time, I know. I got your pictures the other day of you and Ann. Only you, Wood, could pull something like that off. On top of that it happens while you're doing a twelve piece for the Feds. I'm happy for you bro—I really am. Ann's the kind of woman who might be able to pull this off and stick with you all the way to the door. Even if she doesn't she's still a five-star general for having the courage to swim upstream and go after something she wants, despite what anyone thinks.*

> *That's so cool—that's movie stuff.*

> *I hope you understand why I haven't stayed in better touch. Kind of like race car drivers who don't go to funerals, it's just hard right now considering the circumstances. The exciting news for me is this is my year. The way things are looking I should be in Council Bluffs by June!! And just to make sure we're clear, things between you and me are the same as they've been since fourth grade. We're boys—period.*

*Within a year I'll be back in a position where I can help
you. I realize there isn't much I can do, but at the same time I
know there are many little things that can be done—somebody
you can rely on to get those little things done. I know many of
our friends, even the boys have "moved on" and just left you
hanging.*

*I'm going to do whatever I can to have your back through
this thing. There's no cure-all—no easy way out—and it kills
me to think how high your hill still is for you—it's going to be
hard. But one thing I know you're not looking for is pity—it's
something we just got to ride out—one day at a time. Just
know that you and I have never been better.*

*I send you the best bro—take care of that girl, you got the
one you wanted and you know she's worth it—get yourself
right.*

Tom

Tom's letter boosted my mood, as did Annie's second visit. The visiting room rules say you are allowed a hug and kiss when you first meet your visitor, and then again when your visitor leaves. I pushed that rule to its boundary, because when Annie entered I gave her a kiss lasting about two minutes. I figured, legally, if our lips continued to touch it was still one kiss.

"I have some good news," Annie said afterward. "I applied to Bastyr University in Seattle. They have the largest natural health arts school in the country."

"What are natural health arts?" This sounded kind of hokey, but I didn't say that.

"Like acupuncture, naturopathic medicine, and nutrition. I applied for the nutrition program. I had to write essays and go through a number of interviews. It is really hard to get in there."

"But you did?"

"I did."

I gave her a congratulatory kiss, which certainly shouldn't be counted. I saw the guard McDonough walking our way. McDonough was famous for two things: for tormenting inmates and for screwing up.

One night he was manning the fence controls when two Mexican prisoners snuck out of their unit and started throwing rocks at the fence. The fence sensors went off, and he radioed the trucks that circle the perimeter to check it out.

They drove by but saw nothing. Once they left, the Mexicans threw rocks again. It was a windy night, and after a while McDonough assumed that the wind was playing havoc with the sensors on the fence. He shut the sensors off, and the Mexicans climbed the fence and escaped. McDonough was the laughingstock of the compound, which only made him less pleasant.

"Do you not understand the rules, Hopwood? No kissing."

As Annie and I talked, McDonough stared us down from behind the desk. I looked around the visiting room. People were groping each other and some were making out.

Annie came back the next day, too. We were sitting next to each other when McDonough came over to our table.

"Hopwood you're done," he said.

"What do you mean?"

"I warned you yesterday. Your visit's over."

Annie started crying. She had driven eight hours and stayed overnight in the hotel so we could visit for the entire weekend.

"Can you at least tell me what we did?"

"You know. She had her hand on your knee."

"Is this a joke?"

"No joke. Say your good-byes because this visit is over."

Annie was crying more. I tried to calm her down. It didn't work. I envisioned grabbing McDonough by his scrawny neck and twirling him around the way a hunter puts a pheasant out of its misery.

"Don't worry, Annie, someday this will all be over."

I didn't understand why he kicked her out until I was back in the unit explaining it to Bobbie.

"Well, that's easy to see," he said. "McDonough is a hater. You think he likes seeing a beautiful girl visiting you in prison when he can't even get a date in the trailer park?"

Bobbie went on to say that I should expect more of it, that some guards would treat us differently precisely because Annie was who she was.

...

On a Monday I was waiting for news about a new job. I had no plans after the law library meltdown, so I worked out and ran on the track for hours. I wanted to isolate myself, and the track was a good place to avoid interruptions. When I returned to the unit, C-Dog, the leader of the Crips and the guy whose stuff had been hidden in the library, pulled me aside before I could reach my cell door. He had a bad stutter, which got worse when he was angry.

"Sh-sh-sh-shon, can we talk?"

I had no choice.

"I need to know what the k-k-cops were asking you about, man. Tell me how the, the, that all went down."

"What can I say? It was bad. I lost my job. Now I don't know if I can continue with the legal work I'm doing for people."

"And th-th-the other stuff, our stuff?"

Another Crip, Bubba, walked up next to C-Dog. He is about six three with a tattooed money symbol on his neck.

"What up, Shon?"

"Not much," I said. "We're talking about the law library."

Now Bubba did the talking.

"You like to work the cops with all your bull. Everybody knows that. You're good at it. They buyin' what you're telling them. But you don't like to work us, do you? So you need to tell us straight, so we know what's coming down. Either way you answer is all right, as long as it's the troof." He lied.

"D-d-did you tell them where the stuff came from?"

"No. I told them nothing. I told them I didn't even know it was in there."

"What about R-Ryan?" Bubba asked.

"Ryan didn't tell them anything. That's why he's in the hole. I wouldn't worry about him. If anything he's probably going to want to figure out how to put some new deal together with you."

"What deal?" Bubba asked.

"Nothing, never mind," I said.

"Y-y-you saw them taking stuff out? The guards?"

I still worried that maybe they knew, so I didn't want to ensnare myself in a trap.

"I didn't see them take anything out. I just heard it was a lot of weed. Guys were saying it was a lot, and the cops who interrogated me said it was a lot."

"What did you tell them?"

"I said I really had no idea where it came from and didn't even know it was in there until the bust."

"They believe you?"

"They don't believe anybody."

C-Dog stepped back a little. He put his hand into his pocket. I thought I had done pretty well, but this didn't look good. Maybe he was reaching for a shank.

The muscles in my arms tensed for combat. C-Dog cupped his hand and put it out to shake mine. As I grabbed his hand, he slipped me a piece of paper wrapped into a tight triangle.

"Y-y-you done the right thing, dog," he said, pounding his fist against mine.

Folded in the triangle was a healthy chunk of weed. I called Bobbie over and we smoked our worries away. The crisis was over.

I thought about that moment when I was worried

they might kill me. I realized that I really didn't want to die anymore.

For a long time, that's all I wanted, but not anymore. It was a change that had been brewing. It was one more thing to mark the whittling away of that mountain of time. I had finished the doesn't care if he lives or dies years. Annie and the law had done that.

Annie would drive eight hours to Pekin, visit eight hours, and drive back eight hours, all in one day when she didn't have time to do it any other way. That was dangerous, but she wouldn't stop. She considered moving to an apartment in Pekin for a year—until she started school at Bastyr—because then she could work at home, designing catalogs for her father's business and visit me often. Suddenly, I felt truly responsible for her and I lost confidence.

What on earth was a girl like that doing with a guy like me?

It was like I had just woken up. Maybe the stress of the Crips situation had shifted my gears and reminded me who I was.

What I kept thinking was that the worst thing I could do was to place her life on hold for eight years, after which she could expect a future in which I would probably work in car washes—I mean, get real, that's what it would be. I knew I was doing my self-destruct thing again, but the thought of wasting her time got me the most. I had stolen enough things of value in my life; I didn't need to do this to her, or to anyone so kind and innocent. So I decided to act out and to push her off a little. Maybe she would wise up and find a more suitable guy. But first I would need some liquid courage to do it.

If you take a few quarts of fruit juice, mix it with water and sugar, and let it set somewhere warm, in a week or two you will have homemade wine. In prison it's called hooch. It tastes like I imagine Drano does, and isn't much healthier.

Bobbie purchased a whole gallon. I called Annie after two glasses and slurred a tale about a girl I had once dated whom I said could never be replaced. And I told her not to take all my big talk too seriously, because I was who I was.

She was quiet; she was crushed. I called her to apologize, but she wouldn't take my call. Fine. I didn't deserve her and I should let the clean break stand. Just the same, when I woke up the next day, my heart ached. I tried calling a few times again because I couldn't stand it. She didn't pick up.

So I was going to be who I was, a jerk in prison. It occurred to me before the hooch wore off that I was about the only guy in there without tattoos. Being different had always been my way, but just the same you watch guys getting inked and you think, well, if I ever did get one, what would it be?

That question rolls around in your head all the time for years until you finally know what it would be, and what it would look like, and sometimes you look down or around at your skin and are surprised the tattoo isn't there, like somebody stole it. You have your phantom tattoo and it becomes a part of who you are. I would let the thing have its own dignity, its own place in the visible world, and I didn't even have to ask who the best tattoo artist was. It was Reaper, the guy with the swastika on his forehead.

He was a big, strong man whose arms were twenty inches around. He had long but balding hair.

"Stop staring at it, man," he said when I went to sit down with him and talk about something for my back. "I mean, you got one, too, man."

I asked him what he meant.

"I mean, every white person has one of these right here, whether or not they want to think about it or admit it. I just put mine out there so it's honest. I bet you don't want one, do you, Shon?"

"Not a backward one like yours."

"Cut it out, man."

It was our longstanding joke. I had told him maybe a year earlier, when I learned he had tattooed his own forehead, that he had done it backward. He was irate. He had stormed into my cell when he heard that I was saying that around. I was giving him a hard time just because I didn't much like the look of it.

"How do you know, man?" I asked him. "How do you know you didn't do it backward?"

He fell into my trap. He jumped over to the mirror above the cell's sink and he pointed to it. "Because I can see it, man!" he said.

"But you're looking in the mirror," I reminded him. He stormed out. He didn't have it backward, but it was fun to make him check with his friends.

I had stopped torturing him months ago when I first started thinking maybe I would ask him for a tat.

"I was thinking of another design, and on my back," I now told him. I had brought him a candy bar and a pop, which are not inconsequential host gifts. He had about finished both in the first minute.

"I was thinking of just a little Celtic cross and some words around it, like maybe 'my cross to bear.'"

"What the hell does that mean? And why would you want a cross?"

I had been giving guys a hard time about religion. I had been using my legal logic to make mincemeat of their irrational beliefs. But maybe I was one of those people who protesteth too much, and was just covering my own insecurity about my beliefs. It was the tattoo I had come to see in phantom form, and it had a life of its own and wanted a place on my body. At least I wouldn't have to look at it. If I were to get killed in prison and my body was sent home, maybe it would be a final message to my folks, that I had been listening and that maybe they would see me again. And, really, I was still dealing with a lot of guilt and maybe one way to get this behind me was to literally put it behind me. I think there were a lot of reasons.

We set a date a few Saturdays away. He was a busy tattoo artist and he had an appointment book. He needed it not only because he was busy, but because he had been a meth addict and he was very slow to process things. You could say something to him and sometimes he would just stare at you for a while, letting the message move from his ears to his brain in the way that a lazy cat explores flower beds. Eventually his brain would receive the message and it would process it and then send the cat to his tongue. In addition to his delayed responses, most of his bones had been broken in motorcycle crashes.

All that aside, Reaper could be nice if you happened to be white, and even if you were black and he liked you. I never understood how he could wear all those white supremacy tattoos and then be friends with black guys. And I never understood why the black guys even talked with him.

When the day arrived, I watched him clean his equipment as he laid things out on my bunk. That's the thing you worry about, but he had a good reputation for not causing infections or spreading diseases like HIV.

So I wanted to see the alcohol flow all over his homemade electrical tattoo pen. It did.

His pen was like most of the ones you see in prison. You start with a small electrical motor. We used the one from the beard trimmers they sold at commissary. You find a wheel that goes around at about the right speed, then somehow attach a little arm to one edge of that wheel so the arm will go back and forth like a piston on a camshaft when the wheel turns.

The needles were made at the prison metal factory and then smuggled out. They were really just sharpened wire that jabbed in and out when it was attached to that vibrating thing. You run the needle through the body of an old ballpoint pen with the ball removed. The body of the pen is secured with a bracket and often some tape to the motor.

Now you have a pen that, when attached to power,

has a tiny needle stabbing in and out where the ball of the ballpoint pen used to be. You get a supply of tattoo ink that you bought from a guard. Wait, did I say that out loud? I mean ink that you bought from an inmate. You add a few drops of ink in a toothpaste cap, which the artist holds in his left hand if he is tattooing with his right. That's how it works.

Every few seconds you dip the pen in the ink and then go back to the skin. The needle being just a sharp wire, the whole thing hurts considerably more than tattoos received outside prison, but even pain can be a way to kill time.

"When I get right over your backbone, this is going to hurt like hell," he said. "But don't flinch."

"I won't."

We were in my cell, with me facing the door. I was to tell him if I saw a guard coming—my celly, Robby, who had roomed with Reaper a few times, was watching, too.

Tattooing is against the rules, and tattoo equipment is contraband, but many of the guards look the other way. Sometimes, when a friendly guard was on duty, Reaper would tell him he was going to be doing some work in a particular cell and would the guard please stay away, and the guard would agree to that.

Then you hear the buzz of the contraption and you bend over the back of a chair. It's not quite like the sound of a dentist's drill, but I was put in mind of it. Prison is so noisy that it was just another sound, lost in all the clank and clatter and TV laughter and sports cheers and private sobbing..

13
BAD LUCK TO GOOD

Maybe a criminal is someone whose good luck comes from someone else's bad luck. If so, I was a criminal to Annie. Her difficulty with anorexia was probably the one thing that made her need a truly captive audience like me, someone safe, far away, who would just listen, and who wouldn't impose expectations. That was good luck for me. But I hoped, in turn, that my situation had provided some good luck for her. The one good thing about being locked away is that it really did give me ample time to think about her in an exceptional way and know her as perhaps no one else could.

That doesn't mean I have ever understood anorexia. It is a mystery. You can try to interpret it, but the more you know the less you understand. You can see it sometimes in the animal kingdom, where animals deprived of food morph into a panic of overactivity that makes their situation worse.

And, of course, there are cultural and psychological forces that contribute. But anything I might say about it would cause experts, armchair psychologists, and others who have witnessed it to say, no, that's not it at all. It's something else. That may be the answer: it's a lot of things.

I admired how she dealt with it head-on. She studied it relentlessly to hold mental power over it. Sometimes it would sneak back and grab her, but she would struggle away from it again, sometimes just in the nick of time, before there was nothing left.

Part of her just didn't feel comfortable in this world, didn't feel truly loved, no matter how much true love was given. Imagine being terribly hungry for food all the time but never being satisfied by what you receive. It's like that, but the hunger is for love, and the brain is wrongly wired to think that the way to obtain it is to starve the body. We like to think we can just see or hear the truth and it will overrule the wrong ideas in our heads, but that is not the way it works, is it?

It is very hard work to disable our self-destruct circuits, and particularly hard work for some kinds of faulty wiring. Mine was easier than hers: the wrong wires were showing themselves and I was trying to clip them and put them right. It wasn't that easy for Annie, and I was coming to understand that. You have no idea how much courage it takes some people to do things that to all outward appearances seem routine.

You don't admire the courage involved unless you're able to see deeply inside the person. You see a man walk past a bar and don't know that you might be seeing an act of courage and character to rival any decorated soldier's brave acts.

The more I knew Annie, the more I saw her bravery and the more I loved her great heart.

There is a little veterinary clinic on the main road leading into David City. That was her dad's clinic.

He'd raised cattle, horses, greyhounds, sheep, and rabbits for a time, which fueled his interest in animal medicines and nutritional products. He started buying in bulk for his friends who were also raising greyhounds, and that was the beginning of his business. Over time, he started distributing more and more animal health supplies, and KV Vet Supply just grew with the catalog. It's now 550 pages and takes a great many of David City's wives to produce.

The vet clinic is still there, and the family house next to it is where Annie mostly grew up. Her childhood home had a nice pasture in back and some farm buildings, some cattle and horses, and a small trailer park—it still does. Now her dad rents the house because, when Annie was a senior in high school, he built a nicer but more modest one next to it. He could have built a bigger one than he needed, but people in David City don't do that.

It was a long road to success for Annie's dad. Early on, Annie and her mom and sisters sewed their own clothes, including some they entered in 4-H fairs. She said her dad was preoccupied by the business.

Over time he and Annie would become very close, perhaps because they were so alike; she said her dad demanded a lot of himself, too. But it had been rough when she was young. Growing up, she had competed for her father's attention, partly because any kid wants it, and partly to make him happy so her mom would be happier. To become a source of family pride and happiness, she excelled at running, earned top grades, and became a star in dance recitals and musicals—she's a terrific performer. She pushed herself to achieve an impossible perfection. The Catholic school in David City provided a great education, but it also reinforced this idea that she needed to be perfect, that she needed to work harder—and she needed to feel guilty about normal human desires and imperfections.

By junior high, the reaction of other kids surprised her: they thought she had become remarkably beautiful, and she had. At first she didn't agree, but then she accepted it, which just gave her a new avenue to strive for perfection.

Her older sister developed an eating disorder. Annie assured her mother that such a strange thing would never happen to her. At age fourteen, however, it started. It began after a too-hot date at a high school party where she learned a hard lesson about life. Her Catholic upbringing brought shame crashing down on her. She wanted to get rid of her shameful body. She wanted it to be unattractive to boys. She wanted to be sick enough to be able to say no the next time. She believed she was trash in God's eyes, and she wanted to be tiny and pure and worthy of love again, or to disappear.

That's when the endless running and constant dieting began. Her dad caught her exercising to aerobic videos at 3 a.m. and realized he had another daughter in trouble. By fifteen, she was in a hospital.

Religion had been but another system of authority for me to reject when I was growing up. For Annie, it was a lake to drown in.

I was rooting for her as she was rooting for me, but I was quite helpless to really help her. She needed, and

I knew she needed, a lot more than my encouragement from afar. She needed constant love. That is why I had decided to chase her away—so she could find someone who could deliver. She needed someone better than me. Really. I was almost relieved when she didn't pick up my calls. But it was killing me.

...

I soon had a new job, and I tried to perform it well and not think about Annie or about ever getting out. I needed to be in robot mode. Bobbie would ask me if I was depressed. I would tell him I was not depressed. I just wanted to do my job and take my classes, and quit asking me that.

My new position was administrative clerk, filling out time records and monthly paperwork for one of the upper-echelon guards, a guy named Vincent. His wife also worked at Pekin and was my counselor. The three of us were cordial. When I figured how to work efficiently for him, I had spare time to continue my college courses and to study the law, which had become both my addiction and my comfort.

I had lucked out again with a good job. I did the robot work and otherwise made Vincent's life easy. He was in charge of running the compound—the main outdoor areas— "his compound," as he would say. He was supposed to be a tough guy, and he had a nasty reputation. He would stand like General Patton on the compound during the ten-minute moves. When he wasn't making things even tougher on the inmates, his job involved overseeing the picking up of cigarette butts and other litter, and checking inmates for contraband, which guards at Pekin could do at any moment.

His wife, Terri, was the counselor for our housing unit. A counselor is not exactly like a camp counselor, but more like a social worker, school nurse, and stern aunt. There were several women on staff at Pekin.

Terri was nice. Some of the guys stalked her and would stare at her through their cell doors and windows when she was on the move. She took it in stride. They watched her take it in stride.

Terri was in her middle thirties, with sandy blonde hair.

She knew I was on a different path than most, so she would sometimes ask how I was doing.

There is always that line between staff and inmate that you can't cross. If you look too chatty you can develop a reputation as a snitch. Even so, I always tried to talk to guards like equals. I used to tell them that we all had the same goal, which was to make it through our time as easily as possible and then go home. For the prisoners that meant years, and for the guards it meant an eight-hour shift. We were all humans and we were all stuck there.

But I couldn't become too equal, and I was very careful to let the inmates know that I would never talk behind their backs.

14
ANOTHER HUSKER

When 2002 was still fresh, Milan came running up the stairway to my cell.

"Shon, you better get downstairs, because you got yourself another Cornhusker—like we don't have enough."

It was welcome wagon time. I put down my book and gathered some saved-up gifts into my laundry bag: a bar of good soap, a new toothbrush in a plastic case, shower flipflops to keep your feet a quarter inch above the urine and hair and who-knows-what of the shower floor, and a few snacks.

After the rough-and-tumble of county jails and transports, a little welcome basket, even in an old laundry bag, means a lot. The simple and unexpected kindness of it can make a man get teary-eyed, except there are no teary eyes in prison—just allergies or something in your eyes.

I welcomed John Fellers, who was a clean-cut, good looking man who resembled a middle-aged stockbroker. Like a lot of people you meet in there, he didn't look the part. I told him to let me know if he needed anything or had any questions.

Easygoing John settled in. He was the kind of guy

who would smile and stick out a handshake when he saw you coming—not everybody in prison is like that. You could always go to him for sensible advice or a little help. John had been a used car dealer in Lincoln with a good reputation. He worried about how his new wife was handling the business while he was gone.

He was in for a drug rap. He had started using drugs for a short time when he was going through a divorce, and he stored some for his dealer for a short time. He was in prison for giving an honest answer to a couple of deputies who asked him about it.

John started asking questions about the law because others told him I was the guy for that stuff. After his freshman time in a three-man cell, John moved in with Robert Jones, two cells away from me. Jones was rumored to have smuggled pot by the ton into the Midwest in the late eighties.

Despite their different backgrounds, they hit it off. As I was starting a new friendship with John, I received a second letter from Tom, who was out now and had just attended our ten-year high school reunion.

Wood,

I began talking to some people about how it works for you to use the phone in there. I also let them know how you don't get paid squat and yet you still have to pay regular prices for food, hygiene, clothes, etc. The bottom line is bro, these people out here really just don't understand how the system works.

But that doesn't mean they've forgotten about you or don't want to help.

For the next twelve months, we are going to send you a $50 money order every month. We decided it would be better for all *of us to kick in a little each month and spread it out rather than have people just kick in a one-time big amount.*

We want this to be something you can depend on. Ultimately, my goal is to be able to do this for you each year until your release. The names may change, but I have no doubt in my heart that we'll get this done for you. But for now, the following people have given you a one-year commitment. Everyone pretty much agreed we don't want you to feel like you have to call or write any of us. We're doing this for YOU. Call your family, buy yourself some good food, whatever.

The following people are in on this: Cory, Billy, Ryan T., Nate, Ryan L., Jennifer, Shellie, Mandy, Erin, me, and my sister, Kim.

What do you say to something like that? I could not get over the fact that these people, some of whom I had not spoken to in years, were helping me. This one act of grace put me on a different path. I decided if people were willing to help a puke like me, then I should do the same.

John Fellers and I often walked to the iron pile together at dawn. He figured he might as well use his early mornings to work his way back into shape.

A walk in the morning is one of the best moments in the prison day: dewy grass and sweet air make it seem like a walk in a park somewhere. The compression eases off your chest as you breathe and you try to imagine walking in a straight line right through the fence and razor wire to the field of corn beyond.

On the walk one morning John said he wanted to ask me to do something. I could tell it was important. I knew him well enough to know that he would not ask me to cover for him, to lie, to get him an unfair advan-

tage somewhere, or to get him out of a jam with a thug.
I knew that but just the same he seemed uncomfortable.
I was worried that maybe his celly had put him up to
something.

"You know I'm in here on a meth conviction, but I
want to tell you more about it, and I'm telling you for a
reason."

As we lifted weights with a dozen other guys, he gave
me the story.

"I never was one for drugs, Shon," he began. "I
was in the middle of an awful divorce when someone
handed me something to cheer me up and, man, I was
gone. Me and meth were best friends for, I don't know,
a few months. But I was hooked, honestly, after that one
hit. The stuff grabs you that fast."

I had heard enough horror stories from my celly,
Robby, to know what that was like.

"I was soon burning through a lot of money, and
got in a pinch financially, thanks to the divorce and the
way it froze up the car business. So this guy who was
selling the damn meth to me says, if they could store
some of it at my place, then I could have the next bit
for free. That happened. I even sold a little for them,
which was stupid. All I can say was that it was a messed
up time."

I was pressing a barbell on the incline bench. John
lowered his tone.

"Then I shook the habit and told them all to get lost.
I could see where it was going. It was hard to stop, but
I did it, just like that. Anyway, the dealer and a few of
his people were later arrested and convicted. You know

how it is, the only way to get their sentences reduced was to implicate lots of other people, so they put me on the list."

"But the police didn't find any drugs on you? You quit. Or were you still storing it for them?" I asked while curling forty-pound dumbbells.

"No, that stuff was long gone from my life." He was lifting but not concentrating on his exercises. I was a little confused as to how he could have been arrested, with no possession and nothing but an accusation from someone with no credibility.

"So it was your word, a businessman's, against the word of a drug dealer?"

"That's about it."

"How did that happen? Did you confess?" I stopped lifting and stared at him.

"Yes and no. That's what I want you to look at." He set down his weights and came closer.

"Listen, I'm not one of those guys who is moping around prison saying, 'I was framed,' and all that. I did what I did. But I'm looking at twelve years in here. I want to appeal the thing, but I have only about six weeks left to file. I asked my lawyer, and he said it was a lost cause, but he would file an appeal if I would pay him twelve grand."

"The same lawyer who represented you at trial?"

"Yes."

A grand jury had indicted him solely on the testimony of the dealers. A short time after the indictment, the police arrived at his home, and John let them in. They informed him of the indictment. They wanted to talk about the drug conspiracy and John talked, not knowing any better. Afterward they arrested him without finding any drugs.

If a lawyer had been on the scene, John would not have talked. He didn't understand his rights or the seriousness of the situation. Without the statements he made to the police, that would have been the end of it—his word against some drug dealer clawing for a sentence reduction. But he ended up in federal prison. I felt bad for him, because I knew a rich guy with a high-level lawyer would be out on his boat right now, not in prison. The system works great for those guys.

That's what I think upset me about John's sentence. To incarcerate a decent businessman for twelve years due to a short binge during a crazy divorce was not what Congress had in mind when they created the federal drug laws. Okay, he sold something, so how about a few months in county?

"The trial judge didn't do me any favors, and now I have only about six weeks to appeal to the Supreme Court. I don't want a guy representing me who thinks I'm a lost cause."

I still couldn't see where I was going to fit in.

"So what I'm thinking is maybe you could do it for me. I can look up some of the stuff myself, but I really would need your help," he continued. "I'm looking at twelve years in here.

Twelve years away from my daughter if this doesn't get fixed, and you said to come to you if I needed help. I need some help.

Otherwise I'm going to be in here. This is going to be my life."

I didn't want the remaining seven years of my sentence to feature him complaining every morning that I hadn't helped him when maybe he had a chance. Nor did I want to spend those years with him complaining that I had screwed up his appeal because I didn't know what I was doing. It was a no-win situation, unless of course we won, which was next to impossible, and we both knew it. When you're facing a no-win situation, you might as well do the right thing, but I wasn't ready to roll over yet.

I told him what little I knew. His lawyer was right to tell him that the odds were long. Preparing a case for the Supreme Court is like brain surgery compared to the elementary first aid I had been doing. It would take a ton of study.

Could I learn to write a brief like that from scratch? No way.

Not in six weeks. Probably not in six months.

"I know, Shon. What I was thinking was maybe you would take a look at it, just spend an hour looking at it. Your one hour against my twelve years. As a friend."

"John, if your lawyer thinks you have zero chance, you have less than zero with me."

"Well, you know, except for our time, which is a good thing to kill, we got nothing to lose but a postage stamp, and I'll spring for that."

The weight on my chest grew heavy. He watched me lift for a minute. Then he looked around and that made me look around. You must stay vigilant because you never know when something might happen. Like when you're driving a car or bike, you always need to know what is happening on all sides of you. Sometimes you feel like you need to be extra alert. It was like that—a moment when everything might change. But all the dangerous energy was coming from John.

"Listen," he said with an odd burst of a salesman's forced enthusiasm, "I have a good feeling about this. I think you could maybe pull off something amazing. I really do. And wouldn't that just impress the hell out of Annie?"

Indeed. Annie seemed long gone. But the veteran car salesman had me. He had lured me into his office and made me sign on the line. He had used the old impress your girl closing, probably because it always works.

15
THE FIGHT CLUB IN D.C.

I had been thinking a lot about the Supreme Court anyway. History turns on the actions of Congress and the president, and of course on tragedies, wars, booms, and busts. But when you examine the big moments when the conscious decisions of men and women have reshaped our lives, those decisions have often come down from the Supreme Court.

The language of the Court is interesting all by itself. The men and women who argue cases there, and who sit on the bench as justices, seemed to me a breed apart. They are warriors who use words, employing remarkable memories and razor logic as deftly as swords in mortal battle. And lives hang upon their skills. Darth Vader robes and marble chambers aside, there is something fascinating about that. They are almost like more highly evolved creatures. I have never been too easy to impress, but I was constantly amazed as I read the transcripts of these people who think on their feet so brilliantly, with a nation's future or a human life at stake.

If it were a game, which it is not, it would be the best and hardest mental game in the world.

So, like a lost tourist who can't even read the street

signs, I started poking around the Supreme Court law books on behalf of John J. Fellers. But without that law library job, it was hard.

The way I now had it organized, my job with Vincent really took me only an hour a day, so I used the desk time to do my schoolwork and to dig deeper into John's case. Vincent knew I was working on it, and he respected that. The harder I worked, the better I managed things with him and Terri.

When I couldn't be at my work desk, I tried to work in the law library, but so many guys were peppering me with questions that it became far easier to work in my cell, especially as Robby was such a good bouncer for me.

John's case was a puzzle to me—very off-kilter. If I could figure it out, I would be the first to do so. When the police had come to John's house, they told him that a grand jury had indicted him on meth trafficking charges. They described what the dealers had said against him. Then they let silence happen, and John started talking. They didn't interrogate him; they simply created a quiet space for John to fall into. They arrested him and transported him to jail. When he arrived there, they read him his *Miranda* rights and he signed a waiver of rights form. He figured he had already let the cat out of the bag once, so he told them the same story again.

The prosecutors would later say that the police weren't required to read him his *Miranda* rights at his house because they weren't interrogating him, and that the real interrogation came later at the jailhouse—after they read him his rights and he waived them.

I started to read hundreds of *Miranda* cases. *Miranda* warnings are primarily intended to protect your Fifth Amendment right against self-incrimination. If the police take you into custody and they interrogate you about a crime, the Self-Incrimination Clause says you can't be made to testify against yourself. In the *Miranda* decision, the Supreme Court said you must be told that you have the right to remain silent and to acquire legal representation. Lately, the Court is now saying you have to expressly invoke your right or else the interrogation can go on *ad infinitum*.

I found a case where the Supreme Court defined interrogation as express questioning or "any words or actions . . . that the police should know are reasonably likely to elicit an incriminating response from the suspect." That might help John. If he could claim his first confession was legally void, then it might be possible to say his second confession was void also, since John confessed because the police let him assume the cat was already out of the bag, when maybe it wasn't. That is called the "fruit of the poisonous tree" doctrine—and it's fairly well-established law. In a nutshell, it says the prosecution can't profit downstream from an initial illegal interrogation or confession.

But all this had been known by his lawyer, by the trial court, and the court of appeals. The court of appeals had said that John had not been interrogated by the police when they were at his home. And they had said that, even if he had been interrogated at his house, the fruit of the poisonous tree doctrine did not apply to *Miranda* violations. So John was screwed either way.

The court of appeals' decision against John was based on a 1984 Supreme Court opinion called *Oregon v. Elstad*. In that case the Court claimed that *Miranda* was not really a constitutional matter. This point was the subject of a long-running feud between liberal and conservative justices. Sure, *Miranda* protected the Fifth Amendment right against self-incrimination, but the Court concluded that *Miranda* was not on par with, say, a Fourth Amendment right to reasonable searches and seizures, and therefore the fruit of the poisonous tree doctrine did not apply to *Miranda* violations. It had to do with whether a right was written into the Constitution or if it was a derivative thing. The Court has previously said that *Miranda* was derivative, not enshrined in the Constitution itself. If your head is spinning, believe me, so was mine.

The fact that John's second statements were admissible under *Elstad* was a major problem, but one that seemed beside the point unless it could be proven that John was interrogated in his home, an argument that seemed weak. The police said they were there to discuss methamphet-amine, not to ask John about it. Cases often turn on fine distinctions like that.

I rolled the arguments over in my mind a thousand times, always coming back, instinctively, to one of my favorite textbooks: *Modern Criminal Procedure.*[10] Something was missing.

Something else was going on, and I could not put my finger on it. It was like a ghost in the corner of my eye that darted away whenever I tried to turn and see it.

"You'll figure it out, Shon," Robby said to me. He

did let John come into our cell, as John was often bringing us a couple of candy bars and nachos; I was missing some meals because we were running out of time.

John would hover, waiting for some good news, waiting for me to look up and smile. I would say hello without looking up from my reading or notes. Still he would linger, his little daughter on his back, his laundry bag ready for the trip home. This is how I imagined him and why I did not look up.

"Go away, John," Robby would finally say. "Shon here can do it. Just keep the Snickers coming."

I was reading by moonlight one night, late after lights out, when Robby woke up and looked over from his bunk.

"You're going to ruin your eyes. Whatcha reading now?"

I held it up. The moon and the perimeter lights streaming through the barred window illuminated the book's cover: an embossed image of the Supreme Court's pillared front facade.

Robby was half asleep.

"Hell, it looks like a bank, Shon. You can take that mother," and he rolled back into his dreams.

My concentration was making me irritable. I really didn't want to let John down, and I really didn't want to think I was too stupid to figure it out. I was worried that maybe John didn't have a claim after all. Days and nights went by, and I kept other guys at a distance. When I did have conversations, I was unfocused. My notes looked like the disorganized scrawls of a madman.

16
GOING WIDE

I was using parts of my brain that had been previously unused, or at least had not been used in quite some time. In my worst years, when I was in trouble, I experienced a strange phenomenon. The more danger you're in, the more your perspective narrows. Your imagination shuts down. Your empathy shuts down. Your creative vision closes in. Your ability to plan even simple things deteriorates. On some level it is simply denial of what is inevitably coming, a state that forces you to focus only on what is small and immediate and right in front of you—closer and closer things.

I would be unable to solve the riddle of John's case unless I could think outside the box I had put myself in, which was as much mental as it was cement and steel.

Even when I was robbing banks, I was aware of the shutting-down process. Each bank job had less planning and thought than the one before. I was narrowing to a dangerous level.

Right after the first bank job, flush with cash, I had moved to Lincoln and roomed with some guys going to school there.

An old high school acquaintance, Craig, showed up one night. He had been down the same roads, having spent some time in the armed services before coming back emotionally drained. Unlike me, he had had a tough childhood, including trouble with the law as a kid and a stint at Father Flanagan's Boys Town, which is on the David City side of Omaha. He was kicked out of the Catholic school in David City and ended up in the public school, where I met him. Out of the Army, he was sleeping in his car in Lincoln. I asked my roommates if we could take him in. Craig and I had nearly fought in high school, but I couldn't see him sleeping in his car.

When I ran out of money from the first bank robbery, I asked Craig if he wanted to do a bank with me. He was as quick to accept as I had been earlier that year with Tom. It's like that when you're desperate.

I wouldn't let Craig have a loaded gun; he carried an inoperable shotgun for show. I did that because I wasn't sure how he would react under stress, and I didn't want anyone to be hurt. We were in and out of the bank in three minutes, and we didn't lock anyone in the vault. We didn't think ahead enough to realize that, because the bank was so near Lincoln, big city cops would have helicopters to chase us within minutes. We could hear them. We were lucky that morning, but we seemed to always be lucky in taking down banks. The morning fog protected us from the helicopters above.

The $12,000 take was a disappointment to Craig, because it was about enough for each of us to buy a used car. Most of the haul was in small bills.

I paid most of my half to the lawyer representing me for my old failure to appear on the bad checks charge. I handed him a paper bag full of money, mostly ones.

"Tips from my restaurant job," I told him.

Gresham came next, the third bank. It was close to where my grandparents lived, which was awful for them when the truth came out later. We were in and out in less than four minutes.

The fourth bank was in Peru, Nebraska. We were starting to unravel, becoming careless, doing a little less planning each time. I really did believe the end was near, and I had accepted that. In Peru, I went in disguised as a dirty homeless guy and started screaming like the characters in *Pulp Fiction* who rob the diner. We did that to change our modus operandi. This was the year of the meth takeover and of recent casino openings along the Missouri River, and it was a record year for bank robberies. We wanted ours to become lost in the crowd.

Peru is close to the Missouri River, which is also near to the Nebraska, Iowa, and Missouri state line. We sped out of town, nearly were stuck in the mud beside the river, popped up on a road, and crossed the bridge. A mile into Missouri, three speeding state troopers flew right past, heading to block off the bridge.

We crossed into Iowa close to Council Bluffs, made our way back to Omaha, then back to Lincoln. A little while after I dropped Craig off, I was caught in a speed trap driving down "O" Street. I pulled over and handed my friend Kirk, who was in the car, a wad of cash from my pants. My Smith & Wessy and $15,000 were in the trunk. The cops were so anxious to have me on a warrant—the bad checks—that they didn't search the car, which was just left beside the road.

Kirk bailed me out with the cash a couple of days

later. The stuff was still in the car when I got back to it. That was the spring of 1998. With close calls like that, I could feel my time was coming.

My brothers knew what I was doing, as did a small circle of friends. Tyler, who sold us weed and guns and stolen cars, had a rented garage in Lincoln where we would camp out late at night, working on cars and smoking weed. We went out dancing to clubs, where, thanks to fat tips, we were ushered in through the side doors instead of having to wait in line. At the apartment, we slept until noon and played videogames and watched Cheers and Cosby Show reruns. We were lords of a cut-rate Camelot.

The police were circulating a composite drawing of me. It was on the television news a few days before we were caught.

It wasn't a great likeness, but it was close enough to make my father, who saw it at work, lock himself in his office and cry.

Dad wasn't sure it was me, but he thought it could explain a lot of the new mysteries surrounding me.

The beginning of the end was when I received word that my little brother, Brett, and Craig's little brother, Cody, and a mutual friend of theirs, Harley, were planning to rob a bank.

They were all seventeen. I raced to David City to confront Brett. We had a shouting match, but what credibility did I have to tell him no?

I should have gone to Dad, of course, but I wasn't even thinking that way anymore. Besides, what would I have said?

"Dad, Brett wants to be a bank robber like me."

My brain had narrowed down to nothing.

I made Brett a deal. He and his friends could do something for me on the next bank job, certainly not inside the bank, and I would give them a taste of the loot. But never again. And we would all retire from doing banks after that. He agreed.

Like I have said before, bringing in Brett is the moment of my past for which I have the least patience or understanding.

Instead of protecting him, I was asking him to steal a car for me.

Craig and I already had our sights set on a bank at Pilger, Nebraska. Brett and Harley set out to find a getaway car. They took one and hid it at an abandoned farm. It evidently wasn't entirely abandoned, because the car was gone the next day, returned to its owner.

They found another car, but a few miles down the road it ran out of gas. We were all in it. We walked up to a farmhouse to borrow some gas. The people were very nice and asked where we were from. Like an idiot, I said David City. They filled up a jug of gas, enough for us to make it to the nearest station. When we filled the car up in town, we realized none of us had cash, so we drove away. It was like I was begging to be caught.

The next day, the day of the bank robbery, we were on our way to the bank when the transmission went out. Somebody really didn't want us to rob that bank, or certainly didn't want the young boys involved. But we found a third car and were back in business.

I did the bank myself. It was a bigger bank than I

was accustomed to, with three tellers and two handfuls of customers. I had spent all of about five minutes planning the job.

I went in screaming. One man looked at me with an incredulous grin, almost laughing, like he was about to give my performance two thumbs down.

People were running out the back door of the bank. The manager had a .357 Magnum pistol in his desk drawer.

I cleaned out the tills and made my way to the vault. With my pistol, I scooped the cash into a bag. It didn't look like much. I moved across the bank lobby with big steps.

Craig's brother, Cody, was waiting at the curb as my driver. People, including the manager, were running out of the bank. Some were screaming. When I jumped into the car, Cody mashed out of town and sailed over the first hill at ninety, causing us to glide through the air. The rest of the guys were waiting in another car at the edge of town, where we abandoned the getaway car.

We made it to our hideout—Cody's mom's house on an Indian reservation. I started counting the stash. It was over $130,000. I was stunned; we were Midwest rich. It was unsettling, like an extra zero on your paycheck.

We were in Omaha when the FBI started to close in. I went to buy my first suit, an Armani for a wedding I planned to attend. It was the wedding of the dispatcher and my former point guard, whose conversations we had overheard on the scanner after our first bank job. Nebraska is like that sometimes.

A week after the job, Harley was arrested on a minor

charge and had way too much money on him. The dominoes fell quickly. The FBI was mounting evidence against us, such as my palm print on one of the cars. The elderly people who had lent us the gas and who knew we were from David City had talked to the people we had stiffed at the gas station, then to the police. It was coming from all directions.

I was tackled by agents in the lobby of the Doubletree hotel in Omaha, just off Seventy-second Street. From the lobby floor I looked up at the big skylight and it was ribbed like a spider web. I laughed inside. Too perfect.

On my way to Lincoln in handcuffs, I was very angry that the FBI had denied me my Butch Cassidy ending. Rather than go out in a blaze of criminal glory, I'd have to face my parents and see their pain. That had always been the nightmare.

17
THE KNOT

When the Eighth Circuit Court of Appeals had denied John's appeal, one of the judges had written a separate but concurring opinion; he agreed with the verdict of the majority, but he took a different path to get there. I had read his opinion before but not closely, because it said John was not entitled to a new trial. But I was looking at anything unusual that might be the loose thread to unravel the Gordian knot, so I read his opinion again.

In the majority opinion, the other judges had discussed *Miranda* in the context of the Fifth Amendment's right against self-incrimination. That's completely normal. Most people and most courts equate *Miranda* with that constitutional provision. But *Miranda* does more than just protect against self-incrimination; it protects the accused until an attorney can be afforded.

The Fifth doesn't expressly extend the right to an attorney, but it gives you the right to shut up until you have one. The Sixth, on the other hand, explicitly guarantees the "Assistance of Counsel" for a defense. Judge Riley, who concurred with the court of appeals majority, had written that John's Sixth Amendment right was also in play.

The question of whether the Fifth or the Sixth was active in John's case depended on whether the police were just investigating, or whether they had already filed charges. If they were just investigating, the Fifth gave John the right to shut up until he could obtain a lawyer. If the State had already charged him with a crime, then the Sixth was in play, because the State had started, officially, the adversarial process, with the government on one side and the defense, through an attorney, on the other.

Here is the way to think about that: let's say the IRS is nosing around your financial records. The auditor asks you questions. You don't have to incriminate yourself, thanks to the Fifth Amendment. Now, say the government has actually filed charges against you for tax evasion and you are sitting in a courtroom. The prosecutor is not going to go looking through your wallet for evidence of your hidden wealth.

Everything the prosecution does must be carefully requested by motion. The lawyers will make copies, and it's all, well, very courteous and done at arm's length. That's because you are in a trial, the government has started the game, and the game has rules set by the Sixth Amendment.

When the cops showed up at John's house, was it an investigation or was the game already on? It was on, because John had just been indicted by a grand jury. Everything that happened after the indictment was more like a trial, falling under the rules of evidence, methods of disclosure, and so on. The game had begun and the Sixth Amendment applied.

That's what Judge Riley was hinting at. He knew that once the indictment came down the game changed and it had become a formal adversarial proceeding. I couldn't figure why that was important, but I knew it was. I knew the riddle was in that direction. I knew the Sixth Amendment's right to counsel opened a new world of legal protections, but it was a secret world to me.

"Hey, buddy," John said. "You come up with any thing yet?"

I laid it out for him. I told him that we at least knew where the magic cave was, and now we had to explore it. He looked discouraged, like I was going off on a tangent, and we didn't have time for that.

Instead of reading just *Miranda* cases, I had to learn what the Sixth Amendment right to counsel protected and how it differed from the Fifth Amendment right to self-incrimination, which also, thanks to the *Miranda* decision, included a right to counsel.

It was right there in front of me somewhere, but my mind was twisted into knots. I stared at the 1,800-page *Modern Criminal Procedure* book and continued reading.

After lights-out one night, at nearly dawn, something clicked. I could suddenly see it. I had to do a quiet little dance, for in that moment I was indeed the happy genius of my household.

"You all right?" Robby asked, waking.

"Yes, sir."

"Figured it out, didn't you?"

"Yes, sir." I was still smiling.

"Figured you would."

I wanted to wake up the cellblock and send the news

two cells down to John, but in the dead of night I decided that ruckus would not be welcomed by the others. So I tried to go to sleep.

...

"Here's the thing," I said. John had come in, and, to-gether with Robby, he and I were ready to make our way across the compound to the recreation yard.

"Once you were indicted by the grand jury, the game had started," I said as we walked. "An indictment begins formal proceedings, where the State has taken sides against you, and the world becomes a courtroom. Their team can only deal with your team in a very fair and formalized way. Your right to counsel in a formal pro-ceeding is different from your right to counsel if a cop tackles you on the street, and it comes from an entirely different part of the Bill of Rights."

"Keep going," John said.

"Let's say a guy driving a car like yours just held up a liquor store, and a cop sees you and pulls you over—"

"Hey, Shon, they are playing Kid A on the yard," called out Paul, one of my inmate buddies, who hap-pened to be passing by. The inmates would sometimes ask the guards to play requests over the PA system in the yard. Paul had requested Radiohead, which was unusual in a place that preferred rap and metal music.

"Cool, but we're headed to work out."

"All right, I'll catch you later."

Robby, John, and I were halfway across the com-pound. It was during the middle of a ten-minute move, so everyone was out talking to their homeboys housed in different units.

"Anyway, where was I? Oh yeah, so a cop pulls you over and he sees a six-pack of beer and a wad of money on the front seat. He asks you to step out. Maybe he sees part of a pistol sticking out from under your seat. He has you standing in back of the car, waiting for his backup. He will probably arrest you, but until his backup arrives he decides not to ask you any questions. Does he have to read you your *Miranda* rights?

Probably not, at least not until he announces the arrest and cuffs you. But if you blurt out some confession right after your arrest, a judge would probably not think you had been cheated out of your *Miranda* rights. In your case, maybe it was an interrogation or maybe it wasn't—the way they just put accusations out there and waited for you to comment. Let's say they didn't owe you *Miranda* yet. Let's give them that."

John's brows scrunched up. So far I hadn't provided any hope. We made it to the recreation yard and walked to the track for a warm-up lap. The Italians were rolling ceramic balls on the bocce court.

"But your situation was different than the liquor store situation. You had, essentially, already been arrested and cuffed by the grand jury indictment. You'd been already charged with a crime by the State, even before the cops showed up. It's a Sixth Amendment situation, not a Fifth."

"Well, what's the Sixth say?" Robby asked. Now he was curious.

"The Sixth is the right to counsel once proceedings

are under way, like in a trial. Let's say you're in the middle of a trial. The prosecutor cannot meet you in the parking lot and try to start a conversation to bait you into spilling the beans, can he?"

"No," John said.

"If the prosecutor tried something like that, the judge would toss out the confession and possibly the case. But what if the prosecutor instead sends a few cops to hang out with you at your house to see if you spill anything? That's the same thing, John, and that's what they did. And nobody got that. They messed up. The critical difference was that you'd already been indicted."

I looked at them to see if they were following this. I needed to explain it in a way that everyone could understand, because until you can orally drive home your argument, you can't write it well.

Robby and John nodded, but I could see it wasn't quite sticking, and the argument had to be instantly understandable if it was going to succeed. I tried a different approach.

"Think of everything after the indictment as happening in a courtroom," I continued. "You have a right to a fair and orderly jury trial. That's the Sixth. The courts protect that Sixth Amendment right more diligently than a simple *Miranda* violation. Under the Sixth, the courts have said that the State cannot 'deliberately elicit information' without *Miranda* warnings being issued. Under the Fifth, they say you can't be interrogated without waiving your *Miranda*.

Elicitation and interrogation are not the same thing, and the courts have said so. The Eighth Circuit said you weren't interrogated at your home. They were right. But because you had been indicted and the trial had effectively started, the standard should have been the elicitation of information. They used the wrong standard. They were wrong."

"I think I get it," said John. "But are you sure it isn't all too technical, Shon? Is this really something? I mean, is it too academic for them to bother about?"

"No, John, it's real and it's simple. The court of appeals applied the Fifth Amendment standard, which is interrogation, when they should have applied the Sixth Amendment standard, which is deliberate elicitation. It's just that simple.

I'm a hundred percent sure how to do this now."

He was reeling.

"But downtown, they did give me my *Miranda*, and then I told them everything again."

"Oh, you're screwed," Robby said, laughing.

"Shut up," John shouted.

"Well, there's this other thing for that," I said. "It's called the fruit of the poisonous tree doctrine. If the first confession was bogus, so is the second confession, unless some intervening act has occurred that dissipates the taint of the illegally obtained confession." I was surprised to hear myself talking like that.

"What's an intervening act?" John asked.

"A number of different things can qualify, including the time that passes between confessions and whether *Miranda* warnings were issued."

"But they did give me *Miranda* at the jail."

"I know, and under the *Miranda* cases alone, that

would be the end of the matter. The courts would say that the second confession can be admitted."

John was showing confusion again.

"The great thing is that the Supreme Court, unlike the lower courts, has never faced a case quite like yours where the first confession was not just a *Miranda* violation but a Sixth Amendment constitutional violation. The Court treats constitutional claims differently, and based on their previous decisions, the fact that the police read you *Miranda* warnings at the jail might not matter."

I started reciting a string of Supreme Court cases from memory. They could decide that the first confession was out of line, being a direct affront to the Constitution, so that the poisonous tree doctrine applied, despite the *Miranda* warning given later. That is what the Court had said in a different context, where the underlying violation was a Fourth Amendment illegal search and seizure.

"Well, if I'd known the stupid stuff I said at the house couldn't be used, I sure would have kept my mouth shut the second time."

"Exactly. This argument is good, John. I can't guarantee the Court will do anything about it, but the argument is good. It's our only shot, and it keeps your case alive, which is a good thing for its own sake, on the off chance that some other lightning strikes." I was thinking of how, if my own case hadn't been considered final when the sentencing guidelines were changed, I might be packing for home.

"Guess what the name of the leading Sixth Amendment case is?" I asked John.

"I have no idea."

"Massiah versus United States."

Robby suggested that John go say his prayers.

In fact, the odds against the Supreme Court taking our case were even higher than I then assumed. The Court usually grants only about 1 percent of cases that are filed, and far, far less than that for cases that are filed pro se, without the help of a lawyer.

Later I learned that what we were claiming was a simple case of error correction. Normally, the Supreme Court only grants cases on legal issues that have divided lower courts. Rarely, outside the death penalty context, do they grant a case to correct a bad lower court ruling. If they did that too often, they would never have time for cases with sweeping impact. But I was too green to know that.

We did a few sets of push-ups. Before we left the yard.

John patted me on the back. "Hey, buddy, at least we'll go down fighting," he said.

"It's a good argument," I said. "You can win, John. Think positive."

"Say your damned prayers," Robby added.

...

I decided to write Annie. I told her about my breakthrough with John's brief. She had met him in the prison visiting room, and I knew she thought he was a good guy trying to make it home to his young daughter. She wrote back.

While her letter lacked the love of previous letters, it

did contain the warmth of friendship. That would have to be enough.

...

I went to work as if I was on death row and this was my last appeal. I worked right through the quiet nights. The guards were bewildered when they came past for late night counts and I was still up. I pored over other petitions to understand the language and tone that Supreme Court lawyers traditionally use. This was the first brief I would file to the Supreme Court, and I wanted to follow all the rules, all the conventions.

I wrote the appeal, which is technically called a petition for writ of certiorari. The Latin translates to a "request to review" the lower court ruling.

I wrote it over and over again by hand, making subtle improvements. Seven long, complete drafts later, I started typing it on a typewriter; we didn't have computers. At night, I would proofread the copy.

It began with two questions we wanted the Court to answer:

1. Did the Court of Appeals err when they concluded that Petitioner's Sixth Amendment right to counsel under Massiah v. United States, 377 U.S. 201 (1964), was not violated because Petitioner was not "interrogated" by Government agents; when the proper standard under Supreme Court precedent is whether the Government agents "deliberately elicited" information from Petitioner?

2. Should the second statements—preceded by
Miranda warnings—have been suppressed as fruits
of the illegal post-indictment interview without the
presence of counsel, under this Court's decisions in
Nix v. Williams, 467 U.S. 431 (1984), and Brown v.
Illinois, 422 U.S. 590 (1975)?

That was followed by citations from Supreme Court
precedents spelling out the Court's standards for the
right to counsel under the Sixth Amendment. I finished
with a defining paragraph:

From these precedents, it is clear that once a defendant
is indicted the Government may not deliberately elicit
information from him without the presence of counsel. It is equally clear that once a defendant raises a
Sixth Amendment—Massiah challenge, the question
of whether the defendant was interrogated becomes
constitutionally irrelevant.

Exhausted, I had John read it one more time. He
signed it. I then did the unconventional thing—because
I didn't know any better—of writing a personal note in
the cover letter to the Court. The letter said essentially
that I know the Court receives a lot of indecipherable
junk from guys in prison but this one is for real. Please
consider it because the lower court violated about six
Supreme Court decisions.

The Court, in fact, receives tens of thousands of pris-
oner-written briefs, and none of them makes it past the
first stage of review—almost none. Even professionally

prepared cases are rejected en masse. The small handful of cases that are accepted for review by the Supreme Court are generally written by big law firms, sometimes with dozens of lawyers working as a team. Their finished writ is bound into a booklet that includes a complete history of the issue and all the relevant lower court decisions, and these professionally prepared bound books are delivered to the court. John's "pauper" petition was but one copy. Pauper prisoner-prepared briefs are rarely taken seriously.

John provided the postage stamps, as promised, and we sent it off. It felt like applying to college—nothing to do now but sit back and pray.

It came back immediately. There was a letter saying something was missing. As far as I could see, everything was in order, so I just sent it back again with a note saying it had been fixed. The Solicitor General's office, our adversary here, waived response, meaning they thought it unlikely that the Court would take our case, so they wouldn't bother arguing against our brief. They do that 88 percent of the time. It doesn't mean you're dead, but just about.

Then something strange occurred. Instead of denying John's petition, the Supreme Court asked the Solicitor General to file a response anyway. The practice is labeled a Call for Response and it happens when at least one member of the Court is interested in the case; it happens around two hundred times a year. The Solicitor General soon filed the response, recommending—big surprise—that the petition be denied. We filed a short brief in reply to that, pointing out the defects in the Solicitor General's logic.

Months went by. Nothing. John's cert petition was on life support, but not dead.

While we waited, John was transferred to another prison. Guys are transferred when their custody points drop, which can occur for good behavior or because you are closer to release, that sort of thing. John was transferred from our medium- to high-security prison to a low-security prison in Sandstone, Minnesota. He was hoping to earn his way to a minimum-security prison in Yankton, South Dakota, to be close to his daughter. His crime was nonviolent and he had served some of his sentence, so that's why his points were low.

I really missed his company. I tried to forget about the petition. Of course I couldn't. But something happened that made me forget everything else.

...

Near David City, Annie's mother, Rita, took a drive to nearby Columbus for a salon appointment. Her son, Danny, was coming home from school in Florida for a long weekend of family fun. Rita pulled out onto a two-lane highway and didn't see a semi-truck coming. She had just looked the wrong way, or looked and not seen it, and an instant later she was dead.

Annie didn't know what to think. She felt like she was in a free fall, completely out of control.

"Annie, I am so sorry," I said over the phone. "If there is anything I can do, I will."

"I want her back," she said, crying. "I want her back."

"What happened?"

"I don't know. I talked to her thirty minutes before it

happened. She seemed distracted about something. She gets that way sometimes." She paused. "I wanted to be the one who could make her happy," she said.

What can you say in a moment like that?

We talked and then corresponded. I wrote letters to her every day and sent a card to her dad. I told her I would love and care for her always, even though we were just "friends."

But it was not enough. Within weeks her weight dropped dramatically and she was hospitalized. Then she was back in the Tucson treatment center. She never made it to Bastyr, never made it to her dream school.

Dear Shon,

Thank you for your beautiful letter. Yes, I guess what I need and want now more than ever is love. I want to be held and nurtured. I want to be held and have my head caressed . . . to feel loved, important, safe, and cared for.

My mom was my whole world, and I feel like part of me died with her. Now I am left to try to heal without her, and I feel so scared and lonely. My heart feels so broken and empty. So much happened this year. . . . I resorted to the anorexia as the only coping mechanism I have known. It has been my faithful companion for almost fourteen years now.

Love,
Annie

It was incredibly frustrating to be so far away from her when she was crying out for an embrace. I think helplessness might be the worst of all emotions. It felt like Annie was on fire and all I could do was stand by helplessly while she burned.

So I did what I could do. I wrote and called and prayed. I was surprised to hear myself praying. It was, I guess, a remnant of my upbringing that I could not kick.

A couple years earlier in the snow, Tom had said I was his bad luck charm. Maybe that's who I was to everybody. All that came back as I worried about Annie.

Since I couldn't help Annie, I focused on accomplishing what I could with those around me. One time I was on the phone with a lawyer who was representing a prisoner friend of mine. I had prepared a solid post-conviction motion and we had mailed it to the court. The judge believed it contained enough merit to appoint an attorney pro bono, and my friend had been assigned this clown. This guy believed the motion had been filed too late. Although the court had received the motion after the deadline had expired, that didn't matter, as there is a provision in the law called the "mailbox rule," which says that motions filed from prison are not late if they were mailed on the day they are due. Prisoners, after all, can't jump in a cab and drive their motions to the courthouse, nor do they have access to overnight delivery services.

This lawyer didn't know or had forgotten about that provision, and he was about to accept defeat. I couldn't believe it. Rarely did I allow myself to become angry, but I let this guy have it. He deserved it.

From a few things he let slip, I realized he had probably done this on purpose to end this court-appointed case. In other words, it was worse than incompetence: he was throwing the fight, and if he got away with it, the cost would be years in prison for my friend.

I threatened a lawsuit and a bar complaint. I don't

remember the words, just the message. He finally relented and agreed to do the right thing. As a result, a guy from Iowa would go home early.

My body was trembling from the confrontation when I hung up.

I scanned the dayroom and everyone was staring at me, even from the railings. I must have been shouting. In a way, I was screaming at myself.

"I should talk to my lawyer like that," someone called out from the railing, and laughter followed.

18
SOMEONE RUNNING AT ME

At 6:30 Wednesday morning, March 12, 2003, I was on my way to the iron pile when I saw someone running across the yard toward me yelling my name—screaming, "Shon, you're going to die!" over and over.

My first thought was that I was about to be in a fight. My adrenaline surged, but it was Wade, a guy I knew pretty well, sprinting toward me. He wasn't looking for a fight; he was waving a newspaper.

"You gotta see this, Shon!" He was getting closer. "You're gonna die, man!" He had a smile full of white teeth, an uncommon sight in a place full of smokers, coffee drinkers, and drug addicts.

He pushed the newspaper into my hands and pointed to an article with his shaking finger. "There, man, right there, is that our Johnny boy? It is, isn't it! Has to be!"

The Court had accepted the case. The odds of them accepting it were, well, it was the equivalent of winning the legal lottery.

Washington (AP)—The Supreme Court is taking a fresh look at police questioning and when officers must recite the "Miranda" warning to suspects they're preparing to arrest. Justices said Monday that they will review an appeal from a man who claims he was tricked into talking to officers. John J. Fellers' case provides an unlikely test of the landmark 1966 Miranda ruling which led to the familiar refrain beginning "You have the right to remain silent."

He filed his appeal without an attorney. The Supreme Court receives thousands of such cases a year, but only rarely agrees to hear one.

Guys grouped around to see what was happening. The crowd was completely mixed in terms of race, gangs, and types. Any sort of news about court action that might send someone home transcends everything. If someone is about to stab you in prison, just say, "Did you hear about the big Supreme Court decision today?"

Wade shouted as he strutted around me: "Shon here got John's case to the Supreme Court. What do you think of that?"

Everyone was happy, especially John's former cell-mate, Robert Jones, who, once I was back at the unit, was slapping me on the back so hard I had to hang onto my breakfast. Robert was serving his second decade, based in part on a previous conviction for possession of drugs that local deputies would later admit had been planted in his house by a dirty sheriff. Robert and I had been fighting this bogus conviction for years, but, remarkably, the trial judge and the state prosecutor fought it every step of the way. In addition to honest happiness for John, the Fellers case reignited Robert's willingness to fight for himself—a fight he continues to this day.

I ran into the unit to find a phone and call John's mom; there was no way to call John at Sandstone. Beverly thanked me, and we talked about the next steps. She knew and I knew, win or lose, this would be a life changer for John.

I had to call Annie at Mirasol. I waited on the line a long time after I asked for her. I panicked in those few minutes, thinking someone would come on the line and tell me some bad news. But when I heard her voice on the line I sighed and said a silent thanks.

In her beautiful, quiet voice, she congratulated me and offered up encouragement. Of course, she assured me, the Supreme Court would grant my petition.

That evening I called home to David City. John Fellers' mom had already called my parents. Dad answered. There was a long pause. "Congratulations, Mr. Famous." He then said he was proud of me. It had been a long time since I had heard anything like that. If the rift between us was over, well, we were both glad about it.

My dad was a big believer in rules—his own, of course, but also rules generally. He was the best umpire I've ever seen on a ball field. When I once volunteered to help him ump some games, he sat me down first with a rule book and told me how it worked.

"You need to memorize this book. When you are out there, you are the book. People will argue with some of your calls, but you just have to stick with it. You are the rules. But that puts a real obligation on you to get it right. You must be better than anybody else in watching the game, but you also must be better than anybody else in knowing what's in this book. You owe them all the best you can deliver. A bad umpire is just a waste of everyone's time."

He was a law man on the ball fields—baseball, basketball, football. Hundreds of kids relied on him to get it right for them. Of all the law men I had defied, he was the best. He was Wyatt Earp, mustache and all. I was seeing that now. He was excited that I was into the rule books now—the big ones.

For him there was only one bigger. Rules, to him, were the wellspring of character, honor, civilization itself. I couldn't have hit a better home run for him than this thing, win or lose, in the Supreme Court.

...

The next step was to find someone to argue the case. Lawyers from both coasts realized John didn't have representation, so a flood of them contacted the Minnesota prison where John was located. Arguing a case in front of the Supreme Court can make a lawyer's career.

The heavy hitters who frequent the Supreme Court are not the kind to come begging, but they are the ones you want. A new breed of Supreme Court advocate had emerged in the 1990s—proficient at writing briefs that read as smoothly as novels and skilled at standing before the black-robed Nine and answering rapid-fire hypothetical questions without hesitation. They can cite the Court's relevant precedents—sometimes going back over two hundred years—by memory, including obscure cases the justices will pull out of the blue sky. They can also argue policy matters as delicately as any politically polished senator. They do all this with a natural skill for explaining and storytelling, so that common sense, or what certainly feels like it, settles down with good humor over the courtroom—although a million pages of legal history spin invisibly in the air above them.

There is but a handful of Supreme Court specialists who routinely argue cases during each Supreme Court term. Names like Paul Clement, Carter Phillips, Tom Goldstein, Patricia Millett, Jeffrey Fisher, and Ted Olson may be unknown outside the D.C. Beltway, but when issues of the moment affecting our daily lives come before the Court, they are the ones presenting the case.

Seth Waxman is one of them.

Like several, he served as a United States Solicitor General before moving to private practice and therefore is at home in this country's highest courtroom. His path is familiar: Harvard for undergrad, Yale Law School, a clerkship for a federal judge, then working as a trial lawyer.

In 1994 he took a job at the Department of Justice, ultimately rising to Solicitor General under President Clinton. As Solicitor General, he represented our federal government in all litigation coming before the Supreme Court. After his government service, Seth became head of Appellate and Supreme Court Litigation at the law firm WilmerHale, one of the largest and most prestigious firms in the country.

Few attorneys ever have the chance to argue a case before the Supreme Court. Fewer still argue multiple times before the High Court. Yet Seth had stood at the podium and said, "Mr. Chief Justice, and may it please the Court" over seventy-five times.

When things are meant to happen, answers often arrive from several directions at once. The National Association of Criminal Defense Lawyers (NACDL) frequently files amicus curiae ("friend of the court") briefs with the Supreme Court.

An amicus brief is a supportive argument offered on behalf of one side of a case or the other. For example, if a developer was suing a community for refusing to let him develop a parcel because it was an important wetland for birds, a Sierra Club lawyer might file an amicus brief to advise the justices on issues that might not be raised by the litigants. So criminal law cases that might affect thousands of criminal cases will often merit an amicus brief from the NACDL. Someone working for the association saw that the Fellers case had been granted without the assistance of a lawyer and sent a note to Seth Waxman, asking him to investigate. John Fellers' previous attorney had received a recommendation from another attorney, saying that Seth would be great for the case.

John got brave and just called Seth Waxman, and somehow Seth ended up on the line and said he would look at the case. And he did. When John Fellers telephoned his office, Seth was still in the first years of his post-government career with a slight hint of gray in his temples, an athletic face of an avid runner, glasses, and a very wide smile.

I received a letter from Beverly Fellers a few days later:

*I just got a call from John and he told me the attorney's name so
I looked him up on the Internet and got this information. Sure
hope he is reputable and will do a good job for John.*

Seth had accepted the case with one caveat: that the
Shon Hopwood who wrote the brief would stay involved
with the case.

Once again luck and the grace of good people had
come my way. To be clear, Seth Waxman did not need
my help. I doubt few attorneys with his pedigree would
have taken input from a federal prisoner, let alone
requested my contribution.

Had John obtained a different attorney, there is little
question that my involvement would have ended.

In our first phone call, Seth was full of good things
to say about the petition I had written. I was having a
pinch me moment talking to a guy who had a lifetime of
education and experience whereas I had none; I had yet
to even earn an associate's degree. Seth told me that I
would be on the team with him and his associate, Noah
Levine. I jotted down Noah's number and we were set
to go.

For me, the trick would be persuading the Pekin staff
to allow me to be involved in the case. You can obviously be in touch with your own lawyer and do your
own research, and you can assist guys in the law library
if you want, but this was something altogether different—a top flight attorney requesting assistance from
a federal prisoner on another prisoner's case. The test
came soon.

"This is a prepaid phone call from a federal prison,"

the automated voice said. "To accept the call press five now; otherwise press one to block this call."

On the other end, Noah pressed five.

"Hello, Noah, this is Shon Hopwood."

"Hi, Shon, it's nice to meet you, even if it is over the phone," he said. "I guess the first question is how this will work. Any thoughts?"

"Well, I don't have access to a computer or computerized legal research. Plus, I figure you guys have the legal issues covered. But I do know the record very well."

The record is all the lower court files, which included the trial transcripts, the transcripts from the suppression hearing, the docket statement, and all the pretrial motions and rulings.

"Okay, so when we finish drafting the brief, we will send it to you and you can make notes in the margins about anything from the record you think should be included or any other questions you may have. When you're done, send it back to us."

Once a Supreme Court case is granted, an entire new round of briefing occurs, arguing only the merits of the case, as opposed to why the Court should accept review, which is what I had done in the cert petition.

Noah soon sent me a draft, but since John Fellers' name was on the cover of the brief, the prison considered it another prisoner's legal paperwork—off-limits to me. I argued that it was no different from my photocopying a case with another prisoner's name on it from the law library, but reason and logic often have no place in prison.

I went to Terri, the counselor, the wife of my boss.

She was aware of what had happened with the Court; indeed, the entire prison knew about the case.

"These guys are like the top lawyers in the country, and they are allowing me to be a part of the defense team."

"I get that, Shon. It's very impressive."

"They are trying to send me a draft of a brief. They want my input," I pleaded. "And sometimes there will be conference calls that they'll want me in on, and they might call at times that don't work with controlled moves. I don't know if you can do anything about that for me."

"It might be a problem."

"You could think of it as a part of my education."

There was a silent moment as she thought about it.

I could see she wanted to help but was wavering. Rules were rules.

"Cornhuskers are supposed to help other huskers, you know," I said. She was from Broken Bow, Nebraska—140 flat miles west of David City.

Terri rigged things so that the coming flood of legal mail appeared as if it had come for my own case. The packages came directly to her, skipping the rule-heavy mailroom. She opened the envelopes—sometimes boxes—in front of me, searched for contraband, and then handed everything over.

My cell and my work desk soon looked like a paper recycling center.

Seth and Noah said they wanted to revise the questions I had presented in the cert petition. I asked if, legally, they could really do that, and then I realized they probably knew better than I that they could do that. Duh. Seth responded with a polite "I think so, Shon," but not in a condescending way.

School was in session, and I was soaking up everything I could.

"Noah, why do you always base legal arguments on things other than the Court's precedents?"

"Because, at this level, precedent can change in an instant," he said. "It's not enough to just say the Court should do it our way because of this case. We must show the Court that our way not only keeps with prior precedent but also is the better way of handling these types of issues."

"Okay, that makes sense."

"Shon, I have a question for you. What is a normal day like in there? You always seem so positive."

"There are no normal days in prison. There are lots and lots of boring days, but no normal ones. And if I sound positive, it is because there are things to look forward to when I get out of here."

I explained what those things were: my family and Annie, although I couched her in terms of a "good friend" rather than something else.

Noah always took my calls and spent time explaining things. He never once asked me about my crime, which I found strange, but I appreciated it.

He started telling me about his life, including his engagement to Lauren, a woman he had met during an internship at the Solicitor General's office—where he had also met Seth.

I honestly couldn't comprehend why he and Seth

were so generous to me. That there is a world of educated, smart, successful people out there who, in fact, are kind and generous was a revelation. I had stumbled into the crystal cave and had magical mentors. Any young attorney would dream of having such mentors, and I was far from being an attorney.

Noah and I conducted a massive review of *Miranda* decisions, Fourth, Fifth, and Sixth Amendment cases going back half a decade. We had to have an answer for hypothetical questions that could be thrown at Seth; we had to coordinate with another set of attorneys on two related cases that the Court had also granted; we had to coordinate with the people who would be filing amicus briefs supporting our side. Well, that was what Seth and Noah needed to do. I was just helping around the edges. At least, being where I was, I didn't have to get the coffee.

People around WilmerHale had a funny nickname for me: I was called "in-house counsel." As in the "big-house."

When the *Fellers* briefs were finished, Seth prepped for the oral argument. We would do some of that over the phone.

"Terri, I need a big favor," I said. She looked up from her desk like this must be the millionth favor.

"The attorneys want me involved in a conference call. I don't think I can make that work from the regular phones in the unit."

She squinted at me before rolling her eyes.

"When, exactly, did I become your administrative assistant?" she asked.

The call happened a week later in her office. Seth introduced me to the other attorneys on the phone. Most of the call covered details of the briefs, and I participated here and there. Then Seth asked me what questions I thought the justices might ask.

I was dumbfounded that he would ask me that. He knew these people; I didn't. But it was a law school moment. The professor was asking me to think fast on my feet.

"Seth, really, I have no idea," I said. I heard some chuckling in the background, then I started laughing. I would rather get a laugh like that than spout off about something I knew nothing about.

Seth asked seriously if I could think of anything we hadn't covered. I said I thought the first question, the one about eliciting information versus interrogation, was a no-brainer, but the second question, about the legitimacy of the second confession, still worried me. Everyone agreed. That would be the tough spot.

Through his research Noah had concluded that Justice O'Connor would probably be the key vote on the second question; Noah had clerked for her back in 2000.

Then that was it. Everyone wished Seth good luck. My participation in the case of John J. Fellers v. United States was presumably over—all but the waiting.

19
THE MORNING OF BATTLE

It was an overcast morning in Washington, D.C., thirty-six degrees and breezy. A drizzling rain was on its way.

I pictured Seth and Noah stepping out of a cab in front of the Supreme Court and walking up the forty-four marble steps.

In the news that morning, Al Gore had announced he would not make another run for the presidency, and was throwing his support behind Governor Dean. Suicide bombers were killing people in Iraq and Moscow. The new premier of China was visiting the United States.

I had an idea from talking to Noah how it would begin. He and Seth would be whisked in past the tourists on the north side. The clerk of the Supreme Court, William Suter— known around the Court as "the General" on account of his background as an Army lawyer—would meet Seth and Noah just inside and escort them to the lawyers' lounge, which served as a sort of green room, where refreshments would be served and quill pens handed out.

I had read all about the famous courtroom itself: it is small and elegant, with only a few rows of seats that resemble church pews. Everyone stands as the court marshal yells "Oyez, oyez, oyez" and plush red curtains open. The justices file in and take their seats behind the slight curve of the long dark wood bench. There are four marble columns behind the bench and the justices. A clock, not some symbol of justice, hangs oddly between the middle columns. It may as well be a stopwatch: one hour will be given to John Fellers' future: thirty minutes for Seth to argue for his freedom and thirty minutes for the government to argue against it.

I knew I was going to be fairly useless that day. Breakfast didn't sound good at all, so I just worked out longer and ran the track continuously, trying to imagine exactly what was happening 700 miles to the east and forty-four marble steps up. I guess for as long as Seth was arguing the case, I was running. Toward the end of the scheduled hour, I wanted to be at my desk in Vincent's office, which is not far from the phone in Terri's office. I heard it ring a couple times, but Terri didn't come running for me. The third time was the charm.

Seth was on the phone. He had just hung up with John Fellers. Seth said he thought he had aced the first question. Mr. Michael Dreeben of the Soliciter General's office had argued against our case. One of the justices had characterized Mr. Dreeben's assertion that the first confession was not a violation of the Sixth Amendment as a "rather extreme position."

Seth had surely won that argument. He was unsure of the second, that the second confession was poisoned. Seth and Noah agreed that the second question would likely result in a 5–4 split, and how it would go was anybody's guess.

The legal knots that I had untied in my cell had now

been untied in the minds of the Nine by Seth. Perhaps. The Court doesn't just vote and that's it; after oral arguments they work on the case, write opinions, write minority opinions, and it all takes months. We would have to hold our breath. But it sounded like it had gone very well.

...

On a Monday in late January of 2004, I was writing in my cell when I heard my name called from the dayroom below. It was counselor Terri. I went to the balcony rail.

"Shon, you have a phone call," she said. I was unsure what it could be. Doomsday scenarios played out with my every step. Was I going to the hole for something? Had a family member died? Had someone told the cops they wanted to kill me? All I knew was that Terri rarely came into the unit to summon people for a phone call. I ran down the steps and walked across the unit with her.

She led me to the center office. That was odd. I looked at her. She gave me a nudge and then smiled.

"It's your pal Seth Waxman on the line," she said.

"Shon, how are you?" Seth said.

"Good. I take it a decision was handed down?"

"On the first question: nine to nothing in our favor. The second question was remanded back to the Eighth Circuit. Justice O'Connor wrote the opinion."

"We won nine to zero?"

"Yes, unanimously."

The Court's decision meant that although John might

not be going home immediately, his case was back on track, and he stood a decent chance of earning a retrial.

We congratulated each other. Seth told me his firm would represent John at no cost in the Eighth Circuit, which would hear the issue of the second confession. He said that Noah would take the lead on that case, and I would be helping him if I was interested. Of course I was interested.

I sent Annie a letter with the news. She was still in treatment at Mirasol. Lately our letters had been more sporadic, but I continued to worry about her. Sometimes when I was most up, she was most down and vice versa.

> *Dearest Annie,*
>
> *When things seem tough and the days seem endless, remember there is someone praying for you and waiting for the day you get healthy. I'm impatiently waiting for the day when both our struggles are over, and we can see each other. Won't that be a glorious day!! You healthy and me free!!*
>
> *Much love,*
> *Shon*

Two weeks after the big victory came a big scare. I called home for my weekly talk with Mom and Dad, and I could tell by Mom's hesitation and lack of focus on the conversation that something was bothering her. I asked her what was up.

"Your dad is having pain in his stomach and they found a mass of cells below his abdomen," she said.

"What's that mean?" I asked.

"Well . . . nothing at this point. They are going to operate on him in a week to see if they can figure out what it is. There is a good chance it is a benign tumor. Even if it's cancer, there is a chance they can remove it surgically."

She handed the phone to Dad.

"Don't let your mother worry you, Son," he said. "Whatever it is, they will get it out of me next week."

"But you're going to be okay, right?"

"Don't worry. I love you."

When I left the phone I bumped into a big black guy as he grabbed the phone next to me—he was a new arrival. He had the largest set of arms I had ever seen. His name was Big Meeks.

He came from Chicago and was plugged in with the Gangster Disciples. Instead of just selling drugs, like most Chicago gangsters, his crew would steal them with the help of two Chicago cops. He would take the two police officers to a dope house, and together they would rob it. He had been convicted of interstate robbery and sentenced to forty years.

What made him stand out in prison was his strength, even among guys who worked out all the time. He could bench-press over 500 pounds and rep 225 around forty times. Nobody could touch that. Guys would gather around the weight pile to watch him bench-press.

With strength comes respect and Meeks had plenty. He was on the higher rung of the Gangster Disciple crew, Pekin's largest gang.

One day he approached me and I hoped it wasn't to fight.

I wouldn't have taken him on with a baseball bat.

"You the law man," he said.

"My name is Shon. And, yeah, sort of."

He had a few questions he hoped I could answer. I could and did. I later proofread a few letters he sent to law schools hoping to recruit help.

One day he and I were in my cell discussing the merits of challenging his indictment, when I heard counselor Terri yell, "Hopwood, telephone call."

I went back in my cell to gather a pen and paper. John's case was at the Eighth Circuit, and Noah was probably on the line about it.

When we made it to the office, Terri said, "It's your mother."

"They couldn't get it all," Mom said, crying. "They found a big tumor below his stomach."

"What is it?"

"It's cancer, lymphoma, wrapped around the big artery that goes to his lower half. They took what they could and closed him up."

His prognosis was fair. Lymphoma is often a deadly disease, but Dad had his youth, forty-seven, and modern medicine on his side.

...

The Eighth Circuit Court of Appeals, as instructed by the Supreme Court, ruled that John Fellers' first confession was null and void. They then heard Noah's arguments that the second confession was therefore poisoned. We were waiting for their decision when big news came from Washington: the Supreme Court had ruled on another case potentially affecting tens of thousands of prisoners.

In the biggest criminal law decision in perhaps forty years, the Court threw out the Federal Sentencing Guidelines. Their decision was based on the reasoning they had established five years earlier in *Apprendi v. New Jersey*. The new case, *United States v. Booker*, ushered in a dramatic change. No longer were sentencing judges required to stick defendants, especially nonviolent drug offenders, with decades of imprisonment under the old guidelines. They could still do it if they chose to, but advisory guidelines are much different from mandatory ones.

I had been tracking *Booker* and several other sentencing-related cases for the better part of a year. I was helping a guy named John Davis, a Nebraska farmer who was in on drug charges.

John was so angry at the "criminal injustice system," as he called it, that he soon picked up the nickname Hater. His conviction for possessing and distributing meth was based solely on the testimony of drug addicts who cooperated with the government to reduce their sentences. Although Hater was a decorated Vietnam vet and had never been in more trouble than a traffic stop, he had been sentenced to life plus ten years.

His appeal had been denied by the Eighth Circuit, and now he was facing a deadline if he wanted to take a final appeal to the Supreme Court. The petition was due by the beginning of June 2004. He asked me to look into it.

"What happened with John Fellers was a fluke," I told him. "I can't really help you."

He called me names that I will not repeat. But his

anger, though taken seriously by others, was a joke between us—he had become a friend.

My every prison day now had a set pattern and he had become a part of it: I woke up to the normal symphony of clanks and flushes and guys talking. I worked out first thing, then showered, then went to Hater's cell for coffee and to hear his stories before starting on cases and then heading off for my work in Vincent's office.

Hater's cell, near mine, was the established coffee place.

It was like the small-town breakfast joint where farmers stop for a cup of coffee and to share bad jokes and donuts.

"How are you today, Hater?"

"I'm surrounded by idiots, but it could be worse," he said, patting his stomach.

He was older than I was and had stories about being left for dead a few times during the Vietnam War. He had stayed in Southeast Asia after his enlistment and worked in Thailand flying for the CIA's Air America. One evening in Vietnam he woke up in an opium den with a Vietcong soldier across the room from him, his AK-47 rifle propped against the wall. They stared at each other for a long time. Instead of fighting it out, they continued smoking. Hater was a good storyteller and had hundreds of stories to tell.

He had become a farmer after his time overseas, before he got caught up with drugs. Dealers later fingered him to prosecutors to obtain a plea deal. If it sounds just like John Fellers' case, you must understand that there are cases just like that all over the prison system. The drug laws and the plea system place an incredible amount of pressure on people to fabricate exaggerated or outright false accusations.[11]

I called Noah and told him about Hater's case. He asked if I had been following the sentencing case that an attorney he knew, Jeff Fisher, would soon be arguing before the Supreme Court. I researched that case and could see that if the Court agreed with Fisher, the decision would also call into question the federal guidelines. That was a train we wanted to get aboard.

We filed a cert petition two weeks before the Court issued its momentous decision in *Blakely v. Washington*, holding that any facts that increase a sentence under the Washington State sentencing guidelines had to be proved to a jury beyond a reasonable doubt. *Blakely* was simply an extension of the *Apprendi* decision, which had led me to the law in the first place. The *Blakely* decision caused many lower federal courts to believe that the same reasoning applied to the Federal Sentencing Guidelines. So a couple of months later the Court granted the petition in a case called *Booker*, which said that the Federal Sentencing Guidelines were unconstitutional. All of this opened the door for Hater's petition to be granted, and I had won in the High Court again. Rather than hearing the case, the Court simply remanded Hater's case back down for possible resentencing.

I had filed three cert petitions and two had been granted. That was a terrific batting average for any lawyer, but for a prison inmate with no formal education in the law, it was almost incomprehensible. I felt proud, but unfortunately my record of success was making me the enemy of the other jailhouse lawyers at Pekin.

Noah filed a brief with the Eighth Circuit, arguing

that John Fellers also qualified for resentencing under *Booker*. The Court ruled that the second confession was valid, not poisoned, but, hallelujah, they remanded him for resentencing under *Booker*. As a result, four years were shaved from his sentence. That could not have happened if his case hadn't still been on appeal.

John wasn't exactly packing to go home yet, but he could now see daylight: he had two more years to serve instead of six. And he could yet have a life with his young daughter, Johana.

Those two years went quickly. When he finally made it back to Nebraska, he restarted his car business and was fine.

And his daughter was still a youngster—he hadn't missed all that.

It was different for Hater: the Eighth Circuit ruled that his trial lawyer had not objected to the *Booker* issue back at his sentencing, and the resentencing claim was therefore waived. But we resolved to keep working toward proving his innocence, a cause I believed in. And still do.

20
MY MELVIN MOMENT

The months and cases rolled by. I was cranking out documents like a print shop. I had lots of time to work on cases because my back hurt so bad that I was bedridden on and off for six months. Basketball falls and weightlifting had seriously damaged my lower back.

A prison doctor examined me, listened to my complaints about chronic nerve pain, and concluded that I suffered from psychosomatic pain. He prescribed antidepressants, which I didn't need. Although the medication didn't reduce my pain, it did prevent me from performing legal work because I was walking around like a zombie. Maybe that was the point.

Mom called both of the senators from Nebraska and asked them to contact the prison and order them to give me appropriate medical care, but it didn't do any good.

Noah sensed I was coming apart, that the pain was taking a toll on my mental well-being.

"Why don't I talk to the other partners here at Wilmer- Hale?" Noah asked.

"Talk to them about what?"

"About what options we have?"

"Noah, my mom and dad want to help me, but they don't have the money to hire you."

"Let's not worry about that now."

The partners at WilmerHale decided that Noah should be my official attorney, pro bono of course, and a letter from one of the most prestigious law firms in America arrived at the medical administrator's office. I was taken to an outside neurologist three weeks later.

Coincidence? Probably not.

Mom was happy that I had received medical treatment, but she had something more important on her mind: every time I called home, she gently reminded me that I needed to work on my spiritual side. Since Dad had been diagnosed with cancer, she was less patient with anyone's—especially my own—reluctance to make a commitment. I had been thinking about it. My friend Montreal Dungy was also working on me, as if he had been hired by Mom.

"Shon, when are you going to get real with God? I bet your momma is praying for you right now." Mom's campaign was well known, as my locker had become a lending library of religious books.

"Why don't you just do you and let me do me?" I said. This was a common prison saying.

"That's the problem. You doing you is what got you here." Montreal's religious conversion had come shortly after he had received a thirty-year sentence for possessing a few handfuls of crack cocaine. He was now studying to become a minister, taking correspondence courses from a divinity college.

He wasn't the only one hammering me. Of all people, Robert Lynn Jones, the notorious drug smuggler, had decided to "give his life over to God." He told me one day in his cell that it was "time to make a change." Then he started talking about forgiveness over vengeance. That was an incredible turnaround for a guy who was serving an extra decade because some bogus sheriff had planted drugs in his house. As far as I could see, he had a right to be angry. I thought he was putting me on—making fun of the whole jailhouse conversion scene—but he was serious about it.

...

An interesting test of who I was, or who I might become, arrived in those same weeks. I was offered a deal by a friend of a friend. If I would write an appeal on a difficult case, $10,000 would be deposited in an outside bank account in my name. I could use it for college tuition, to pay down on what I owed the government, or for whatever I wanted.

And it would be mine, win or lose—it would not be a contingency thing. I knew it was for real, because the guy had outside access to major money. I analyzed the case enough to know why he couldn't find a willing attorney. He really didn't stand a chance.

He said he knew it was a long shot, but he was willing to see what would happen. In other words, he wanted some hope—something that might shorten his stay in hell, or at least make it seem to go faster. My friends and his friends lobbied me. I said I would think about it. Everyone knew I was busy with other appeals.

The idea of taking serious money concerned me. Guys were generous with snacks and supplies. Some, like Hater and his father, Herman, showed their appreciation by helping me pay for a couple of college courses on "repay someday" terms—not because they had to but just because they wanted to.

This proposal was different. I was different. For some strange reason, I had come to the idea that I shouldn't take money I hadn't earned, and I didn't think I could give this guy his money's worth in terms of results.

That next day at evening chow a young black kid, Melvin Brown, came up to me. He sort of reminded me of the young guy I had sat next to on the Con Air flight into Oklahoma City. He was a gentle, religious kid with a deep-voiced chuckle that carried nicely through the unit. He said that he had a not-so-good lawyer and he wondered if I would please look at his case. The deadline for his appeal was in two weeks.

Two weeks just doesn't work for motions of that magnitude, so I almost blew him off, and would have if not for his courtesy—uncommon in prison. He hadn't had many breaks in life. Not many people had said yes to Melvin. He had a history of the petty crimes that come with growing up in poverty. Most recently he had been busted with four grams of crack. Smoking crack was bad for you, of course, but I could never understand why black man's crack cocaine merited a much longer sentence than white man's powder.[12]

The two-week deadline was the biggest challenge. A law had been pushed through in 1996 after the Timothy McVeigh bombing: the Antiterrorism and Effective Death Penalty Act.[13] It limited a prisoner's right to a habeas corpus appeal to within one year of sentencing or the denial of direct appeal. Death row prisoners generally had two capable attorneys assigned to them, so having a year to prepare a habeas motion was doable. But for petty criminals like Melvin who were unable to afford an attorney and were probably in prison because the attorney they did have was incompetent, the deadline was daunting if not impossible. Such guys would be lost in the law library, trying to figure it out for themselves. Instead of education, most had mental illness, and the law books might as well have been written in Latin, which they kind of are, especially habeas law.

The antiterrorism bill not only shortened the time available; it also added to the complexity of the undertaking, creating more hoops to jump through or you forfeit the right of appeal.[14]

For most of that year Melvin had been moved around in county jails, where you really have few resources at all, so he was screwed.

I knew I would not have time for the $10,000 case if I helped Melvin. I thought about it in my bunk that night. I had to decide what I really wanted to do and who I really wanted to be, and what I wanted my relation to the law to be. Was I going to be a take-the-money-and-run guy like some of the attorneys I had witnessed? Besides, Melvin was a good kid; the other guy, not so much.

I decided on Melvin, not the money. I felt that the decision could be a turning point for Melvin, and for me.

21
THE FIRM

I dove into Melvin's case, marshaling help from a few guys I had come to trust. In fact, I had what looked like a busy operation going. There was copying, mailing, typing, filing—I couldn't do it all alone. It made the time move faster; this was 2005, and I had three years yet to go, assuming good behavior.

My typist was Glenn, one of the Wagner brothers—two brothers who shared a cell. In their early forties, short, unscathed by exercise, they were a bit Jekyll and Hyde: Glenn was clean-cut and educated; Frank looked like a troll from under a bridge.

Drugs had done a number on both of them. Before they were arrested, Glenn was doing the books for an Omaha dealer in exchange for crack—Glenn was a former accountant. The two of them had smoked crack all day long. They were victims more than criminals, but drugs do that.

Frank and Glenn took care of each other. I knew two other sets of brothers at Pekin, and they did the same. The Petty brothers, two skinny African-Americans, spirited so much food from the kitchen that their sandwich operation made them a small fortune. They were happy guys, big Eddie Murphy smiles, selling their sealed baggies of patented Petty Sandwiches for three or four stamps each: fresh Wonder bread, bologna, lettuce, tomato, cheese, all fresh-stolen, plus little packets of mustard and mayonnaise.

Melvin bought me a new typewriter ribbon and a prepaid card for the copy machine. That set him back about $14. We called it square. Although he had been arrested with a very small amount of crack, his sentence was over sixteen years. It was long because he was treated as a three-strikes career criminal.[15] How someone could be a career criminal at twenty-four was beyond me. One of those three arrests had been for possessing a tenth of a gram of crack with intent to distribute. But when he pled guilty they had dropped the distribution part of the charge and he was convicted for simple possession. For him to be classified as a career criminal, he needed two prior distribution offenses. With the one charge dropped to simple possession, he did not have the two priors, and he should not have been sentenced as a career offender.

His lawyer had missed that distinction, so the kid had been sentenced to sixteen years instead of probably five. I wrote the brief over the course of a day; it was easier than I had anticipated. A month later his sentencing judge agreed with our contention, and, for his $14 and his courtesy, Melvin was resentenced to five years and some change.

When he made it back to Pekin after resentencing, he gave me a big hug in the middle of the compound. That was not your standard prison protocol—a guy showing real affection to another, let alone a black and white guy hugging. But neither of us cared.

Most of the black guys in my unit were ecstatic that Melvin would be going home. Big Meeks gave me a rare smile and thumbs-up across the dayroom. It was a really big thumb. Getting John Fellers his day in the Supreme Court was maybe my first big legal victory, but Melvin was my first pack-your-bags-kid-you're-going-home victory—well, it was almost that: he had two years to pack, but he would be going home a decade early.

...

While I was still in the glow of that victory, I received two important packages. The first was the equivalent of a legal care package, compliments of Noah. I had asked if the firm had any extra briefs around, because reading other people's briefs was how someone who couldn't attend law school could learn. Noah had rounded up a box of Supreme Court briefs. I was grateful that Noah had taken the time to gather them and ship them to me. I was also grateful for the encouragement Noah had given me. He strongly advised that I pursue law school when I was released.

The other package came from my mother. In it was another Christian book, and stuck inside the book was a written speech my dad had given at church:

> *I know I would have never gotten through this last year without having faith that God was in control. Cancer can be a lonely disease. You sit in a doctor's office, you sit in scanning machines, you sit at home sick, a lot of times by yourself, for hours. But God impressed upon me during those times that when*

He is all you have, He is all you need. It was during those lonely times that God drew me closer to Him, especially through His word and through prayer.

I didn't always get what I prayed for and sometimes God said no, but God was changing me and because of that I have been truly blessed.

I am not thankful to have cancer, but I am thankful that God has brought me through cancer treatment and continues to strengthen me both physically and spiritually. I am richly blessed.

When I read it, I thought, wow, that was quite a perspective from a guy I had heard crying in the background during a phone call after a particularly hard radiation treatment. He hurt so bad that he was unable to talk to me on the phone, except for whimpers and grunts to acknowledge what I was saying.

Dad's cancer was now in remission for the second time, and Annie was out of treatment and back home. Dad told me he had seen her one day when he was playing a round of golf. She was visiting the nearby Catholic cemetery where her mother is buried. Dad finished his round and waited for her at the gate. They had a nice talk. He invited her to come visit them sometime, but she hadn't. He gave her a lot of credit for my turn-around. She was too humble to agree, but he made her feel like family.

As it turned out, they were both just taking a short break from their illnesses. I wrote her after Dad's report of that chance meeting, but she didn't return my letter or take my call. She was soon in California in another treatment facility.

...

Long ago Bee Dog had warned me that I had to be
mentally ready for the time when I would be tested
physically, and that I would be redefined by my reaction.
I figured that just wasn't going to happen to me, that I
had circumvented that trial by defining myself the way I
had, but my time finally came in the chow line.

"I gonna smash that bitch. I gonna smash that bitch
good—know what I'm sayin'?" He went on and on,
talking and rapping to nobody in particular.

Dray had dirty dreadlocks, man breasts, and a reputation for talking too much and starting fights that
he rarely won. Backing down from him—losing to a
loser—would send me into precarious waters.

He was a few men ahead of me in the chow line.
He glanced back at me, continuing his verbal taunts.
It was all about some "bitch" in the unit, and how he
was going to smash that bitch. The week prior we had
had an altercation over one of the televisions. At the
time he'd just stared me down and then the next day
he had bumped into me on purpose in the chow line.
Now, in the line again, he droned on and on, rapping
to himself and moving like he had headphones on.
"That bitch is going to get it, and you know who I'm
talkin' about."

In prison, the epithet refers to a guy who is regularly sexually abused, a submissive, a guy who will allow
another to walk all over him, a guy who garners no
respect from anyone. If a friend calls you a bitch, it can
be a joke, but there was no joke going on here. The guys

in line understood that I was the target. Everyone was tense. I was nauseous because I knew I had no choice.

I had to react *appropriately*. And soon. If I didn't, I knew what would start to happen because I'd witnessed it before. Maybe someone else would start calling me a bitch and then someone else would think I really was. Next, they'd ask to borrow something and wouldn't pay me back. Eventually they'd no longer ask; they'd take. Thus, would begin the long slide down until I finally fit Dray's description of me. The difference between the streets outside and prison life is considerable, but it's nothing compared to a fall from the upper levels of prison life to the lowest circles of its various hells.

Big Meeks and the other gang leaders I'd helped legally were my friends now, but that could change if they saw me shrink from a righteous confrontation. Meeks preyed on weak guys. He'd go into their cells and say he'd heard they'd been bad-mouthing him. They'd shake. He'd do it right when they had come back from a commissary run, with their pillowcases full of goodies. They would just hand him the bag to make peace and save a beating. He would do that when his locker got a little bare. Sometimes he would ask me what I thought about one guy or another. I knew what he was doing: he didn't want to mess up a friend of mine. So I tried to spare as many guys as I could by saying they were friends, even when I didn't like them.

I knew that no matter how good I was with a law book and even if it took a year of sliding, I would eventually be on the receiving end of someone's terrorizing if I backed down from Dray. In prison, if you can't maintain a modicum of physical respect, nothing else really matters. A man's body is his castle, and if he doesn't defend it with his life, it gets looted and burned.

And whatever respect I had earned on the basketball court or football field was ancient history—with my bad back and law work, I hadn't played lately. Prison credibility has a shelf life of around three years, with all the people who get transferred and released.

After chow, during the ten-minute move, I took a couple deep breaths through my nose and marched to his cell door. His cellmate wasn't back yet, but that wouldn't have mattered. I would have gone ahead as I did. I stormed in and threw a straight right into Dray's jaw. His glasses flew across the cell. I pushed him with one hand under his chin and the other on his gut, working him against the back of the cell. He turned his back toward me and beat his fists on the bars and clear glass to summon help from the guards standing outside the unit.

I moved away from him and went to the cell door to see if guards were running our way; I didn't want to end up in solitary or lose good behavior time if I could help it. Not to mention that I had a good job, a good cell, and plenty of guys depending on me to do their legal work. That was what I was thinking about during the fight.

No guards were in sight. As I turned back toward Dray, he sprung up and caught me in the eye. I felt blood rush down my face. In the few seconds I'd given him, he had tucked a padlock into the web of his fist like a brass knuckle.

His punch flayed the skin around my eye. There was no way the fight would be unnoticed now.

We were already outside his cell, in the wide-open space of the dayroom where everyone was watching. He swung and caught me again. I landed a right to his head and grabbed his dreads. The guards came running. I knew if I stopped right then, serious discipline against me would be unlikely, but I also knew my standing in the yard would suffer. So as the guards started to pull me away from him, I yanked on his dreads to jam his face into my knee. The guards tackled us both.

We both landed in solitary for three weeks. But in the screwy world of prison where status is everything, I'd purchased enough safety to maybe last through the three years I had left.

I didn't get off on violence; some guys really do live for bloodshed. They have plenty of time to psyche each other out, plan revenge, probe vulnerabilities with little taunts and dramas, and find opportunities to climb the ladder of respect at someone else's expense. If you had a summer camp for kids with extreme anger management problems, and you took away most of the adults, added weapons, and you didn't let anyone go home for years and years, you'd have a U.S. prison. It's strictly *Lord of the Flies*.

I was in solitary for only a short time. I watched solitary confinement, which was often doled out in months rather than days or hours, break strong men. It made them go crazy. No imagine what it does to those already suffering from mental illness. Most of the people placed in solitary confinement will one day be released. And that's after we've made their mental illness worse instead of better. Scary thought.

In solitary, I reread my stack of letters from memory. That connection with the saner world always helped me think above the pointless dramas of prison life. I had time—three weeks in solitary confinement is eternity— to think about how prison had changed me. Had it worn away the good part of me or the bad? Maybe that wasn't the best way to think of it. It had pounded the young idiot out of me, for sure. Maybe I still had a bit of the De Niro gangster cool in my official persona, but it was kept now as a form of protection, not as something I valued in any way. I couldn't let it go too fast—looking too soft was probably what had landed me in the predicament with Dray.

I probably had forgotten where I was. I was thinking I was some young lawyer and wasn't paying attention. I kept telling myself now: I am an inmate in a prison. The hard shell needs to be very hard, or men will mess with you. The fact that someone had proved I hadn't kept the shell steely enough. But it didn't matter, I thought. I could picture myself having lunch with Noah and Seth now a lot more easily than I could picture myself punching a guy out in a prison cell. My former life was diminishing with each calendar year, but I couldn't let this happen again. I had to be the tough prison guy, even if it was just something of a Halloween costume.

The time alone also made me see the whole future with Annie clearly again. I stopped thinking of myself as some jerk wasting her time. Nobody could love her as much as I did. I felt I was good enough at a few things, and I could figure out how to support a good life for us. I wanted to heat things up with her. I decided to write more letters and have faith that she would read them, even if she didn't answer them. And in my cell alone I prayed she and my dad would remain safe.

22
GATHERING CLOUDS

I had a lot of catching up to do on the legal front when I got out of solitary. Deadlines were approaching for quite a few briefs, so I worked like a first-year Biglaw associate.

Like I said, not everyone in Pekin was happy about my legal victories. The unhappiest was a Nation of Islam fellow who wore the standard pillbox hat and had an attitude about everything. He took himself seriously as a legal expert—though he was not an expert by any stretch of the imagination.

He would take paragraphs from one opinion and use them with paragraphs from other opinions, as if legal opinions were made of LEGO blocks that you could take apart and rearrange as you pleased, without regard to context. I tried to talk to him about things like that, because it bothered me that he was ruining some guys' one chance at legal relief, but he was just insulted that I might think he needed any help.

With each of my victories there came a longer stare from him. One day in the law library we were on opposite sides of a bookshelf, and I could see his angry eyes over the tops of the books.

"You don't impress me, cracker," he said. "You got outside lawyers helping you."

That was very true; I was regularly calling Noah to ask questions.

"But I do what I do all from here," he said as he poked his own temple way too hard, knocking his cap sideways and making himself wince. "Don't be takin' on no more brothers, because they don't need your help. You been warned, whiteboy."

His words stung a little. I had been operating an equal opportunity firm.

He was affiliated and had a very powerful band of brothers. I thought about what to do. I could stop helping black guys, or maybe I could stop the legal work altogether and just concentrate on my classes. I gave it a moment's thought and then decided to just ignore him.

Then another danger sprang up. A new guy arrived. His nickname was Kaos. In our circus world, he was a star freak. He was an olive-skinned white guy who was missing his front teeth. That was fine, except he celebrated the look by tightening up his upper lip to reveal the hole in his smile and then sticking his tongue through it.

"What up, Shon?" he said, smiling. I had been friendly, watching him operate, but I didn't want anything to do with him. I had my newly hardened steel shell on.

I walked past him.

"Oh, you don't have time for a playa," he cackled behind.

"Well, f-you then," he said.

He ran his mouth like that constantly. Overhearing

him one day, I realized he was the nightmare I had been dreading all my years at Pekin. He was telling stories about his former cellmate, Tyler. I recognized the name and the stories.

He had been cellmates at another prison with my Tyler, the drug dealer from Lincoln who had provided the guns and the stolen cars for my bank jobs, and who hated me for taking a plea bargain. Kaos looked at me as if he knew the story, like he was carrying Tyler's anger, like he had finally let the thing slip out within earshot so I could start worrying.

Kaos looked at me like I was the enemy. All my codefendants, as I mentioned, had pled together except Tyler, who insisted on playing a losing hand. We were not obliged to go down in flames with him and spend our entire lives in prison. I didn't consider myself a snitch, but the wrong words can paint you as one.

My hard work to earn and keep some respect seemed at risk now. Kaos could start trouble. We circled each other for weeks, waiting for the other to start it up. He was a Latin Disciple.

The group included both Hispanic and non-Hispanic white guys. My good friend and basketball teammate Joe was a Latin Disciple, as was Milan. The leader of the LDs was a Puerto Rican named Jay, who was also my friend and someone I had helped with a habeas motion. If Kaos and I fought, those friendships and loyalties would be tested, and it was more likely than not that I would be on the losing end. It might break some guys' hearts to go against me, even to hurt me, but they could not and would not turn their backs on their gang.

All I could do was keep my eyes open and hope it didn't come to that.

So there was this dark cloud above, with Kaos and the Nation of Islam guy, and then—rule of three—we got this new inmate with an electronic voice box, presumably installed after losing his larynx to cancer. His flat, electronic voice was a strange addition to the prison sounds, but that wasn't the problem.

The morning he arrived I was working with John "Hater" Davis. We were going through a box of forensic evidence from his trial.

"Take a look at this," Hater said as he handed me a document. It was the sworn statement from a guy who had said, under oath, that he had been at John's farm and bought some drugs.

"Look at the name of the guy."

I looked at the name on the statement. I had heard that name just recently. Where? It was the new guy who had come into the unit.

"You got it," Hater said. "It's Voicebox. He's the guy who signed this, and it's nothing but lies, because I've never seen him before this morning."

"But you've seen him now?" I asked.

"I saw him when he came in. Complete stranger to me."

"You have never seen him before?"

"Never, Shon, I swear."

So one of the people who had framed Hater was in a cell less than fifty feet away.

I was worried that Hater would do something out of anger, so we devised a plan. We would pay Voicebox a visit when his celly, Bernie, and my celly, Roger, were around as witnesses.

That evening, Hater, Roger, and I walked to the cell. Bernie and Voicebox were reading.

"Hey Bernie," I said, hoping not to alarm Voicebox.

Bernie was on his bunk with a novel resting on his belly. He's a big guy, so he had a good place for the book. Hater stepped in.

"Hey, do I know you?" he said to Voicebox.

Voicebox scanned his face.

"No, I don't think so."

"Are you sure?" Hater said.

"Were you at the holding facility in Oklahoma?" Voicebox asked.

"No."

Voicebox was puzzled.

"I don't think we've met, then."

Hater pulled the signed statement from the pocket of his khaki pants.

"Then how come you said you bought five pounds of dope from me at my house?"

The cell was quiet. I checked the floor to make sure Voicebox hadn't urinated on it. He made noises, kind of whiny-like. His body was heaving, first a little and then big heaves. His eyes, which I could see because I was now sitting beside him, were flowing.

He handed the paper, shaking, back to Hater. He looked on the bed for the voice device. He held it to his throat, slowly took a deep breath, and looked at all of us. His rasping voice was interrupted every few words by his heaving and sobbing.

What he said was that Hater's codefendants had put him up to it. They wanted someone to verify their lies, so they had concocted the scheme in county jail. One of Hater's codefendants had paid Voicebox $2,000 to do it. He said he had always regretted it, and, crying, he apologized to Hater in his robot voice.

But how do you apologize for a life sentence? Well, you just do.

We left. Hater had stayed calm. The guy had agreed to recant and sign a new affidavit. He was still shaking when we left. I thought it was a mix of remorse and fear. He had been worried for so long about this moment that he didn't understand that the storm was blowing over, and his agreement to sign a new and accurate affidavit would bring a new start. It might not bring forgiveness, but it would be a basis for coexistence, which is half the battle in such places.

But his fear overwhelmed him. He wanted out of there.

The only way out was for him to say Hater had threatened his life. That is exactly what he claimed, and he checked into protective custody the next morning. He even had the gall to write Judge Kopf to say Hater had threatened to kill him.

Just like that he was gone. Hater's best ticket home had just slipped away. I wished we had stayed longer in the guy's cell and settled him down, but it was what it was. At least we had witnesses who would sign affidavits as to what everyone had said.

Though the Supreme Court had granted Hater's petition and sent the case back down, he was denied resentencing by the court of appeals. We filed a habeas motion to Judge Kopf, raising a number of claims, relating the evidence we had about Voicebox and others, and attaching a number of affidavits. Judge Kopf rejected the motion. He didn't believe us. So Hater is still there. It kills me. How would you feel if one of your friends was stuck in a bad place for life and you couldn't help?

...

By the summer of 2007 I had about a year and a half left. I wanted no trouble from anyone. I had made contact with Annie and was fanning those coals as best I could.

She needed love and I could now almost see the day when I could be with her and hold her. I was doing sit-ups on a cold morning when the Nation of Islam guy appeared. It was a little after everyone else had headed off to their jobs. I had some extra time and wanted to boost my heart rate. He saw me and left without saying a word.

It somehow shook me a little. Since there was still a controlled move under way, I headed back to the unit to start my work for the day. There he was again on the compound with a couple of his gang buddies, looking all business. They were just standing there up ahead, in my way. I kept walking toward them, which is all I could do. Getting seriously messed up this late, this close to getting out, would be justice in a way. That thought helped me smile as I got closer. And yes, I had just taken on a new black client in clear defiance of the warning not to.

I was within a couple of feet of them when they stepped completely off the sidewalk to let me pass. I should have kept going, but I was perplexed. As I stopped, I saw a shadow.

Someone had been walking behind me. It was Big Meeks. He had cut over from the clinic to the weights to work out, but he had seen me and thought he might be of some assistance. He knew the issue.

"You dogs good?" he said to them. They nodded, looking up at him. "That's good. Shon here is my law man, you know. You all understand that, don't you?" They nodded. The Nation of Islam guy turned and started walking away. That was that.

The Kaos thing was still hanging over me, but I could handle one thing hanging. I minimized the risk from Kaos by just staying far away from him.

23
THE LAST VISIT

My release to a halfway house was set for October 2, 2008, still a little over a year away. I was in the home stretch. I was focusing on completing my college courses so I could get a degree as soon as possible after my release. My job search would depend on it. Annie and I continued to correspond. Some days she could not wait for me to come home, and others, well, she seemed to be wising up. She told me how two guys, both of whom she had dated, had proposed to her and she was debating what to do. My suggestion was that she dump both, even though she hadn't really asked for my opinion.

She started visiting again, but when we were holding hands I could feel the uncertainty. She was the center of my future life—that much I knew. I resolved to be patient and easygoing, whatever she needed.

Dad's cancer had returned. He came to visit the week after his prognosis. I could tell that this go-round with the disease was scaring him. When I asked what the doctors had said, he changed the subject. But I pressed him to promise to still be home when I got there, and he promised.

My brother Brett was well on his way to a successful life. He was getting married that summer to his longtime girlfriend, Katie. They already had one son, Nathaniel, and they were expecting another. I wished I could be at the wedding to share in my family's joy.

On an August evening when Dad and Mom had just returned from the cancer center in Omaha, I called home. Mom was crying. Dad took the phone, but then he broke down, too.

"The doctor said there is nothing more they can do for me, Son."

"What . . . there's nothing they can do?"

Dad and I had discussed at length that the day might come when he would need to be selfish—because he deserved the right to stop his treatment, to go out his own way.

When we had talked about it, I never thought things would reach a point where he would really do it. But four years of chemo, radiation, and stem cell transplants had taken a toll as great as the cancer.

"What are the doctors saying?"

But Dad couldn't answer. He passed the phone back to Mom, who told me that the cancer had advanced into his liver and other organs. They would do a radiation treatment to reduce the discomfort and pain, but there were no more solutions.

"The doctor said it's inevitable," Mom said. "I just will thank the Lord for every day I still have with him."

I'm sure they were holding hands.

...

Against the doctor's orders, Dad decided he needed to come see me one more time. Bringing him to Pekin would be challenging. He needed an IV drip with large doses of pain medication and replacement fluids in his arm almost all the time. And the expense of the trip seemed impossible; the medical bills had depleted the family savings. But word had spread in David City and in Shelby, the nearby town where Mom and Dad had started out. To their complete surprise, envelopes started arriving in the mail with best wishes and checks in small amounts to help with the trip.

You just can't say enough about the people of David City and towns like that. They knew Dad was an honorable guy, and that was enough. He had a right to see his son one more time.

...

My mom and my sisters, Kristin and Samantha, rolled Dad into the visiting room in a wheelchair with an IV suspended above it. The bones in his face were sharp under his leathery, yellowed skin. Even the whites of his eyes were yellow; his liver was failing. I was not prepared for how he looked, and I almost broke down when I saw him.

"How are you doing, Son?" he said.

I hugged him and kissed his cheek. We sat at a table and he wanted to know all about my latest legal efforts and my progress toward a degree. He told me he was proud of what I had become and proud that I was helping people. That, he said, is what life is all about. He said he was sorry that he would not be around to help me when I was released, but that others would help if I came back home.

We played cards—a few games of Spades like when I was a kid. Dad nodded off a little. My sisters and I would talk, and the game would restart when he woke up. There were long silences.

He told me that he wanted me to take his place when my sister Kristin was married, to walk her down the aisle for him. In saying that, he had accepted me back into the family, showing me he trusted me with its responsibilities.

When Mom and the girls were in the back of the visiting room buying food at the vending machines, Dad leaned toward me and said, "I want to see you in heaven."

I told him I would see him there, but he shouldn't look for me too soon. I told him I wanted to have a new life with Annie, and I thanked him for being a good father to me.

"I'm sorry for everything," I said. "I wish I could go back and change things."

Dad smiled. "Don't we all, Shon . . . some of it. Not all of it." I promised to spend some years back home in Nebraska once I was released. I told him I would be there to take care of our family and to give Mom the love of a son that had been denied her for a decade. I said I hoped I might be able to go to law school when I was released, but, after that, I would come home to the family.

The trip had already worn him down, so I took Mom's cue and pushed him toward the door. His tired eyes were moist, as were mine. I gave him a hug and kiss and told him that I loved him. His frail arms wrapped around me and he did not want to let go, nor did I. The finality of everything was unbearable.

Mom rolled him out. He glanced back and waved his wrist. I had caused him a lot of grief, but he loved me deeply. I walked back into the unit with red eyes and tears collecting on my khaki shirt. I didn't care who saw them or if they thought I was soft. I didn't care about much that day.

Two months later my new counselor—Terri had been reassigned to another cellblock—came up to my cell. "Hopwood, Hopwood, are you awake? . . . Shon, are you awake?"

I already knew what it was. Dad passed on Sunday, October 14, 2007. Six hundred people attended the funeral.

My best friend, Tom, read a short eulogy, stopping briefly in the middle to collect himself before finishing the words I had sent from prison.

All day I could hear Dad's voice. I remembered the time we were out at the farm and he was riding the quarter horse chasing cattle around, with his arm in a sling. He had broken it, I don't remember how. When we were finished sorting cattle, he said, "Not bad for a one-armed fat man." It was a play on the John Wayne line from True Grit, one of his favorites.

Shon,

Just know that I am carrying you in my heart, saying lots of prayers for you and your family, and I promise to be here for you and help you in any way that I can, both now and in the future. Although you haven't asked this of me, I have grieved hard this week, both because of my own sadness and for you. I sobbed so hard and felt such sadness as I also grieved the loss of the hopes and dreams of experiences you were counting on having with your dad after your release. I know that sadness myself as I, too, had to deal with the overwhelming shock of my mom being yanked from my life and the shattering of all the dreams of experiences we would have together throughout my life. I guess it wasn't meant to be that way for you and me. It is strangely ironic that five years ago, you were there for me when I lost my mom and now I am here for you as you have lost your dad. We are very blessed to have each other, indeed.

I love you, Shon. And your family loves you. We are all praying for you and looking forward to next October.

Peace and Love my dear friend,
Annie

She was at Pekin the next week—a beautiful angel to support me in my grief. After the visit, I knew I wanted to marry her. I would have married her right then if I could have.

24
EVIL SPIRITS

Horn arrived in 2008. He was about twenty-five and tattooed from head to toe, with big bulky shoulders, Mad Max energy for mayhem, and a total dedication to white supremacy. He had transferred from a high-security federal pen and considered himself the leader of white supremacists everywhere. I was now in my early thirties and he was like a little kid to me. He sat at the tables where the Aryan Brotherhood, the Skinheads, the Dirty White Boys, and a few Hells Angels and other bikers congregated. He was stirring up so much racial trouble that the staff started leaning on him to cool down. They threatened to send him back to a maximum-security prison. Over dinner after that threat he tried to force all the white guys at his table to back him up. He told them that the guards couldn't send them all away if they stuck together. They balked at the idea and tried to calm him down. He picked up his food tray.

"I'm not sitting with you rats."

He scanned the room. He looked over at our table, the Nebraska and Iowa guys. We were known for something different, mostly for keeping ourselves out of the limelight. Maybe we looked easy to a newcomer. He came over and sat down.

"What are you doing here?" I said. If we accepted him at our table, we would have trouble with black gangs and everyone else within a few weeks. Most of us had worked hard to keep good relations.

"What do you mean, what am I doing here? I'm eating my dinner."

"Not here," Bobbie said without looking at him.

"You're saying I can't sit here?"

"You're trouble, man. You can't sit here," I said. Horn was stupefied.

"Let's go outside with this," he said.

He trailed Bobbie out. I hung back behind them both.

"So you two are saying a peckerwood can't sit at your table?"

"Peckerwood" is a term white guys use to describe other white supremacist gang members. I don't know where it originated.

"No, we're saying you can't sit at our table," Bobbie said. "You bring too much heat."

"So let me get this right." Horn inched toward us with his hands in his pockets. "You saying I positively can't sit there?"

The last thing I wanted to do was start a fight with this moron in the middle of the compound. I wasn't scared of him or the knife he was pretending to have in his pocket; I was scared that Bobbie and I could lose good time. We were short timers now.

"That's exactly what we're saying," Bobbie said. "If you try it you know what will happen."

"I don't fight. I use them things," Horn said, motioning an arm as if he already had his blade in hand. "We'll see what your homeboy Toro says."

Toro was a fellow Nebraskan, tough, intelligent. I often worked out with him and another Nebraska boy named Jimmy.

Horn thought Toro was tight with him because they sometimes talked on the yard.

"You can talk to him now," I said.

Toro and Jimmy happened to be nearby. They could tell what was happening, based on the positioning and body language.

"What's happening, fellas?" Toro said to Bobbie and me.

"You better tell your boys to back off before I cut one of them," Horn said.

Toro looked over at us and laughed.

"And why would you do something so stupid?" he said.

Horn laid out the problem. But Toro told him he should respect the traditions, that he should not sit somewhere if he wasn't invited. What went unsaid was that if Horn started something it would be all four of us beating him. That was the end of it.

Two months later Bobbie and I were walking through the yard when Horn came running past, chased by two white guys. One tackled him. They took turns kicking and stomping him with their boots until enough guards arrived to stop them.

I asked Bobbie if he thought we had ever been that stupid, back when we were starting our sentences.

"We were stupid," he said, "but not that stupid."

...

Davey was my last celly. He was about seven years older than I was but decades younger in some ways. It felt like having a teenager in the cell. I don't have the expertise to diagnose things like obsessive-compulsive disorder, multiple personality disorder, or schizophrenia, but to my layman's eyes Davey exhibited symptoms of all of them.

He would watch TV programs like 24 or Prison Break and be so wound up in them that he was sure they were real and he was a part of them.

"Shon, did you see the way Jack Bauer took those guys out?"

I was in bed and ignoring him.

"Did you see it?"

"Davey, I'm writing a letter."

He would then launch into a word-for-word recitation of the entire episode.

He was short, slender, and gullible to the point that guys would set up elaborate jokes to mess with him, like telling him a system-wide prison escape was being planned.

When these hoaxes came along, I tried not to discourage him all the way, because he needed hopeful things to think about at night to fall asleep. Otherwise he would often become lost in the horror of what had happened during his one-day crime spree. If he couldn't sleep, sometimes I couldn't sleep, because he would be twitching around and half talking and moaning.

Davey had robbed a bank. He was in love with a

girl who left him because he never had any money, and there was some other guy who did. Davey, then twenty-two, figured he needed some big cash so he could win her back. He took a single-shot 12-gauge shotgun into an Illinois bank—he had never fired a gun in his life. He wore a ski mask and camouflage Army pants with the big pockets full of shotgun shells.

The vault was closed, so he took a customer as hostage and went back to the vault area with the manager and demanded he open the thing. I expect everybody in the bank could tell that he wasn't quite right. The guy he was holding was a nice guy, a father of two who had brought his blind mother to the bank to make a deposit. When the vault door swung open it bumped Davey's elbow and the gun fired, sending the good man's brains all over the place and all over Davey. He surrendered shortly thereafter, crying.

In his cell, trying to sleep, he was often wiping himself because he still felt blood and goo all over him.

He was going to be in prison for most of his life. Deep inside he knew it was justice; he felt awful about the man and his family. Just the same, he missed freedom and would have done anything to be out and leave the horror of his old life behind. He was a miserable kid; though he wasn't really a kid: he just seemed that way.

After listening to the adventures of the latest television thriller, I went back to writing Annie.

Dearest Annie,

It's after midnight and the unit is quiet. It's best at this time. No screaming, no arguing, no rapping to music videos, and no dumb legal questions. Just me, my radio, my pen, and notebook. Not perfect but close. If only I could smuggle and then snuggle you in here for a night.

Love,
Shon

I looked over at Davey sleeping. If he had had a better lawyer, I expect he would be in a high-security mental facility. Many prisoners suffer from severe mental illness and receive no treatment. The best they can hope for is friendship.

25
RACE RIOT

The new year was still fresh when some Hispanic guys tried to kill each other on the yard, triggering a four-day lockdown. In a world of attention-craving narcissists, lockdowns bordered on cruel and unusual punishment.

For me, however, these occasions had become reading and writing retreats. I wrote Annie, read biographies and novels, finished briefs, wrote short stories, even opened Mom's books. Lockdowns were a respite from the multitude of legal questions from guys who regularly mixed up words like "retroactive" and "radioactive."

I saw that there would be one more legal storm coming before I left, and retroactive was, in fact, the word. For years the federal government had made a distinction between crack cocaine and powder cocaine. A person could receive a ten-year mandatory minimum sentence for possessing over 50 grams of the former, but it took possessing over 500 grams of the latter for someone to receive the same ten-year sentence. Obviously, more African-Americans were dealing affordable crack than expensive powder, and due to these policies, black men were locked up for disproportionately longer terms than whites.[16]

The U.S. Sentencing Commission had rethought that policy and changed the punishment levels. I prepared detailed, one-size-fits-all motions that could be plugged into brief after brief. When the time came and the Commission finally did, in fact, make the change, I would be ready. I researched a way to argue for larger sentence reductions than even the new regulations might provide, and those arguments worked, even though the Supreme Court would reject them some three years later.

I filed briefs in courts all over the country leading to decades' worth of new lives. It was my going away present for everybody. The Wagner brothers—my typist and his brother—could go home three years early.

...

Bobbie packed up and cleaned out his locker. There's usually sort of a pot luck when a guy leaves: he'll distribute this and that, a few cans of pop or Vienna sausages, some books and magazines, cheese crackers that might be a year or two out of date, some shampoos and shaving cream, and other items of junk that just accumulate. Some things have probably been passing from locker to locker since the joint opened.

"Don't go back to Champaign and the old crowd," I told him again as he sorted and packed.

"Does Davey have a reading light? I never used it much."

He handed it to me and I tucked it under my arm for Davey.

"Who is coming to pick you up? Your sister?"

"No, I decided to take the cab to the halfway house." He'd decided that going to the halfway house in Peoria was a better plan than returning home. "I will see my sister once I get there."

"Don't let the guys at the halfway house punk you out. I hear they're tough," I said.

"See, this is what I won't miss. You messing with me." He tossed away a half-squeezed tube of hair gel.

"Remember, when you get there, start looking for a job immediately. You should be able to find a machine shop in Peoria." He had learned to be a machinist at Pekin—they did give him that.

"Yes, Mom. You want these multivitamins?" His real mom had died of brain cancer two years earlier.

"You should take those with you."

He agonized over each piece of junk.

"Just toss it, Bobbie, nobody wants to touch your crap."

I gave him a hug before he left the cell. We waited together in the dayroom until a guard yelled his name and another one arrived at the unit to escort him to the main building for processing out. He had made a lot of friends, so it took some time for him to get through the dayroom handshakes and backslaps, good lucks, and keep your head ups.

It was weird not having him around. I had gotten used to tormenting him and now I would have to spread it around. When a friend leaves, you are of course happy for them. But it is tempered with loss. They leave, and you just sit down, read a book, and try not to think about it.

He was soon making decent money outside. His sister needed a kidney, and he gave her one of his. Even though he was trying, it's hard when you get out. The temptations are sometimes greater than before. It's always a struggle if you were born for trouble in a tough place. I kept in touch with him—I still do—to encourage him, but the waters are always high around him. It hurts me not to be close enough to be a better pal, which is what he needs.

...

Pekin was changing. America's prisons were being flooded with illegal aliens, and very tough Hispanic gangs were coming in with them. It didn't happen overnight nationally, but it hit Pekin that way.

When any new guy arrives, there is of course the awkward moment when he has his tray of food in hand and is looking for a place to sit. He instinctively knows, even if it's his first time in prison, that he may not be welcome at some tables, that they are reserved for cars or gangs or just friends, even if some seats are empty.

The new Hispanic guys suffered a little of this and then decided to take action. They planned to rush to the dining hall when the controlled-move alarm sounded and just take over some tables. My friends and I walked in and saw that the Latin Kings had taken our table and some others. There was a staring contest; nobody was going to start a fight right there. But something had to be done. A whole system of respect and coexistence was being challenged.

I no longer had the stomach for starting a confrontation over a stupid prison table, but I didn't want my boys Pete, Toro, Jimmy, Richie, Pat, and Josh doing battle without me.

"Take a bite of your dinner, man, and get out of here," Jimmy said to me. I didn't get it.

"Go, Shon," two others said.

"How many weeks you got, Shon?" Jimmy asked. "This isn't your fight, man. You're short. Get out of here. You need to go home."

Jimmy was thinking past anger and about me. I held my tray with one hand and downed what I could. I had good friends.

"Don't let us catch you out on the yard," Jimmy joked, pounding his fist into his other hand.

"Talk to them," I said to Jimmy as I left.

That's exactly what happened. Jimmy and the others talked to the Hispanic guys. They worked it out. Everybody understood that everybody else was armed and dangerous and willing to fight. Nobody really wanted to fight over that awful food. We got our table back but didn't reserve more seats than we needed. It worked out. Nobody lost respect.

That episode was the final one of my remaining days in Pekin, the place where I had been housed for nine and a half years. Although it had never been home, I did, in many ways, grow up there. And I grew up enough to understand that I never wanted to go back.

The federal prisons used to be places where bad people went for doing bad things. When the federal prison system was created, its primary concern was rehabilitating people. Not anymore. There are now over two million prisoners in this country at a cost of over $68 billion a year. The federal system is now mostly about warehousing drug offenders and forcing them to work in prison industries—factories owned by the wealthy and well connected. It's big business.

I figured rehabilitation was possible, if you wanted it bad enough. But for every guy I knew who would come out better, there were twenty more who would come out worse. There was no real effort made to motivate the unmotivated. It was, as I said before, a Lord of the Flies situation with damn few grown-ups in sight—among either the staff or the prisoners.

I hated leaving Hater. I had grown fond of that old man and couldn't stand the thought that he would spend the rest of his years inside. I promised to help him continue his legal fight, but we both knew it would be tough. He was more concerned about his 90-year-old father, Herman. I promised to go visit him.

There were a lot of other guys, too, who needed a break and a ticket home. The longer they stayed inside, the poorer their chances would be for a productive and decent life. Once you miss the appeal deadline, you're lost in the abyss. I had tried to catch some of them from falling over that cliff, but I felt guilty now for leaving. New kids would be arriving, and maybe someone would help them but probably not. I wished I had done a better job of leaving something like a legal clinic behind, but other than my friend Josh Boyer,[17] I wasn't sure there was anyone capable of stepping up to the task. Surely I could help from the outside. I thought of ways I might do that, even if I never made it to law school. It was like that show Lost, where people are stuck on an island. I was leaving but I wanted to come back and help them out, too, if I could.

I packed and repacked my letters and books in the last weeks. A book my mother sent, called *The Purpose Driven Life*, kept ending up on top, maybe because it was the right size or maybe because I kept sneaking peeks inside, even though its title was short a hyphen, which bothered me.

And maybe I kept scratching around that book because I was wise to the fact that most of my life had been characterized by chaos, not purpose. If I had had some sort of calling back then, the robberies wouldn't have happened. I could see the appeal and the organizing convenience of having a purpose in life. Helping others had been an excellent endeavor for me, but I would soon leave all that behind.

Out in the world where you must make a living, you can't be a jailhouse lawyer living on thank-you snacks. I'd soon find out if I had a future working in law. One way or another, the whole purpose thing sounded like the right question to be asking at the time.

Could I win Annie once I got out? Now there was a purpose. But that would be answered one way or another. What purpose after that? I had come in here thinking I would leave with a new life plan. I had just a few weeks left to find one.

I had resisted any corny behind-bars religious conversion. I didn't like the idea of living as a stereotype of some prison script. I had seen a lot of guys misuse religion as a way to hide from who they were and where they were. It's easy enough to put all your mistakes on some altar and say, poof, I'm absolved. I'm brand-new. Not likely.

I had digested some of my guilt and knew part of it would be a knot in my stomach for the rest of my life; I still had lots to repay on that account. I didn't want to hide from that or from anything. But a real theory of life and living, a purpose that might thread together the thousand beads of disorder that would otherwise spill over the floor—that I could go for. So I read and pondered.

I thought most about the grace that had come my way, the kind people who had given me their time and love for no good reason. I still was not ready to take credit away from them by saying it was all from God. But I was seeing a sort of layer of love out there that kept sending me the right person and the right opportunities. Noah and Seth? All that because I didn't like my kitchen job and complained to a guy watching TV with me? Ann Marie Metzner—the holy grail of my youth? Good grief. Sometimes it was too much.

I knew the standard Bible stories from when I had learned them as a kid, like the Old Testament story of Job, who was saddled, time and time again, with horrible losses. His children were killed, everything went wrong in his life, yet he held to his faith. My situation was the reverse: love and generosity and other blessings had come to me in amazing ways, one after the other, yet I clung to disbelief.

I was not looking at my Pekin surroundings with

Jimmy Cagney eyes anymore. I could see that many of the guys were decent at heart. Even the worst of them had suffered greatly in their lives and they deserved some understanding.

The very worst of them were receiving my pity instead of my anger. I wasn't getting softer—you must be hard to survive in prison—but I was seeing past the anger. I was mostly seeing that I was moving toward love and away from fear. That is a big move.

My upbringing was Christian and my sensibilities were Christian, so it was natural for me to start to process things in that frame. I could imagine Jesus himself in Pekin, maybe a few cells away. I had met his love many times in the kindness of friends. I wanted to make that relationship more real. I wasn't ready for some big come-to-Jesus moment, but I was becoming friendly with the whole idea that we have worlds within our worlds, mansions within our prisons, and friends who are very powerful in helping us do the right things. How many more good things would have to happen to me before I caved and admitted that I believed?

26
THE RELEASE

I was thirty-three when two guards walked me out. It was October 2, 2008. Prisoner #15632-047 was free—at least free to live in a halfway house near Omaha for a few months. My days and nights would be carefully controlled.

Any trouble and it would be back to jail. There is a well-known inmate superstition that says it is bad luck to look back at the prison as you leave. It means you'll see it again. But I stood and stared at what had been home for so long. And I didn't mind the idea of coming back, if it was as an attorney who would help some people marooned in there. I hoped, in fact, there would always be enough friendly help coming to people in prison to give them a chance at redemption. I couldn't even count all the good things and nice favors that had come my way, even from the first day. Good old Bee Dog, my first friend and celly, who had served his sentence, been freed, and then got snagged for something again, was probably at some faraway prison being nice to some new kid.

My brother Brett picked me up. I didn't recognize him because he was wearing mirrored sunglasses and a hoodie. He gave me a quick hug, then punched me in the arm the way brothers do. A few people had wanted to take me home, including Annie, but I was worried about freaking out, and I wanted to be with someone with whom I could feel most comfortable. That was Brett. We settled in for the eight-hour drive.

He told me all about his beautiful wife, Katie, and their two boys, Nathan and Marcus, and his blossoming sales career in St. Louis. He had made it—made it through the rough patch of youth.

You can't imagine what it feels like to get out after a decade locked up—the wide views, the kaleidoscope of striking colors after so much black and white—it's sensory overload.

I looked at people in the other cars and saw them talking and smiling—content. It had been a long time since I had witnessed that.

We stopped for gas at a convenience store and I went inside. I hadn't had a stick of gum in over ten years and it sounded good. A girl cashier with pigtails studied me. I glanced down to make sure I wasn't still wearing prison khakis.

Jack Klosterman, my dad's good friend from Grass Valley Farm, had sent me some new clothes for the trip. The gum and candy aisle presented too many colors and choices, which required decisions. I sort of panicked, then quickly picked out something and paid. I would feel the same state of anxiety for about a month.

On the road, I looked around and let the new world soak in. I asked Brett what it was like to be married, to raise kids. I was proud of what he had become.

"The last time we were in a car together we were

going pretty fast," he said. That was true. We had been in a getaway car.

...

We finally drove across the bridge into Nebraska—the Good Life. We went to a restaurant in the Old Market, in the downtown area of Omaha, where my family was waiting.

My beautiful sisters, Samantha and Kristin, were there and let out a cheer. Mom was waiting. My brother Brook was waiting. And Jack Klosterman was waiting.

I walked over to see Big Jack and behind him was Annie. In the last months before my release I could not get a bearing on her feelings. Maybe she was a little afraid of dealing with me as a free man instead of at a safe distance. I wouldn't push too hard, but I had this resolute belief that what I hoped for would happen somehow.

She sat beside me, smiling. She held my hand under the table. When the party broke up and we were outside talking, she told me she had something for me out in her car. I walked her to it, and she turned and kissed me. It was like that first kiss, though now she was the aggressor.

Mom and the girls drove me to the halfway house. The accommodations were worse than prison. I could handle a couple months of anything, I figured, with so much freedom around me to take the sting out of it.

27
CAR WASH BLUES

It took me a couple days and some patient help from my sisters to learn the intricacies of a cell phone. Portable phones were expensive things with a retractable antenna when I had gone in; now they were cheap and everywhere.

I even saw young kids talking on them at Walmart, which kind of freaked me out. Everything freaked me out in those first days.

I could now communicate with Annie whenever I wanted; she was right there in my pocket. We spent the evenings talking, without the fifteen-minute limit or high rates.

She drove me to my job interviews. I was turned down as a car salesman, a retail store clerk, an administrative assistant, and a factory worker. It was the start of the Great Recession, and jobs were scarce for everyone, let alone an ex-con.

We stopped at one more car dealership. I walked in and asked the owner if there were any openings. His eyes were stalking a husband and wife looking around the showroom as if they might be the only new car buyers in America that week. They might have been.

"Do you have any experience?" he asked without looking away from his prey.

"No," I answered.

"Where was your last job?"

"Federal prison."

"Follow me," he said. I thought my search was over. Nope. Just outside, where he could still keep a bead on the couple through the glass doors, he told me to leave and not come back.

While I was being kicked off the property, Annie was taking a call from California. A job she had applied for a few months earlier had come through, a counseling job at a very prestigious eating disorder clinic in Malibu. All her research, her master's degree, her nutrition work with her father's company, and her own personal experience had shaped her into an expert. She had studied nutrition and eating disorders as diligently as I had been studying law. It's interesting that we both had intensely studied the things that had tripped us up in life.

They wanted her, and it was her dream job. When I returned to the car, she seemed almost drugged. She gathered herself, listened to my rant about the car dealer, then told me.

She would not accept the job, of course, she said. I told her she really had to. Of course she did. I hated it, everything about it, but it was her dream. I encouraged her to take it.

The week before her move, she started pulling away, which is what you people do. We would just do what we had to do for now. But it was awful, and I was walking around feeling sick.

So I did what any lovesick guy would do when his girl was leaving; I called my mother. I explained the disappointing job prospects and blurted out that Annie was leaving me.

She said something about being selfless.

"Yes, Mother," I replied.

Annie flew out to Malibu and was having difficulty finding an apartment. At one point, she texted me. She wanted me to call her so she could escape from a talkative guy with a room to rent.

She texted again the next day and said that she just wanted to come home, and for a few hours I was hopeful that she wouldn't find a place to live. But she soon sent me a picture of her apartment with a caption that said, "my new home." That hurt.

We could write and call, sure. I had to trust that things would work out. They always had for us. But the prospects looked bleak. She had flown to California. She was gone.

...

My first job was conducting political surveys over the telephone—fifty calls an hour. I was so good that I lasted nearly the whole first day. The next day I landed a new job washing cars at a local Chevy dealership.

I needed a car to travel between that job and the halfway house. John Fellers was in the business, so I called him. He wanted me to meet him at a county building, which seemed odd.

"We're here to put the title to this car in your name," he said. He was standing beside a long black 1989 Mercedes Benz in mint condition.

"I can't afford it."

"This car is from me and Bev and Johanna. It's our thank you for getting me home early."

It beat the hell out of a Snickers bar.

I really couldn't believe it. What a great thing for him to do. I drove around, talking to Annie on the phone and feeling somewhat like a normal person.

To some stares, I arrived at that cruddy car wash job each morning in that big boat of a car—almost a limo.

I used my spare time to search for better jobs at an Iowa workforce office, which was right across the river from Omaha in Council Bluffs. I needed to find a different job before the first freeze, when car washing would end.

I spotted a "document analyst" job. It probably meant proofreading. That I could do. It wasn't writing briefs and it wasn't working for attorneys, but it would do for now, I thought. The job was with a printing company in Omaha. I recognized the name; I had seen it stamped on the bottom of Supreme Court briefs along with a 402 telephone number; the area code had drawn my attention because it was a reminder of home.

There are only a few companies that specialize in printing Supreme Court briefs. It is very exacting work, with no room for typos. A small book is published as part of the appeal; it includes an appendix of lower court opinions relating to the case. Forty copies are sent to the Supreme Court—several for each justice and the clerks, and the others for places like the Library of Congress.

Omaha's Cockle Legal Briefs is, in fact, one of the nation's largest Supreme Court printers. For my purposes, it seemed odd, almost a miracle, that they are located in Omaha and not in D.C., but miracles seemed to be happening for me.

I sent them a résumé. When you read it, the first thing you would notice is the ten-year work history gap. I did mention that as an "independent" paralegal I had written briefs that had made it to the Supreme Court, which the people at Cockle would know rarely happens. I also mentioned that I had worked with Seth Waxman and others.

28
GIFTS AND FRIENDS UNDESERVED

Seth is kind of a rock star in the world Cockle Legal Briefs inhabits. When they saw my reference to him in my résumé, they were reasonably sure I was a lunatic. They called me anyway.

They had already found a good candidate to fill the job before I even applied. They were about to make the phone call to complete the hire when my résumé arrived.

Cockle is located in a tiny, nondescript building at the western end of downtown Omaha. It is a short walk to the federal and state court buildings. It is directly across the street from the biggest box of money in Omaha, the Federal Reserve Bank.

Cockle was started in the early 1920s as a regular print shop, but because its owners, Albert and Eda Cockle, had law degrees, they veered into the business of printing legal briefs. Their grandchildren, Andy Cockle and Trish Billotte, run the company today. The basement still has the old lead ingots and buckets from the days when type was set in molten lead. Also in the basement are box upon box of Supreme Court briefs that have changed modern U.S. legal history. Cockle has had some involvement in nearly every major Supreme Court case going back to the 1980s. It is a rather remarkable place, given its modest environs on a standard Omaha street. You might think it was any other printing company, but it is not.

The fact that Cockle is called a printing company is kind of a misnomer. In fact, with high-speed copiers and pneumatic paper cutters, the printing is the easy part. The mental work is the important part. Lawyers from all over the nation are on the phone with the folks at Cockle, letting these careful, cheery Midwesterners calm them down and explain how to prep their arguments for the big show. It's about the only place in the nation where my knowledge of brief writing and the Supreme Court could possibly find application, and it was but a few miles from the halfway house.

My résumé landed in the e-mail in-box of Renee Goss, the office manager. Renee, almost because she thought it was funny or at least awfully odd, showed it to the boss, Andy Cockle.

Andy is a man of moderate height and build, who is charming and quite funny. He would appreciate a madman's résumé, maybe suitable for framing. He read it with a wry smile and then asked Renee to schedule an interview with "the crackpot."

She called to set up a date and time for the interview. When she spoke, her statements were bordered with "please" and "thank you"—a form of communication completely foreign to someone stepping out of prison. She asked if I would please e-mail her an attachment of the letter of recommendation from Mr. Seth Waxman, if I didn't mind.

The Cockles had long been trying to capture Seth's

attention and a portion of his business. They had sent him countless marketing letters and had never heard back. I had used just the right magic name to open the drawbridge. This was another miracle, if you're counting.

When I finished my shift at the car wash, I drove to the workforce center where a secretary tried to help me scan the letter into something called a PDF, so we could attach it to an e-mail. But we had no idea how to do any of that, so I decided to just take the folded, dog-eared letter with me to the interview.

...

The day before the interview I drove home to David City for the first time since prison. I had skirted around the visit for weeks, not wanting to face the reality that Dad would not be there.

The closer I came, the more my stomach knotted. By the time I passed the sign announcing that I was entering Butler County, I needed to pull over. I called Annie in California. She was bummed that I was making the trip without her. We had talked for years about the first trip to David City.

"How is the new job working out?" I asked her.

"It's okay. I am still waiting to be moved into the role as primary therapist. That's where I'll really help people. For now, I'm supervising people during mealtimes and leading group exercises. I'll start the therapy sessions as soon as I prove to them that I can handle the eating part."

Part of the therapy there, which she had to participate in, was to set a good example, by eating what seemed like huge portions of food. And she didn't like cilantro. California food is half cilantro. I tried to calm her down about that. And, yes, I know, how can you not like cilantro?

I had been sending Annie a constant stream of encouraging letters, because I knew how fragile she was. And also because I desperately wanted her to succeed, even if it meant we would remain separated.

Dearest Annie,

I really believe that this is your last big step toward full recovery. And I know you can do this. The food stuff will be challenging and so will dealing with people on terms not of your own making. It will test your resolve but you will persevere because deep down beyond the sensitivity, you are an incredibly strong woman. A woman who amazes me on a daily basis.

I hope you are beginning to settle into your new apartment. Just remember your home is with me, Annie.

Bye-bye cutie,
Love Shon

It was cold and rainy in David City. My first stop was two miles outside of town at my father's grave. My breath produced big clouds that drifted over my father's tombstone.

I kneeled and prayed for him. I cruised into David City, my knees wet from the grass. As I entered the street next to the Thorpe Opera House, I saw a man walking, head hunched over but making good time against the cold wind and some raindrops. It was Dr. Kaufman, the man who had written me letters while I was in prison.

He visited with me on the street for a minute, but it was cold so he suggested we sit in my car. I thanked him for his letters and told him how much they had helped. He said he was glad. He knew all about my law work, about how Annie and I had met, and about how my mother was faring after Dad's passing. Before he got out, he put one hand on my shoulder.

"Let's say a little prayer, Shon." We bowed our heads.

"Lord, thank you for protecting Shon in that place and for sending him home safely after such a dark time. Give him what he needs for a new life now. Help him to live for your purposes and not the world's." He patted my shoulder and said good-bye.

Before he walked away he leaned into the open door. "Shon, I knew your father well. I know he was proud of how you changed. He was very proud of you before he died. You go over there and see him." I told him I just had.

"Good, good." He patted the car and was on his way.

For a few minutes, I did not feel like driving. I just sat and let whatever had been given sink in. These people had every right to think of me as a monster. They could have harassed my family out of town. They could have tried to erase me from the town's memory. But they came with love and kind letters and even little donations instead of torches and pitchforks, and it made such a difference to the shape of my heart.

These random happenings were starting to shake the foundation of my disbelief. What were the chances that Dr. Kaufman would be the first person I'd see in David City? It was hard not to see these things as hints of something bigger at work.

29
MY RESUME GAP

I had only a few minutes to spare. It was my lunch break from the car wash job, and I was still dressed in mud caked clothes. It was time for my interview at Cockle.

I couldn't find a place to change, so I pulled into the parking lot of Channel 7, undressed, and then dressed inside my dark-windowed car. I took a sponge bath with a jug of half-frozen water—at least I would be awake. I straightened my tie in the rearview mirror.

"Your résumé has a rather large gap in it," Renee said as we all sat down in Andy's little office, where bright paintings, an old bucket of lead, an antique cigar poster, a voodoo doll, and an Opera Omaha poster caught my eye.

"You also say that you were a paralegal and that you wrote several Supreme Court briefs, but that you are not an attorney. How is that possible?" Renee asked.

Before I could answer, Andy and Trish started arguing about whether nonlawyers could file petitions on cases other than their own. Then they remembered the meeting we were having.

"Were you able to write and file briefs as a paralegal?" Andy asked. My résumé had somewhat glossed over the gap with a summary of my legal accomplishments.

"It's a long story," I replied.

"Well, why don't you tell us," said Trish. Straight to the point, she would have made a good trial judge. I took a breath.

"I wrote those briefs from prison, where I was locked up for over ten years for robbing banks when I was twenty-two," I said in one breath.

There was, of course, silence. Andy smiled but it was not the smile of humor. It was the smile of a curious man. He caught himself and looked serious.

Renee's smile was frozen. I probably could have produced the same reaction if I had removed my shirt to show the jailhouse tattoos on my back.

Trish broke the silence: "Did you use a gun?"

"Yes I did. I didn't ever fire it, but I had a gun."

Then I told them everything, right down to John Fellers and the Mercedes outside, and my goal of someday becoming an attorney.

They asked me, as they do with everyone, to read a snippet from a Supreme Court brief. It was a literacy test of sorts. I read every word perfectly, stopping only to ask them if they wanted me to read a legal citation as "JA" or "Joint Appendix."

"You know, Shon, we have conducted a lot of interviews over the years," Andy said. "No one ever knew what 'JA' stood for."

After that I pulled out my crinkled copy of Seth Waxman's letter, unfolded it, and handed it to Andy. I also gave them Noah Levine's telephone number.

Renee asked me why I was coming back to Nebraska if I had such friends.

"Why not New York or Washington?"

I said I owed my mother some good years with her son.

She bit her lip a little, so I guessed that was the right thing to say. It was the truth.

At the end of the interview they said they would contact me. I thought they were giving me the "don't call us" script. The interview had not gone as well as I had hoped; I had hoped for the job. But I had, after all, hit them with a sledgehammer of sorts. No one could be expected to react positively to a story like that.

I didn't know it, but as I walked down the street their heads were huddled in Andy's little window to see if I had the Mercedes or, more likely, a shopping cart. But there it was—thank you, John—my big black Benz.

...

I returned to the halfway house to learn we had a new boarder. Tyler's brother had arrived. He had been in prison for selling drugs. I wondered if Tyler's hatred was somehow following me. It had not boiled over at Pekin, maybe because I had so many in my corner. Now I was going to be sleeping—and with my eyes open—in the same room with Tyler's brother?

I asked the house manager if something could be done.

We were moved to different rooms at least.

"Do you know who I am?" I asked when we ran into each other in the basement bathroom.

"I do."

"Look," I said, "we both just got out of prison, and I don't want to go back. I doubt you do either. But we're going to spend some time here in close quarters. If we're going to have a problem, we might as well have it now."

He stared at me but didn't speak.

"I understand it that you don't like me. That's okay. There's nothing I can do to fix that. How about if we just don't talk to each other?"

He looked at me for a few seconds.

"All right."

After the encounter I felt lighter, like there was no danger in smiling, and that I could put away the armor.

...

Hearing nothing from Cockle for a week, I wrote it off and kept washing cars. Annie told me to keep the faith; they would call. She was right.

"We would like to talk to you again," Renee said. They had spent the week researching my every claim. Trish had called Noah and gotten a very good report on my legal skills.

"If you were me, would you hire him?" she had asked Noah.

Noah said he would. He also said that if I visited New York, which he hoped I would, that he would take me into his home and introduce me to his family.

"Oh that's great," Trish said. "Because we really like him." Trish had also placed a call to Seth's office, as she had done before without effect. This time Seth called right back.

He gave an equally enthusiastic endorsement. He told Trish that she'd be crazy not to make the hire.

It was going to happen. I washed cars that day singing out loud to the iPod that rarely left my jeans pocket— my favorite new gadget. Maybe my career had begun. Maybe I had been killed at a bank or in prison a long time ago and this was the dream I had had while dying. Maybe it would all blink out any second.

...

On my first day at Cockle, I met behind closed doors with Andy, Trish, and Renee.

"What do you think is the best way to handle this?" Renee asked. "Do you think we should tell everyone now or

wait?"

I looked at Andy and Trish, who offered no hint as to which solution they preferred.

"If people get to know me before they find out my past, it seems to work better. They see me as a normal guy," I said.

"So you aren't normal?" Trish joked.

The joke felt welcoming.

My coworkers were a curious bunch, and every time I seemed to know something Court-related they asked how I had learned that. Giving fuzzy answers became uncomfortable for me. I wanted to come clean, but I felt I had to duck and dodge for a while longer. Lunchtime was the worst, as everyone wants to chat. I would eat lunch in my car, claiming I wanted to listen to a game or NPR on the radio while I ate.

Shari trained me on the publishing process. Details that are minor in most jobs are vital at Cockle. Due dates are the most important. Fortunately, the staff at Cockle had compiled a book of notes for each type of Supreme Court brief.

Shari kept heaping these books on the desk. Here is how it works. The lawyers send the text of the brief in electronic form, unless they are old school and snail mail us a hard copy. More often than not the briefs are full of errors. We help the attorneys cite the cases correctly and ensure that the lower court opinions are reprinted in the correct order. The main arguments have to be clear, concise, and compelling. Sometimes they arrive mushy and convoluted or they are missing parts, and you have to try to reach the lawyers on the phone and work with them to fix the next draft. The final project sometimes involves hundreds of pages that must be absolutely error-free. The brief is then printed and nicely bound, and sent to the Court in a timely fashion.

Sometimes it is a round-the-clock crash course where everyone has to be finely tuned to their respective job.

I was coming in as a guy who barely knew how to operate a computer.

"Shon, good grief, don't retype that whole section. Just cut and paste the change into place," Shari said to me one day. I had no idea what "cut and paste" meant or how to do it.

Renee, who had become my work mother, helped to take the prison edge off my language and manners. Not that I was going around mean-mugging and punching people, but my vocabulary had some rough spots.

My coworkers, all women, were helpful and patient, but they couldn't imagine what planet I was from.

One problem, which wouldn't have been a problem to anyone but me, was wearing zippered pants. For a decade I had worn khaki pants with buttons. But now, coming out of the men's room, I had to remember about the zipper. When my first day was finished, and I was back in the confines of the halfway house, I discovered a problem. I had been open for business all afternoon. I didn't sleep well that night.

But each day was a little better.

Two weeks in, Andy and Renee assembled the entire Cockle crew in the main workspace.

"We called everyone to this meeting to talk about Shon," Andy said. "We think you all should know that we hired Shon because he has a lot of experience with the Supreme Court. Well, his experience comes from writing briefs while he was an inmate in federal prison."

"Ya, right, Andy," Sandy said, shaking her head. "What's the real reason for this meeting?" She thought it was very funny. Andy can be very funny.

I looked down at Sandy and winced. "No, that is the reason," I said.

I explained where I had come from and why I was there. To my surprise no one later complained to Andy or Trish. They all treated me the same as they had before. I was okay. Maybe more interesting, but okay.

What are the chances I would find a job in Omaha that involved something I was uniquely qualified for? And a place where I was accepted, ugly warts and all?

30
INITIAL DISCOMFORTS

Although I had been out for a few months, I was still in the precarious waters of my new life. I had been fortunate to secure a great job, given that so many others at the halfway house were sitting there day after day, unable to find one. There was one guy in particular who begged the staff to drive him to a job interview, because he had no family or friends to do it. They said no. He never found a job.

The halfway house staff said I needed to obtain a bank account so I could have my wages direct deposited. Then, after payday, I could pay them the 25 percent of my gross earnings—the amount they charged everyone.

So I drove to a bank in downtown Omaha and was met by a young bank manager in a pink-and-blue polka-dot tie. He asked for a picture ID and Social Security card, which I gave him. He ran the numbers through the computer.

"We have a problem," he said.

"What's that?"

"The credit agency says you are deceased. Is this the correct Social Security number?"

"Yes."

He ran the number again. I could tell he was starting not to believe me—especially after he asked if I had an account elsewhere and I said no. Who has no bank account?

He called the Social Security office, who said that according to their file I was alive. That was a relief.

"Is there something missing?" he said. "I don't understand why the credit bureau says you're deceased."

So I told him I had just been released from federal prison after serving a decade-long sentence.

He started punching more keys on the computer. Probably letting security know so they can escort me out, I thought. I was becoming frustrated, because I didn't know that credit agencies run everything these days. I had a valid ID and Social Security number. Wasn't that enough?

He kept glancing over at me while he was typing information into his computer.

"You can ask me if you want to," I said.

"So what did you do?"

I looked around to make sure no one else would hear us, because I didn't want someone to hear the word "robbery" and press an alarm.

"I robbed five banks."

"No way." He looked around and then whispered, "How much did you get?" Maybe he didn't like the bank's retirement plan or something; for one reason or another, he seemed suddenly delighted to meet me.

I left with no bank account that day. It took me weeks to straighten out the credit agencies. Then I walked back into the bank and was greeted by my friend, the young banker.

This can be such a funny planet.

Annie was miserable in Malibu. She didn't like working at the treatment program and decided to part ways and find something else in the area. I wanted her to come back, but she said she liked California, liked her little apartment, and liked the independence. I think she liked the isolation.

Her depression worsened, and I was worried to the point where I considered contacting her father. Instead I tried to just lighten things up.

I called her one day and told her to play three songs in a row that I knew she had on her iPod. While she played the songs, I sent her a series of texts telling our story together, including passages from notes we had sent to each other.

Maybe it was a lame romantic gesture, but she called afterward and thanked me for it anyway. It was the best I could do, given I was a broke former prisoner living in a decrepit halfway house. Legally, I couldn't leave the state to go cheer her up.

She came home for the Christmas holiday. My family gathered at my sister Samantha's tiny apartment in Omaha. It was a tight squeeze for the twelve of us, but Annie fit perfectly with my family.

The next evening we went to Aromas, our favorite coffee joint. It was our chance to be quiet together. For a long while we didn't say a word. She just turned her paper coffee cup around and around and looked at the room, out the window, at me, smiled, and looked around some more.

"I'm going to move home," she finally said.

"And?"

"And I think we should find a place together. I want to be with you."

I have asked Annie many times what had helped her turn the corner. And, much like her answer to why she wrote that initial letter to me, she never has a definitive reply. Part of her reluctance had come from the fear that she would love me too much and I would hurt her. Or that if we moved in together, I would see all her imperfections. I had the same fears.

I think no one thought we would succeed, not even our families.

...

Annie and I met with her father, Ray, at Panera Bread to break the news that we were moving in together. I felt bad for Ray. If I had been in his place, I probably would have punched me.

We told him. Actually, I told him, since Annie was more nervous than I was. He started stuttering: "Okay, ah-hum, ah-hum," but he took it better than I would have. He had seen this worst-case scenario hovering over his daughter for eight years now and had steeled himself for the possibility.

While he didn't know me, he did know my family, especially Mom, and he knew my dedication to Annie. I had to hope that was enough for now.

"I want you to know that no one will love your daughter like I will," I said outside while we were moving Annie's airport luggage from my car to his.

Ray is all midwestern courtesy. "I appreciate that, Shon," he said, and he shook my hand.

...

I was officially released from Bureau of Prisons custody on April 9, 2009, which meant I could leave the halfway house and move into the apartment Annie and I had rented.

I opened the door to my new home and she was sitting in a corner wearing pajamas, tilting her head and smiling in a welcoming way.

In the weeks following, I borrowed an engagement ring from Annie's sister, Angie. I had waited long enough. I had let Annie think that a proposal was months, if not years, away. I created the subterfuge because if I couldn't afford to make the proposal grand, the least I could do was to make it a surprise.

We went to the Whole Foods Market near our apartment and hit the salad bar, as we often did. We took our food to the seating area. There was one table alone near the window that looked unusual. It had a tablecloth, a bouquet of pink roses, wineglasses, and elegant dinnerware.

"Let's sit there," I said. Annie was a little off balance. "It's okay," I said. "It's for us."

She looked down and saw the card on the table: reserved for Shon Hopwood.

A group of ladies who worked there, who had conspired to set up the table for me, watched from a distance. Annie started fanning her face with both hands.

CHAPTER 30

"While you haven't earned a marriage proposal, you have earned a nice dinner."

Her smile was replaced with something else. We sat down. Once she relaxed a little and was no longer expecting a marriage proposal, I went down on one knee. I asked her to marry me.

She said yes. Let me repeat that again. She said yes.

...

I hoped the worst part of returning to society was over. I had steady income at a job I enjoyed and was engaged to the one person I felt destined to be with. I thought I could glide for a couple of months and settle into this new world. I was wrong.

Annie and I had never planned on having children. We even questioned the sanity of people who were "trying"—as if purposely having children was a sign of insanity. After years of battling anorexia, doctors had warned Annie that her chances of conceiving were not good. And I was fresh out of prison so the responsibility of a child was not on the agenda.

But three weeks into our new life, I arrived home to Annie's ashen face; she was pregnant.

This was not supposed to happen. We had waited all these years to be together and now a child was crashing the party.

Annie called Ray about the new development, just as she had after the engagement. I was worried he would stop answering our phone calls. His support, however, remained steadfast.

In the weeks ahead, Annie suffered through days and nights of sickness. She lost weight, a lot of it, and our friend and baby doctor, Mark Carlson, considered hospitalizing her. She was supposed to be gaining weight now, but she was shriveling before my eyes.

Annie's health wasn't our only concern. I had been out of custody for all of a month. I had nothing. Annie had been working part-time and trying to finish her internship, but shewas too sick to continue either.

"We are short on bills again," Annie said. "I can pull some more out of savings if we need it."

I shook my head. "That's your money."

"It's our money, and if we need it we'll use it."

One income was barely paying the bills for two people, let alone three.

Annie and I decided to attend marriage counseling with Marty Barnhart, the former pastor of my family's church, and he agreed to meet with us regularly.

Marty explained what it means to live a life together with God as our focus. Usually when someone mentioned God or spirituality, my mind would be off to whatever sporting event was nearest on the calendar. But this time I listened. Marty said that I could be forgiven for everything. "Yeah, even you, Shon," he said.

On the car ride home, Annie and I discussed what Marty had said.

"What did you think?" I asked.

"I have never heard anyone talk about having a relationship with God. It is . . . I don't know."

"Me, either."

That night in bed I thought about it. I could no longer

pretend all my good fortune came from chance, from some random action of the universe. Had I landed in the law library by accident? Then there were the Supreme Court petitions that had been granted—they were the equivalent of winning the legal lottery, and there was the fact that it had happened twice. Had I met Seth and Noah by accident? How about finding Cockle in downtown Omaha? And surviving prison? And Annie. How had all that happened?

Surely I was not that lucky. And certainly it had nothing to do with merit. It felt like unmerited grace. But from where?

I also couldn't escape the feeling, the intuition, that we are more than flesh and bones. And that this life is not the whole show. If that is true, I wondered what my priorities should be.

I just couldn't argue myself away from God any longer. To be honest, it was never that I didn't believe; I just didn't want to follow. I wanted to do things my way. Still do. But that attitude was not going to help my wife, it would not help my child, and it sure wouldn't prepare me for whatever was to come in the next life.

The more I thought about it, the more I realized I needed faith. I needed a ground for the electrical current of a society telling me that getting my own way, doing everything for myself, and trying to appear important are the keys to true happiness.

It was the same happiness I had chased while robbing banks. To put it differently, I needed a baseline structure—much like the Constitution acts for our government—that would guide my life.

I knew I believed in God, and I knew that His purpose was for me to help people through the law. It felt like my personal rehabilitation required Jesus and my professional rehabilitation required service. I prayed, and I prayed, and I worried what my future wife would think. But then I prayed some more and felt peace with my decision.

Annie and I argued about it that night. She was concerned that I had taken a leap off the Jesus cliff and was going to make her jump, too. She believed that the guilt and fears instilled in her by the religion of her childhood had contributed to her anorexia. She didn't want any more of it.

But she accepted the idea that it was the right move for me. It was a gradual process. In time, she wanted it for herself. Later, her faith would go stronger than mine.

We decided that we would organize our life around love and service.

On the most important things, Annie and I were as one. So we had that in common right from the start, and everything else grew with time.

...

I had been working at Cockle for nine months when it was time to send out the wedding invitations. My workspace at Cockle is an open office, surrounded by hardworking women who excel at their jobs.

One afternoon I swiveled around and announced we had set the date for the wedding, and I needed their addresses for the invitations, because they all had to come.

Tiffany, who bears the burden of sitting next to me

every day, cheered, but it was Sandy who was first to write down her address.

"Here you are, Shon." She paused. "But I just want you to know that we really have nothing much of value in our home."

There was an awkward silence. Mary Anne was the first to crack up, then Tiffany, then the room erupted.

31
LOVE IS A LIFESTYLE

I once heard my father joke that it's hard to get Hopwood men all the way to the altar. That proved prescient for me. Two days before our wedding one of my teeth broke down to the gum, and the soft root was exposed. Annie took me to the emergency dentist and they extracted what was left. I was given some pain pills.

I woke up late on the morning of the wedding. The side of my face was throbbing. Without thinking, I gulped down a few of the pain pills along with the usual nerve medication for my back. Bad idea.

Twenty minutes later I was all pins and needles and sweating profusely.

"You all right" Brett asked. He was at the apartment to babysit me until the wedding.

I staggered around the apartment. I drank some water and immediately vomited.

"Wake me up in thirty minutes."

Three hours before the ceremony, I was taking a cold shower, slapping myself awake.

I later learned, through a Google search, that the two medications I had taken should never be mixed. I was experiencing an overdose.

Annie intuitively felt that something was wrong and

she called me. I didn't answer. When I felt slightly better I called her back and told her what was happening.

"Do you need to go to the hospital?" she asked.

"No, I'll live," I said with one arm on the wall holding myself up.

"Are we getting married today?" she whispered.

"I will be there, that's a promise."

"It's okay, you know," she said. "If you need to go, you should go."

"I will see you in an hour."

It took every ounce of energy to put on the tux. But by the time I reached the wedding site, the overdose was wearing off.

We were married on the steamiest day of the year. Brett and Brook, John Fellers, and Tom stood with me as my best men, and to catch me if I fell. Tom had made the long trip from Phoenix, where he runs a business and is raising his son.

"Thanks for making the trip, brother," I said, wrapping my arm around his head.

"I wouldn't miss it. Is Ann really going to go through with this? With you?"

"I sure hope so."

Tom and I had not been together since 1999, when we were in a county jail for a few weeks after sentencing. Things had come full circle for us. We were both out of prison, both defying the statistics of recidivism, and soon we would both be in the parenting business. And we are still pals today just like we have been since sixth grade.

When Annie first appeared in her wedding dress

the people gathered for the ceremony gave a collective sigh. She walked down the aisle with her father, Ray. He smiled, we hugged, and then he handed his daughter to me.

"I love the way you became reacquainted again," Marty said; he was presiding at the service.

"You began by writing letters, then visits, then more visits, time spent together—when you couldn't wait for the day that you had talked about, this day. It would be really consummated by you, Shon, when you gave Annie a ring and said, 'Will you marry me?' and she said, 'I will, yes,' and so happy that she did. I can remember you guys saying it was worth it, worth the wait."

Marty finished with a slogan that basically summed up the new life we planned together: "Love is a lifestyle."

That will always remain the happiest day of my life.

...

The fall months saw new clothes, an expanding waistline, and nervousness about being a parent. And that was just me!

About a week after the wedding, Dr. Carlson told us that we would be having a boy. We celebrated that night and picked a name. I had promised my dad that if I ever had a son, I would name him Mark, after him. We also took Annie's dad's name, making it Mark Raymond Hopwood.

My mom cried when I called and told her the name. There would be another Mark Hopwood in the world, and that was worth a few tears.

...

Annie was due on January 7, but she and Dr. Carlson believed the baby would come early.

One of the worst blizzards in Omaha's history hit on Christmas Eve, and it kept us from driving back to David City to meet with the family. The interstate was closed, and most of the city was shut down. We enjoyed a quiet dinner at home and we sat on the couch in our pajamas talking and watching the snow fall in sheets.

A few hours after dinner, Annie said she felt "weird."

"What's new?" I said.

"No, seriously," she said. "I feel very strange."

Ask any man who has lived with a pregnant woman and he'll tell you the situation was probably not cause for alarm. Throughout the pregnancy, Annie had not felt well. Of course she felt weird; she was carrying a small alien inside her.

But Annie was right. Three minutes before midnight her water broke. An hour later I was driving us through six inches of snow and ice in a little Toyota Corolla. We were the only car moving through the white fog of blowing snow and city lights. We made it to the hospital—barely.

Mark Raymond was born in the early morning hours of Christmas. I cringe when I think about the blessings we would have missed without him.

32
A TALE OF TWO EMAILS

I continued to work full-time at Cockle, where the learning curve was steep. But I was picking up computer skills more quickly than anyone, myself included, had imagined.

The one thing I came to the job with was eight years of studying the Supreme Court, and that came in handy when I had to speak with clients. I could at least talk shop.

Some briefs were prepared by big law firms and others by law professors at top schools. The one lesson that seemed almost universal was that the more competent the lawyer, the more he or she listened to advice.

I got to work on some of the most vexing issues to face the Supreme Court. One case involved the Confrontation Clause. That portion of the Constitution requires that before the prosecution can use testimonial evidence, such as statements made by a witness to the police, the prosecution must bring forth the witness so the accused can confront him or her through the crucible of cross-examination.

The counsel of record in this case was a well-known

Confrontation Clause scholar, Richard Friedman, from the University of Michigan Law School.

One day I told Rich that I had followed one of his prior cases and he asked why.

"Let's just say I have an interest in criminal law cases."

A couple months later when Rich had another brief, we talked about the merits of the case for twenty minutes.

I think the ladies at Cockle were somewhat concerned that I was discussing legal doctrine with one of the clients.

"Are you an attorney, Shon?" he asked.

"Not really."

"Then why do you know about the Confrontation Clause? It's not something people choose to study."

"It's complicated. I will tell you the story in an e-mail."

The next weekend I spent an hour writing an e-mail to Rich. I was worried he would read it, realize that he was entrusting his Supreme Court briefs to a former convict, panic, and call the Cockles demanding that I no longer work on his cases. Despite the concerns, I felt compelled to tell him, like I was meant to tell this guy my story. So I did.

Rich, to his credit, didn't panic over the e-mail; instead we became friends. Two months later Adam Liptak at the New York Times contacted Rich asking questions about the case he had just argued before the Supreme Court. Rich e-mailed him back and after discussing the case, he broached a different subject.

I wonder if you know the name Shon Hopwood. He works at Cockle. I'd never dealt with him before this case, but I have found him unusually engaged in the subject matter. Turns out until he joined Cockle about a year ago, he served 10 years in federal prison, during which he wrote a successful cert petition, Fellers v. United States, argued successfully by Seth Waxman. He just sent me another cert petition, on which he claimed to be the principal author, and it was a very professional job; apparently he has a string of appellate cases on which he's worked successfully. He's married, kid on the way, trying to finish up a college degree and go to law school. Thought you might be interested.

I don't think Adam Liptak believed that some guy just removed from a decade-long prison sentence was working for a Supreme Court brief printer and had prepared two cases that had been granted by the Court.

Who would believe such a story?

Adam interviewed me, and on February 8, 2010, the story ran: "A Mediocre Criminal, but an Unmatched Jailhouse Lawyer."

Soon I was doing radio and television interviews, and agents were calling from Los Angeles and New York. Annie and I were just learning how to take care of a newborn, and between the lack of sleep and the media barrage, we were overwhelmed.

I answered every single one of the hundreds of e-mails that flooded into Cockle Law Brief Printing Company. Many were from former prisoners and from parents whose kids had done something bad when they were young. To both groups, my story represented some hope, which made me feel good.

But there was some negative reaction. Some of the people I'd robbed were upset that I was receiving publicity and that I seemed to be moving into a successful life. I called the people who'd been quoted in the local paper and those who later wrote me at Cockle. It wasn't easy, and I was sick after each call, but I knew it was something I had to do. To make amends. The personal apologies were long overdue.

I can never take back what I did to the people in those banks. I can only say I am sorry. My hope is that they will see that the immature guy from over a decade ago has long been buried.

...

Not everyone, unfortunately, makes a decision to change, either because they can't or because circumstances drive them back into the old life. A week after the Times story, a local television station interviewed me. Annie and I expected the story to run on a Friday night. While watching the news that night we listened to a story about a guy who had been out of prison for only nine months and had already robbed a bank and been sentenced to seven more years of prison.

When they showed his picture, I recognized the guy. He was the one who had been begging the halfway house staff to lend him a ride for a job interview.

Around two-thirds of federal prisoners are re-arrested within three years of release.[18] Dropped into a recession with few resources and no job skills, most don't stand a chance. That could easily have been me. I thanked God that night for the blessings he had given me.

...

Annie and I were guests at Harvard University in the spring of 2010. We spent a day walking down the cobblestone streets of Harvard Square, not quite believing where we were.

Annie is a stellar student, having just finished her master's in counseling with a 4.0, so this kind of place was right for her. But I felt out of place, for sure. I didn't even own a sweater vest, a piece of attire that seemed to be the standard uniform for male students there.

I was to speak at Harvard Memorial Church and then Lowell House, an undergraduate dorm that has housed Justices Harry Blackmun and David Souter, stars Matt Damon and Natalie Portman, and countless others. I was also set to meet Seth and Noah for the first time in person.

We met at an old restaurant just off Harvard Square. Seth was as charming as I had imagined. When we spoke to a group of students that evening, he graciously deferred questions to me. No wonder the Court likes him.

Noah and I had talked so many times on the phone about the law and our families that he felt like a long-lost brother. We embraced like brothers.

Noah had been a constant presence in my life, even after the *Fellers* case had ended. His friendship led me to believe in myself, to believe that I could find success in the law.

When you've done something terrible and you're at the bottom, a little encouragement goes a long way.

Seth and Noah, in their generosity of spirit, had opened a new life for my family and me, and had helped make possible some happiness for my father before his death.

Before we left Boston, Seth and Noah encouraged me to apply to law school. It was the obvious next thing, although it was not a "for sure" thing, given my background.

Start studying for the LSAT, they told me. It was already on my calendar.

...

Another winter settled over the Great Plains: so much snow to slush through, so much ice not to slip on, so much cold to bundle against. Then the sun started to come back. We were a little family now, and Mark was walking. He already had a rebellious streak, which I attribute to his mother. Okay, a small part of it may come from me!

Although I was out of prison, my mind was often there. I thought about my boys back at Pekin. I tend to think about them on Sunday mornings when I'm at church. I think it's because church reminds me to be thankful, which reminds me of where I came from.

I wondered what they were doing on this day. They probably woke up late, as most do on Sunday mornings, before wandering out to the rec yard for a workout. I wondered if they were thinking past the present and to the day when they would be let go. The ones who do better are the ones who prepare each day for their eventual release.

I also thought about Bobbie, because I had received a phone call from him the day before. He had been in a yearlong in-patient drug treatment program, and the last chance before the probation office sent him back to prison because of his drug and alcohol addictions.

"Hop-woood, what's happening?"

"You wouldn't believe it if I told you, Bobbie." Bobbie had missed my son being born, the Times article, the speaking engagements, and my spiritual decision. I told him about it all.

I tried to encourage him, oh, I tried. But a month later I learned that he had violated parole and was headed back to prison—for two whole years.

I prayed for Bobbie and my boys at Pekin.

...

In early January of 2011 I received an e-mail from my wife. I was working at Cockle, talking on the phone with an attorney, when I opened the e-mail. The subject line read, "Hmmmmmm . . . " The e-mail had a picture of three pregnancy tests saying:

"Yes."

"Positive."

"Pregnant."

The e-mail said: I am scared out of my mind only about things unknown, but yet I feel peace that God knows I/We can handle this and that if this pregnancy would go full-term that it would be another one of His amazing blessings in our lives.

I told the attorney that I would need to call him back. At least I think I told him that!

We had talked about having another baby, but the timing didn't seem right; I was hoping to start law school that fall.

"Son, there is no convenient time to have a baby," my mother said, congratulating us. She was looking forward to another grandchild.

So we would have two young children while I attended law school. It couldn't be that hard.

A few months later Dr. Mark told us we were having a baby girl. God has given us so much grace that the name was easy to pick. Grace Ann. But to us—just Gracie.

33
BEYOND LOGIC

Losing a case bothers me as much today as it did in prison. I become friends with the people I help. I hate the word "clients," as if the law has to be some kind of unattached profession.

I have never been able to place my name on the cover of a brief, even the briefs I wrote in prison. Because I am not a lawyer, my friends in there filed the briefs with their name placed on the front. Even now, when I write a brief with an attorney my name is never mentioned.

I wondered whether I'd ever see my name on the front cover of a brief as Annie and I visited the Supreme Court on a cloudy spring day. We had always wanted to visit the Supreme Court, and it worked out so we could do that on a day when Seth was arguing a case.

As we neared the Court I squeezed Annie's hand a little harder. I find it difficult for certain moments to live up to the expectations built up in my mind. For eleven years, I had dreamed of visiting the Supreme Court, dreamed of walking up the steps to the great white marble pillars.

We entered the building and headed to the Clerk's office. Through Cockle I regularly speak on the phone with the Clerk's office—a wonderful group of incredibly competent people who run the day-to-day operations of the Court. I am usually asking them about the application of the Court's rules to a case that we are preparing. And I wanted to stop by their office and say hello in person.

Annie and I were waiting for one of the clerks to arrive when Annie said, "Oh, my gosh, it is great to see you again."

I turned around and Seth was standing there, smiling.

"And why wouldn't I see Shon in the Clerk's office?" he said.

We watched him argue a case that day, and he was masterful. I was surprised about how small the courtroom is and how close the arguing attorneys are to the justices. It truly is an intimate setting.

We exited the building that day in awe. On the front of the Supreme Court there is a famous inscription: equal justice under law.

The Court has certainly treated me equally. It has granted petitions that I have written, and handed down fair decisions that tangibly affected my life, both in prison and out. It is the Court that has literally changed my life.

...

Applying for law school is not easy. You study for the LSAT in between full-time jobs, and you proofread law school applications until you fall asleep on top of your computer and your wife or your son wakes you. You place way too much pressure on yourself and at times you think, why bother? But you do it, then you take the test and you send in the applications and, like too much in life, you wait.

I wondered if the admissions people just laughed when they read the bank robbery part. I could imagine them looking at it twice, then looking at the stack of young applicants with 4.0 GPAs and ridiculously high LSAT scores, and then dropping my application into the reject pile. When I could see it clearly like that, I just felt stupid for wasting my time and theirs. And from there I started to think I was pretty stupid for believing I was going to get in.

Then the rejection letters began to arrive in business-sized envelopes with a single sheet of paper neatly folded inside.

Annie tried to make me feel, well, less rejected. I felt like an idiot.

My letters of recommendation from Seth and Noah and Rich probably would have nudged me ahead of the competition if I were in that pack of upstanding young applicants with strong academic credentials. But I was a convicted bank robber, and there is just no letter that would fix that. I could see that now—that I had been delusional.

Besides, I was responsible for a growing family, and I didn't have a way to pay for law school even if I were accepted. Oh sure, I could borrow us into a hole for tuition and books. But what about living expenses? I had been living in a fantasyland.

"Did you order something from the University of Washington?"

Annie asked. She was holding an envelope that looked like it contained a big brief.

I bolted across the room.

"I got in!"

I ripped it open. The University of Washington School of Law, one of the top law schools in the country, was sending me the big packet.

Instead of "we regret to inform you . . . " the letter started with "Congratulations."

I kept looking to see if in my distress I had mistaken some subscription offer for a law school acceptance. It looked like the real thing. It was.

My dream of attending law school—a fantasy created and driven by Annie when we first started our friendship—was now a reality. And we would be going to Seattle, a great place for Annie because of her love of hiking and the outdoors.

I e-mailed Eric Schnapper right away. He is a Cockle client who teaches at the UW School of Law and takes employment law cases headed for the Supreme Court.

After he had read the Times article, he had encouraged me to apply there. He deserved my thanks and more. There was still the issue of money. I didn't know how I was going to swing it. I didn't think they would give a loan to a bank robber.

I had learned about a UW program where the Gates Program underwrites law school for students who agree to serve in public interest jobs for five years after graduation. I applied and a few weeks later I was flying to Seattle to interview for a Gates Scholarship. The William H. Gates Public Service Law Scholarship

Program had been started by Bill Gates to honor his father, William Gates Sr., a retired attorney and grad of UW.

Since public service is exactly what I want to do anyway, this seemed like the perfect opportunity. It seemed like God was tapping me on the shoulder and saying, Here's your chance to give back some of those blessings you've received.

I returned to Omaha and settled in for the wait. But there was no wait—the phone rang. It was Michele Storms, the executive director of the Gates Program. She told me how excited UW and the Gates Program were to have me.

I wondered if she had dialed the wrong number.

...

It was that time of year, late April, when snow still holds to the shadows, but the more aggressive trees are already budding green. We drove back to David City for Easter to visit my grandparents, Dale and Sandra Schmid. We passed the great fields of Grass Valley Farm. They were dark with snowmelt, waiting for maybe one more week of sunlight—the soil, half a foot down, should be around fifty degrees before the steel plows and new seeds can begin everything again.

Near our family house I stood up in the threshold of our car and looked around to see how far I could see. Where was the cloud of desperation that I had seen so often hanging over this land? How had I ever seen it, when there was nothing really there but blue sky and kind people and all the opportunity that a free country could provide?

Before the corn comes up you can see a long way. Maybe I still couldn't make out the Golden Gate or the Empire State building, but I couldn't see any obstacles, either.

The obstacles weren't ever there; they existed only in my mind, imagined in the folly of youth. But God's grace, the years, the law, and Annie had replaced all that with love.

34
HOME BIRTH

There is a palpable fear that permeates the first day of law school. It starts with students scurrying around with a paper printout in their hand to find their classroom. One woman was so focused that she ran into me partially spilling my cup of gourmet Seattle coffee so she could get the best seat in the classroom.

Most heave around a big backpack with thick and heavy legal casebooks inside. The weapons of the day are yellow legal pads, highlighters of various colors, and MacBooks—rather than the shanks and daggers I was accustomed to in prison.

Law school is a peculiar mix of people at various stages of life. There are those who've had it together since they left the womb. You know, the 22-year-old who graduated high school early and then went straight through undergrad never earning anything less than an "A" minus. It was hard not be envious. When I was their age, my idea of planning was picking the right cornfield to hold an impromptu beer party—without getting shot by a famer or chased by the cops.

I was older, starting law school at 36 and with a little more life experience than most of my classmates. Maybe too much life experience.

There was a woman in her 50s, who started law school as a change of career after she became an empty nester. Most of the older group—me especially—were just happy to be in law school and not working.

Then there were the gunners. Every law school has them. The gunners invariably took seats in the first rows closest to the professor.

I sat directly behind a gunner for one of my courses. I was forced to see the professor by rubbernecking around the gunner's arm that was like a piston constantly pumping up and down. Sometimes his arm would fire into the air before the professor even finished asking the question—as if he was participating in a game show and trying to hit the buzzer first. Gunners are generally despised. Still, they were present and oversharing their thoughts on every legal issue in class.

I took a seat in the back, wanting to be invisible. But the law school had posted profiles of my class of Gates Scholars. Everyone at the law school knew I'm a convict, yet I knew nothing about them.

"How was your weekend, Shon?" a classmate asked.

"It was good. I had to take a few phone calls from my buddies inside."

"What are they up to?"

"Mostly plotting crimes against their former lawyers. A little murder and mayhem. But I'm sure the lawyers got it coming! You know, ineffective assistance of counsel and all."

"Really?"

"No. I'm just messing with you. Most guys are too worried about how to operate the Internet and find a job when they get out. The last thing they are thinking about is their lawyer."

Some were visibly uncomfortable at first. Others couldn't have cared less. Most were just happy to have someone around who had read caselaw before law school and could say what parts were important.

I could get through the mountains of reading quickly. There is an art to skimming caselaw—to discern which facts and legal propositions matter and which ones don't. It turns out that having read through 3,000 judicial opinions while in prison was a real plus in law school.

Perspective also helps. When other students would get stressed out over the onslaught of reading assignments, I'd try to remember that law school was easier than reading cases in my cell, where I kept a padlock close by in case someone came rushing in with bad intentions.

...

The second day of law school started out normally. I had torts class in the morning with a professor whose mind was fascinating. Professor Elizabeth Porter was passionate about the law and, if you got her talking about torts or class action lawsuits, look out. She could rapidly fire off points of law and ask pointed questions almost simultaneously. She forced you to keep up with her; she pushed you to think about more than bone-dry legal holdings. She was welcoming and funny, and I took as many of her classes as I could while in law school.

I was in the middle of my afternoon class when I got a text from Annie.

"I hate to bother you, but I think you need to come home. My water just broke. I can drive up to the school and come pick you up."

That was Annie—worried about interrupting me.

I raised my hand in class even though the teacher hadn't asked a question.

"I'm sorry but I need to leave home for a family emergency," I said.

"Is everything okay?" the professor asked.

"Yes, it looks like we are about to deliver a baby girl today."

"That is a better excuse than the dog ate your homework."

The classroom laughed. I packed up and left. Annie drove to the law school, about a 10-minute drive from our house, and picked me up. When we got home, we walked over to the grocery store with Mark, and we bought all the ingredients for me to make pasta for dinner. We were having company over.

We had not been in Seattle long enough to know anyone who could watch Mark during the delivery. We didn't want a hospital delivery where Mark would be separated from us, and Annie decided to do a natural birth (for you guys, that means no drugs). She found a naturopathic doctor and a mid-wife to deliver our little Grace, and she decided on a home delivery.

I helped the doctors deliver Grace and when we placed her little head on Annie's chest, I had to control myself from crying.

Grace arrived with a full head of dark black hair and little high-pitched whimpers to let us know how precious she was.

When we left Nebraska for Seattle, we had to pay for pregnancy expenses out-of-pocket because we didn't have maternity insurance. I had often talked to Grace through Annie's tummy.

"You should really wait to arrive after law school starts," I said. "Because then the delivery will be covered by insurance we are getting through the law school. You could save daddy a few thousand dollars."

It was the first, and perhaps the last, time she ever listened to me!

...

The saving grace of law school was my small section. Most law schools separate people into sections for the first year when all the students are taking the same classes. At UW, students were separated into groups of 25 students.

I was assigned to Section 5. My section-mates were all younger than me. But that didn't stop us from sharing knowledge. They'd teach me things like how to take a picture of a classmate using Snapchat and then draw a rudimentary-looking penis on that person's picture. I instructed them on how to make a shank out of a toothbrush.

We kept each laughing all the way through our first year. I don't know how I would've survived law school without them.

...

After my first year of law school was finished, I went to work at the unlikeliest of places. I had applied to several internships in Seattle, but the place I prized most was to work at the federal courthouse for a trial judge. But I understood that working for a federal judge was unlikely for many reasons including that I had just finished federal supervised release, which is the federal equivalent of parole.

I applied anyway. Just for kicks. Then I got a call from a district court's office saying they wanted to setup an interview.

Judge John C. Coughenour had gone to the University of Iowa College of Law. Afterwards he went into private practice as a trial lawyer. President Ronald Reagan nominated him to the federal bench in 1981, where he once served as the chief judge of the United States District Court for the Western District of Washington. Judge Coughenour also taught trial advocacy at my law school. The class met early in the morning and was enthusiastically referred to by students as "Coffee with Coughenour."

He was known around Seattle for being quite intimidating. If a lawyer showed up in his courtroom unprepared, or if Judge Coughenour smelled a whiff of gamesmanship, he wouldn't hesitate to let it be known. He was a judge's judge and he had a short fuse for bull.

One of my advisors at the law school said I should be wary of working for Judge Coughenour because he sometimes yelled in court and he might yell at me. I laughed, explaining that I'd been in the Navy, federal prison for over a decade, and I had two kids. Yelling was the only world I knew.

After my interview, Judge Coughenour hired me and I learned a great deal in three short months in his chambers. He'd often crack jokes. And if he yelled, it was for me to come into his chambers to get his order for the sandwich shop down the street. Then he'd give me his credit card.

"You've got to be the craziest judge in America," I said.

That got his attention.

"What do you mean by that?"

"Only you would hand your credit card over to the former bank robber!"

We both laughed. That was Judge Coughenour. If he liked and trusted you, he was all-in.

Judge Coughenour challenged me in both my written work and when I watched the trials that took place in his courtroom. Sometimes justice occurred; sometimes not. The one thing I learned was that predicting what a jury would find compelling is largely a fool's errand.

He spent more time on sentencing than any other matter that came before him. He felt strongly (and I believe correctly) that federal sentences are set way too steep. When I'd watch one of his sentencings, I'd sweat profusely and my skin would tingle in the same way a reformed drunk must feel when they pass by a liquor store.

One day I was riding the elevator to chambers in the

federal courthouse when my former probation officer saw me.

"Shon, what are you doing here? I thought your supervision ended a few months ago," she said raising her eyebrows. She probably thought I had gotten into trouble.

"I work here."

"What? What do you mean?"

"I work in the building. A few floors above you on the 16th floor. Judge Coughenour hired me as an intern."

"How did that happen?"

"I applied, he interviewed me, and then he said yes." Just like everyone else gets the job, I didn't add.

"Really," she exclaimed. "Congratulations."

I thought it was long past time to begin changing the narrative about former prisoners and what they can accomplish.

...

The start of my second year of law school began with Annie losing 15 pounds. She didn't have that much to lose. She seemed to feel worse every day. Emotionally, she was all over the place, and she only felt good when she was outside.

I had worked through the first year of law school ghostwriting briefs for other lawyers and law firms. We used that money to pay for the restitution I still owed for the bank robberies, and for round after round of medical tests. The doctors couldn't figure out what was wrong with Annie.

She was slowly fading away.

Was it the stress of raising two young kids with a husband in law school in a faraway state without any family around to help pick up the slack? Or maybe it was the accumulated toll of our marriage? The first few years of being out of prison were hard on Annie. I had been locked up with nothing but dudes for over a decade, and then I moved directly into living with Annie. That wasn't easy. I wasn't easy.

In prison, you never deescalate conflict. If you do, people view you as soft and they try to take advantage of you. But the general rules for maintaining stability in prison don't transfer well to a marriage, which is based on mutual respect, caring, and sacrifice for your spouse.

Just when I started to think I could be a good husband, I'd blow it. I'd come home stressed out and want to decompress, and my wife—who'd been home with two young children all day long—would want some adult companionship. Instead of engaging, I'd withdraw, which in turn made her withdraw. Even when I wasn't withdrawn, I was still working through some of the trauma I'd experienced in prison. Heck, I still am.

While we were trying to figure out how to crawl out of this awful rut, the medical test results came in. God gave us some answers. Annie was a complex mess of several illnesses, many of which have crazy names like SIBO, Hashimoto's, or MTHFR mutation. These illnesses led to her having allergic reactions to almost everything she ate and being sensitive to toxins.

After many months of aggressive treatment, Annie

slowly started feeling better. We learned several years later that she was also super sensitive to mold spores. With all the rain in the Pacific Northwest, I'm sure that is why she never felt good in our Seattle apartment. Well, that and the strain we were under living in a new city, being broke, in law school, and with two young kids.

35
JRB

"Please repeat after me, 'I swear to uphold the United States Constitution as interpreted by the Federal Public Defender.'"

This was the shtick performed by Tom Hillier, the Federal Defender for the Western District of Washington. He was swearing all the summer interns into the public defender's office.

When I thought about my future with the law, I always hoped and believed I'd become a federal public defender. They are the saints of the law. They work long hours for little pay, and too much of society views them with contempt.

Oh, you represent those people.

How do you represent those monsters?

Almost every public defender has heard these types of comments at some point in his or her life.

There are very few absolute principles I believe in. The Sixth Amendment to the United States Constitution provides those who are indigent and facing incarceration with appointed counsel. No matter what horrible crime someone is charged with, they deserve a lawyer to represent them.

We, as a society, all too often have believed someone was guilty only to find out they were innocent.[19] We've done it enough to draw the conclusion that the right to counsel is one of the most important provisions in our national charter. All the other rights that our Constitution promises to those charged with a crime—those who might have their fundamental life or liberty taken away—don't mean much unless you have a lawyer who knows how to enforce those rights against our criminal justice system.

So there I was in the summer of 2013, stoked to be working with these saints. It was the summer of sequester and Congress had slashed the federal defender's budget. The office was short several lawyers, and they were ecstatic to have an intern with some federal criminal law experience.

My supervisor, Michael Filipovic, gave me several challenging projects that summer. I argued at several sentencing hearings, usually defending a person who had been released from prison and then (allegedly) committed a violation while on supervised release. Basically, I was arguing to federal judges that they shouldn't send my clients back to prison.

One day I had to argue before Judge Coughenour. The assistant federal defender introduced me to the court and Judge Coughenour pretended as if he didn't know me and I didn't exist. I expected that.

I cross-examined one of the government's witnesses. When I was introduced as a law school student, the witness smiled. He was the psychologist who had treated my client. From his smile and the way his body relaxed, it was apparent he didn't view me as a threat. Great.

Twenty minutes later he was stammering and stalling while answering my questions. By the end, he wanted to kill me right then and there. I took that as a sign I had done something right. The federal prosecutor came over after the hearing and shook my hand, smiling and telling me I had done a good job.

I had trouble sleeping before and after the hearings. Before the hearing, I was always scared about not being prepared enough; after the hearing, I'd wonder whether I could have gotten a better result for my client. And part of me felt anxious about being before a federal judge at a sentencing hearing. It was like reliving my own sentencing over again and again.

It is gut-wrenching to stand next to a client when you know just how much punishment they are about to face. I knew in a way most lawyers would never know. And I also knew the punishment only begins when you enter prison; it continues long after you're released.[20] To relive that punishment day-after-day on top of my own would have been too much to bear.

After the summer, I decided that, if the State of Washington gave me a law license, I should find a different career path. If I wanted to be a good husband and good father to my children, then becoming a federal public defender might be just too hard on me.

Of course, after the intensity of that summer wore off, I convinced myself that I could handle the stress if I had to. I later applied to become a public defender for the State of Maryland. My guilt always has had a way of convincing me to reconsider.

...

A federal clerkship is one of the most sought-after legal jobs. Law school students apply in droves for a few coveted spots with a federal trial or appellate court judge. For those who score such a job, they get to interact with their judge and assist with researching and writing the judge's orders and opinions.

Federal appellate clerkships are the most prestigious and most coveted for several reasons. A law clerk occupies the enviable position of seeing how the sausage is made—how a judge goes about the business of deciding an appeal and then convincing her other two colleagues to join her (most federal appeals are heard by panels of three judges). Seeing that process and working so closely with the judge—someone at the pinnacle of the profession—tends to make a clerk a better lawyer. And it is the rare job that gives young lawyers with so little experience a chance to work on some of the most pressing and interesting issues of the day.

Federal appellate clerkships are also coveted because a law firm, government organization, or non-profit who has two candidates to choose from for a position, will, all things being equal, most likely select the candidate with the federal clerkship over the candidate without. Put differently, these clerkships are door openers; big law firms payout large bonuses for people who've recently clerked for a federal judge—one firm gives a $175,000 federal appellate clerkship bonus.

I had little chance at obtaining a federal appellate clerkship. I didn't go to Yale or Harvard. Most federal appellate clerkships go to students from the very top schools, and while UW is a very good school, it doesn't have a reputation for sending many of its graduates to federal appellate clerkships. Although my grades were good, I wasn't sitting at the very top of my law school class. And then there were those pesky federal felonies I had committed. No one was going to hire a guy like me.

When I told people that I was applying, there were some skeptics. Heck, I was one of them.

But apply I did. And I disregarded the prevailing advice I had received from several people. They said I should not apply to Republican-appointed judges because those judges wouldn't give me the time of day.

Yet I was trained as a lawyer to move past clichéd generalities, so I questioned the premise. Why wouldn't a conservative judge appreciate a redemption story? And why wouldn't a judge want someone in their chambers who had some real litigation experience? And if I didn't apply to Republican appointees, then practically speaking, I'd be eliminating about half of the available spots. I applied broadly.

One morning Annie was driving me to the law school when I got a phone call. A clerk from Judge Alex Kozinski's chambers called and asked if I'd be interested in clerking. I could tell you all the things Judge Kozinski is known for—his epic opinions, his writing style, his libertarian streak. But for all that, he's probably just as known for his use of law clerks.

Within minutes I was on the phone with his judicial assistant. She said, "Just so we're clear, Judge Kozinski expects his clerks to be at the office early and to stay late."

"How late?" I asked.

"Usually clerks leave around 7 for dinner and then they come back around 9 and work until midnight. I'd tell you that 14-hour days are the norm."

"Do clerks typically work weekends?"

"Clerks typically work every single day. Even holidays."

"That's a lot," I said.

"Yes, it is," she said before pausing.

She was telling me this because they wanted people to come into chambers with eyes wide open.

Brutal honesty. I liked it. The part I didn't like was that if I clerked for this brilliant judge, I wouldn't see my wife and kids for a year. Still, I interviewed with him. Judge Kozinski is like the guy from the Dos Equis commercials. Who wouldn't interview with the world's most interesting man?

Stay thirsty, my friend.

I also interviewed with a few federal district court judges that summer. And I received some interest from Judges David Ebel and Neil Gorsuch from the Tenth Circuit, the latter of whom went on to become Associate Justice of the U.S. Supreme Court. Both judges were known as staunch conservatives. And both invited me to their chambers when I was in Denver to give a talk at a local law school. So much for Republican-appointees not being willing to give someone a second chance.

There were liberal judges who also were interested in hiring me (Judge Reinhardt from the Ninth Circuit being one of them), so I don't want to give the impression there weren't.

By mid-summer, I had received some interest and was awaiting decisions from judges, but I had no offers. I tried not to get my hopes up. I dug into work at the federal defender's office—a common way for me to deal with stress or disappointment. Start focusing on someone else's life and problems, and yours seem small. So what if I didn't get a job clerking for a federal judge. The world would not end.

Then one day I got a call from Judge Janice Rogers Brown's chambers. Judge Brown was a graduate of UCLA law school and she was the first African American woman to serve as a justice on the California Supreme Court. President George W. Bush appointed her to serve as a judge on the Court of Appeals for the District of Columbia Circuit. After a contentious confirmation process, she was confirmed to what is widely considered the second most important court in the country.

Judge Brown's clerk asked if I could come to Washington D.C. to interview the following week. I stayed overnight at the house of my former Constitutional Law professor, Ronald Collins, who lives with his wife Susan in Bethesda, Maryland just outside D.C. Ron travels to Seattle to teach one quarter each year, and he had become more than just a mentor. Susan and Ron are friends.

On the morning of the interview, Ron dropped me off at the D.C. Metro redline and I rode the train into downtown. At one of the stops, I looked over and couldn't believe who I saw.

"Hey, how are you, Seth?" I said.

"Shon Hopwood, what are you doing here?" Seth Waxman said.

Out of the hundreds of thousands that rode the Metro that day, I just happened to run into my friend and mentor. That chance encounter with Seth seemed to be a good omen for my interview with Judge Brown.

I walked to the court in long purposeful steps. My hands were sweaty and it felt like I was living someone else's life. In my mind, I still had those cuffs and shackles and a belly chain fastened to my body. I could hear the clinking and clanking of the chains as I walked through the courthouse. To be there interviewing for a job with this accomplished judge was beyond the reach of even my most enchanting dreams.

Judge Brown welcomed me into her chambers like we were long lost family. The first thing you notice is her books. She has stacks of books on her wooden desk and a line of books next it. You can learn a lot about someone from their collection of books. Judge Brown devours books of every subject; she is an exceptionally well-rounded human being.

We talked about everything, from the need for criminal justice reform to our favorite C.S. Lewis books. I quickly adored her. The interview was supposed to last 30 minutes, but we were still talking over an hour later.

"It was a pleasure meeting you, Shon, and I will get an answer to you soon," she said.

Twenty minutes after the interview, I received a call from her chambers. I was offered the job and I probably said yes before the clerk could finish his sentence. I called Annie back in Seattle and we were screaming in celebration together. It was a big day for the Hopwood family.

When Judge Brown said yes to me even knowing my past, it mattered. It gave me confidence. It also gave me instant credibility that would have taken a lifetime to earn on my own. I will forever be grateful to her.

36
TOO MUCH CHARACTER

In my last year of law school, I remained in a constant state of panic knowing that even after I graduated law school the fight to get a law license would rage on. That dread would creep up on me in the middle of the night or during a free moment in between class, or when I'd watch my kids run around a playground. The fear and its grip was tightly wrapped around me.

I submitted a bar application and the Washington State Bar Association told me in the spring of 2014 that I'd need to make my case for a law license at a hearing. Because I had a felony conviction, I had to overcome a presumption that I did not possess the requisite character and fitness necessary to practice law.

Felix Luna, a local trial attorney and a UW alumni, represented me on a pro bono basis before the Washington Board of Bar Examiners. The hearing took over five hours. It wasn't the worst day of my life (that honor falls to the day my dad passed away followed by the day I was sentenced), but it was close.

After it was over, one of the Board members approached me and said, "When you first came in, I think most of the panel members were wary of giving you a favorable recommendation."

She paused, "but you convinced us."

The Board made a unanimous recommendation to the Washington Supreme Court. We thought that was a positive development, although we also knew the Court could overturn the Board's recommendation.

A few weeks later, I graduated from law school. My mom, father- and mother-in-law flew into town. This was a family celebration. Wearing those purple robes made me feel almost Jedi-like, as if obtaining the title Juris Doctorate would somehow bestow wisdom and special powers to me. Not hardly.

My kids, Mark and Grace, held my hands as we walked across the stage to receive my Juris Doctorate degree from the University of Washington School of Law. I had even graduated with honors.

I was the first person in my family to receive a graduate degree, let alone a J.D. There aren't any lawyers in my family tree!

...

We moved that summer to Alexandria, Virginia, so that I could begin my clerkship with Judge Brown in the fall. Working for her was everything I imagined and then some. She is an articulate, brilliant, and fearless writer. That is what the public sees through her published opinions.

What the public doesn't see is her genuine humility. Her ability to continually question whether we had the right answer in a case. This is someone who cares deeply about the rule of law and liberty.

Judge Brown treated me the same as any other clerk. She was always gracious.

Her red pen, which would slice and dice the draft opinions I turned in, was not!

I became a better lawyer and a better person working for her.

Later, I learned that a few of my friends with serious felony convictions who had gone to law school had also scored federal appellate clerkships. I don't think that would've have happened had Judge Brown not said yes to me first.

One morning I received an email from the Clerk of the Court for the Washington Supreme Court. Attached to the email was a one-page court order stating that a majority of the Court voted in my favor. If I passed the bar exam, I'd get to become a lawyer.

I breathed a little easier that day. It was like the shackles and chains had been removed.

Between clerking and studying, I barely saw anyone for the two months leading up to the bar exam. Little Grace came into my bedroom one day and told me, "Daddy, I miss you," which nearly broke me. But the long hours paid off, and I passed the exam.

Judge Brown swore me in as a lawyer in her chambers. As I raised my right hand and repeated the oath, Annie and the kids watched. The kids had no idea about my journey to become a lawyer. They were just happy to be in Judge Brown's chambers and playing with her many elephant figurines.

Now it was time to use my skills to help people.

...

We were out walking on a trail that runs along the Potomac River, just as the leaves began to change color. We had abandoned the double running stroller a few months earlier and the kids were running away from us. In between my shouts at them to slow down, Annie said she had an idea.

"Now that the kids are going to school, I've been thinking about what to do with my life."

"Okay," I said.

"I was thinking that maybe we could work together. Work on cases together."

"You want me to teach you how to write briefs?" I asked.

"Yes, but I also thought about taking the LSAT."

"Seriously?" I said. "I think that's a great idea."

We had talked before about Annie going to law school, but I never thought she'd go through with it. As someone who'd written over 100 legal briefs and never been able to put my front name on the cover, I told her that she might want her name on a brief someday.

Annie studied diligently for the LSAT. I'm quite proud to say that she scored higher than I did. As a result, the Columbus School of Law at Catholic University in Washington D.C. offered her a full-ride scholarship. Now neither of us would pay for law school, which is the only way to do it.

...

As Annie started law school in the fall of 2015, I began working as a teaching fellow at the Georgetown University Law Center's Appellate Litigation Program. The Director, Professor Steve Goldblatt, hired me as a fellow to help teach 16 third-year law school students about appellate practice. Several federal courts of appeals would appoint the program to represent indigent litigants. The kinds of cases we received were right in my wheelhouse: criminal law, prisoners' rights, immigration, and civil rights cases.

Through the fellowship, I learned that working with law school students was a hoot. They were smart and eager to become better at researching and writing—the bread and butter of appellate practice. Sometimes one of them would ask me about what it was like to serve time in a federal prison, and I'd tell stories about researching cases with nothing but a prison law library full of books. For students accustomed to online legal databases, my stories sounded like a relic from the dinosaur age.

I watched my students get better. At everything. From their work ethic to their writing. I went to my students' graduation and met their families, and it left an indelible impression on me.

As I practiced law, I felt like the skin of prison was finally shedding. Some days I'd call a federal prison and ask to speak with my client's prison counselor to set up an attorney-client phone call. And some days I'd even remember that I was the lawyer.

...

In the fall of 2016, Steve Goldblatt and I sat on wooden pews and watched an oral argument in Richmond, Virginia, at the Court of Appeals for the Fourth Circuit. We were there waiting for my case to be called next. It was the first time I'd argue a case on appeal.

When a lawyer arguing before us was yelled at by a judge for not answering a question, Steve put his hand over his mouth and told me, "Make sure you answer their questions." It was his way of trying to both mess with and relax me.

What I mumbled back to him can't be repeated.

When it was my turn, I stood at that lectern, grabbed each side of it, and said, "Your honor and may it please the Court."

Arguing a case on appeal and doing it well is as challenging as I thought it would be. You prepare for weeks, trying to anticipate every question and hoping there is no glaring weakness in your case that you discover only after a judge asks the question you didn't think of. That said, there aren't many better feelings in the world than when a judge starts to see the case like you do in the middle of the argument.

A few months later, the court ruled in my client's favor. I had won the first case I argued.

But I lost the second case I argued on behalf of two South Carolina police officers who spoke out about police misconduct and had been fired by their chief of police. As Steve tried to get me to understand, you can't get too high when you win or too low when you lose. I hate it when he gets all sensible on me.

It is hard to express how great a lawyer he is. I

watched him edit briefs without knowing anything about the issues, and he'd pluck the strengths and weaknesses out with ease. I watched him serve on moots and tell the lawyer to reframe the case in a very focused way, and then I'd listen to the arguments and see that Steve's guidance was the key to winning the case. He was like a magician, and I hated him.

I don't really hate him. Just don't tell him I admitted that.

During my last year at the clinic, we got a co-director, Professor Erica Hashimoto. She was a former federal public defender (my people), and I benefited greatly from her topnotch litigation skills and her constant encouragement.

People often come up and ask me questions when I speak at law schools. At one of these talks, a person came up to me and said, "Your pick-yourself-up-by-the-bootstrap story is so inspiring."

But, I think, my story is the opposite of that. Being surrounded by welcoming and brilliant people was not me picking myself up. It was me riding their waves.

37
DANCE PARTY

Judge Kopf—the judge who sentenced me—had been following my story. After he learned about Judge Brown hiring me, he wrote an article on his blog.

"Hopwood proves that my sentencing instincts suck," he wrote.

When I sent him to prison, I would have bet the farm and all the animals that Hopwood would fail miserably as a productive citizen when he finally got out of prison. My gut told me that Hopwood was a punk—all mouth, and very little else. My viscera was wrong.

We have corresponded over the years and when I applied for a law license, Judge Kopf wrote me a supporting letter.

In fall of 2016, I was asked to come speak about sentencing reform at the University of Nebraska School of Law. They gave me two football tickets and I took Mark to his first Nebraska Cornhusker game, a rite of passage between fathers and sons in that state. I had gone to my first game with a different Mark Hopwood back in 1986.

Mark loved it, especially the roar of 90,000 people dressed in red. And the Huskers won. Go Big Red!

It is standard for a law school to have an outside guest speak and then a faculty member to provide comments.

Instead of a faculty member, Judge Kopf provided commentary. It was the first time I had seen him since the day I was sentenced.

He gave me an old briefcase that day. It had been made by a former prisoner who was also Judge Kopf's former client back before he took the bench. The client had killed someone, been released after serving 15 years, and then never committed another crime. Judge Kopf said the briefcase was a reminder of redemption.

It was an emotional day for both for us. I said that day what I've long said before. Judge Kopf gave me the lowest sentence he could under the then-mandatory federal sentencing guidelines, and I deserved to go to prison for what I did. I've never held any animosity towards him.

After the event was over, I saw my son had Judge Kopf's ear. Mark was now six and although we'd never told him (or Grace) about my past, I wondered what he was asking the Judge. They talked for five minutes and I imagined all the things they could be talking about, especially since Mark had just heard me speak about sentencing and prison reform.

Judge Kopf came over to me with Mark in tow. He said, "Shon, I think you should buy Mark an electric-powered Nerf gun for his birthday."

I was worried about Mark asking Judge Kopf about bank robberies and Mark was instead convincing the Judge to come persuade me to buy him a Nerf gun. I admired my son's moxie. He's going to make a great lawyer someday.

...

I don't know when I arrived at a decision to go on the legal teaching market. It wasn't like one day I woke up and told myself that Professor Hopwood sounds nice. No, it sounds strange.

But I enjoy teaching students, and I spend much of my days writing about the law. In that way, trying to become a law professor didn't seem quite so radical. Yet, at times, it could feel wholly foreign. The legal academy is the elite of the elite.

As a new presidential administration arrived in D.C. during the winter of 2017, the faculty of Georgetown University Law Center voted to make me an offer as an Associate Professor of Law. I accepted.

My colleagues are some of the most talented and welcoming people I've ever met and the day I joined them will be a story worth telling my grandkids about.

Perhaps Professor Hopwood doesn't sound so bad.

As with everyone who has placed trust in me, I hope to honor my colleagues by working hard, teaching well, and trying to make the world a more just place.

...

When the news became public, a local television station interviewed me and ran a story on the nightly news. By that point, Mark was seven and Grace five years old. We let them watch the news report and then we had the talk that I've feared all these years.

Mark said, "I already knew dad. It's okay."

"Do you still have the gun?" Grace asked.

"No, I don't."

"Can we have a dance party now?" she asked.

I will always lug regret around with me, but my kids could care less about what I did twenty years ago. In a way, with them and my dear Annie, I've been reborn.

Grace happens. Redemption is possible. Second chances are needed.

#SecondChances

ACKNOWLEDGMENTS

There are too many people to thank here, and I'm sure that I've forgotten to mention everyone. When you're granted second chances in life, they often come from the grace of others. My wife, Annie, is my best friend, greatest love, and the single greatest thing to ever happen to me. Without her, none of this would have been possible. And anyone who has spent more than a day with us understands that undeniable fact.

My family has always been there for me. I'm grateful for my mother Rebecca, my brothers Brook and Brett, my sisters Samantha and Kristin, and their lovely spouses and children. Thanks to Dale and Sandra Schmid and Bob and Joanne Hopwood, my grandparents. And I want to thank my father- and mother-in-law Ray and Luan Metzner for their unwavering support.

Special thanks to Jody Hotchkiss for being my friend first and an agent second. If you're selling life rights and need an agent, call him.

Special thanks also to my good friend and business partner Michael Santos, who remains upbeat and positive after serving 26 straight years of incarceration.

I want to publicly thank my Georgetown colleagues who've placed enormous trust in me. I'm thrilled about working side-by-side with and learning from you.

The Appellate Litigation Program and Supreme Court Institute at Georgetown have been my home for the past two years. It has been the best job I've ever had in large part because I got to work with Steve Goldblatt, Erica Hashimoto, Daurie Simmons, Ruthanne Deutsch, Amit Vora, Dori Bernstein, Irv Gornstein, and several of Georgetown's finest students.

There is a list of friends who have been instrumental in my success. They include Keith and Heidi Lodhia, Marty and Sue Barnhart, Ron Collins and Susan Cohen, Mike and Valerie O'Neil, Ryan and Pam Dorn, and many, many others.

My mentors are a long and distinguished group: Seth Waxman, Noah Levine, Janice Rogers Brown, Ron Collins, Eric Schnapper, Kellye Testy, Michele Storms, Roy Englert, Stu Dornan, Steve Goldblatt, Erica Hashimoto, and many others. Thank you for your tireless work providing wisdom and the nonstop letters of recommendation.

I want to thank my research assistant Claire Cahill who worked on the new version of this book and many other projects.

Bless all those public defenders, advocates, and non-profits pushing for second chances for their clients and friends.

Families Against Mandatory Minimums

I first learned about Families Against Mandatory Minimums—or as most people call it, FAMM—while in federal prison. It was a fledging organization then. Julie Stewart had recently started the organization after watching her brother serve a five-year mandatory minimum prison sentence for a marijuana offense.

Thanks to Julie's efforts, FAMM is now the premiere advocacy group for criminal justice reform in the country. Kevin Ring is the new President and now leads the organization. I encourage you to support its mission for smart criminal justice reform. You can learn more about FAMM at http://famm.org/.

Prison Professors L.L.C.

I recently launched a new business endeavor with my friend Michael Santos. Prison Professors L.L.C. will teach people how to overcome the challenges and ancillary consequences that accompany a criminal prosecution. Our team will help people who are facing prosecution, sentencing, or time in prison. But we will also advocate for criminal justice reform and push correctional systems to increase the educational and life skill opportunities for current prisoners. You can learn more about us at https://prisonprofessors.com/.

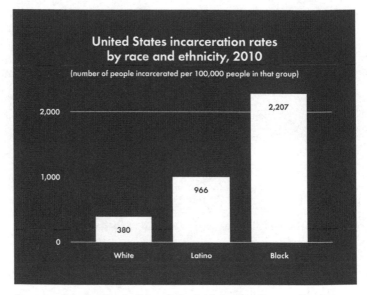

Sources: Calculated by the Prison Policy initiative from Bureau of Justice Statistics, Correctional Population in the U.S., 2010 & U.S. Census 2010 Summary File. 1

END NOTES

1. *See* Peter Wagner & Alison Walsh, States of Incarceration: The Global Context 2016, PRISON POLICY INITIATIVE (June 16, 2016), https://www. prisonpolicy.org/global/2016.html; E. ANN CARSON & ELIZABETH ANDERSON, PRISONERS IN 2015 (Dec. 2016), https://www.bjs.gov/content/pub/pdf/p15.pdf.

2. Visit Families Against Mandatory Minimum's (FAMM) website and either get involved or donate money. Please. The website is: http://www.famm. org/. I recently joined FAMM's Board of Directors because I believe in their mission and the passionate group of advocates that work tirelessly on behalf of all Americans, including prisoners.

3. You can't discuss the American criminal justice system without discussing race. Although people of color makeup only 31% of the population, they makeup 57% of the prison population. *See* ASHLEY NELLIS, THE SENTENCING PROJECT, THE COLOR OF JUSTICE: RACIAL AND ETHNIC DISPARITY IN STATE PRISONS (June 14, 2016), http://www.sentencingproject.org/publications/color-of-justice-racial-and-ethnic-disparity-in-state-prisons/

    Peter Wagner, *Incarceration is Not an Equal Opportunity Punishment*, Prison Policy Initiative (Aug. 28, 2012), https://www.prisonpolicy.org/articles/notequal.html.

4. The Federal Bureau of Prisons' policy attempts to place federal prisoners within 500 miles of their families. Being able to maintain family ties is an instrumental factor in successful rehabilitation. *See* KEVIN RING & MOLLY GILL, FAMILIES AGAINST MANDATORY MINIMUMS, USING TIME TO REDUCE CRIME: FEDERAL PRISONER SURVEY RESULTS SHOW WAYS TO REDUCE RECIDIVISM 19 (2017), http://famm.org/prisonreform/.

5. Crime is mostly a young man's game. Most violent crime is committed by young men between the ages of 18 to 25. But eventually people age out of crime and are no longer a threat to the public. *See* BUREAU OF JUSTICE STATISTICS, VIOLENT CRIMES 2, 4 (1994), https://www.bjs.gov/

content/pub/pdf/VIOCRM.PDF (reporting that 85% of violent offenders are male, and young people ages 16–24 "consistently have the highest violent crime rates"); Marc Mauer, *Executive Director, The Sentencing Project, Testimony to Charles Colson Task Force on Federal Corrections* (March 11, 2015), http://www.sentencingproject.org-/publications/a-proposal-to-reduce-time-served-in-federal-prison/ ("Research shows that after peaking in the mid-to-late teenage years, offending begins to decline as individuals are in their 20s and drops sharply as they reach their 30s and 40s.").

6. Michael Santos exemplifies the type of federal prisoner that was focused on his release every day, even though he was serving 26 straight years in federal prison for a drug offense. Michael earned several degrees, wrote several books, and was a blogger for Huffington Post all from his prison cell. *See Michael G. Santos,* Wikipedia, https://en.wikipedia.org/wiki/Michael_G._Santos; Michael G. Santos Foundation, http://michaelsantos.org/.

7. It is estimated that 37% of American prisoners have mental illness. *See* Jennifer Bronson & Marcus Berzofsky, Bureau of Justice Statistics, Indicators of Mental Health Problems Reported by Prison and Jail Inmates, 2011-12 1 (2017), https://www.bjs.gov/content/pub/pdf/imhprpji1112.pdf ("37% of prisoners and 44% of jail inmates had been told in the past by a mental health professional that they had a mental disorder"). I watched people with severe mental illness go without any treatment during their incarceration. *See also McCreary v. Federal Bureau of Prisons,* No. 1:17-cv-01011 (M.D. Pa. filed June 9, 2017).

8. Adrian Cooper is serving a life sentence without parole for selling over 500 grams of crack cocaine in the early 1990s after having been previously convicted of two drug felonies. *See United States v. Cooper,* 39 F.3d 167, 169 (7th Cir. 1994); see also 21 U.S.C. § 841(b)(1)(A).

9. See Global Tel*Link v. FCC, 859 F.3d 39 (D.C. Cir. 2017).

10. YALE KAMISAR ET AL., MODERN CRIMINAL PROCEDURE: CASES, COMMENTS AND QUESTIONS (13TH ED. 2012).

11. Michael A. Simons, *Retribution For Rats: Cooperation, Punishment, And Atonement,* 56 Vand. L. Rev. 1 (2013) ("For many defendants, the lure of the cooperation departure is irresistible--it is usually the only significant sentencing factor over which they have any control, and it is often their only hope for a significantly reduced sentence. Not surprisingly, the Sentencing Guidelines have ushered in dramatic increases in cooperation.").

12. Congress initially decided to punish crack cocaine a hundred times greater than powder cocaine, even though there is no significant chemical difference between the two forms of cocaine. See Anti-Drug Abuse Act of 1986, Pub. L. No. 99-570, 100 Stat. 3207 (1986). That led to enormous racial disparities in federal sentencing because blacks were sentenced to a hundred times greater punishment than the whites for powder cocaine. Congress finally did something about it and passed a new statute setting the crack/powder ratio to 18 to 1. See Fair Sentencing Act of 2010, Pub. L. No. 111–220, 124 Stat 2372 (2010).

13. Antiterrorism & Effective Death Penalty Act of 1996, Pub. L. No. 104–132, 110 Stat. 1214 (1996).

14. Antiterrorism & Effective Death Penalty Act of 1996, Pub. L. No. 104–132, §§ 101–106, 110 Stat. 1214, 1217–1221 (1996).

15. See U.S.S.G. § 4B1.1 (career offender provision).

16. See note 12, above.

17. Joshua Boyer's 25-year sentence was commuted by President Obama and he will be released to a federal halfway house on August 8, 2017. I can't wait to see him.

18. Nearly half (49.3%) of all federal prisoners were re-arrested within three years of release. See Kim Steven Hunt & Robert Dumville, U.S. Sentencing Commission, Recidivism Among Federal Offenders: A Comprehensive Overview (Mar. 2016), https://www.ussc.gov/sites/default/files/pdf/research-and-publica-tions/research-publications/2016/recidivism_overview.pdf.

19. Currently, 350 individuals have been exonerated due to DNA evidence. See DNA Exonerations in the United States, Innocence Project, https://www.innocenceproject.org/dna-exonerations-in-the-united-states/.

20. There are a limitless number of collateral consequences when a person is convicted of felony. Those consequences lead to punishment long after someone has finished serving time. Someone with a felony conviction can be legally discriminated against in employment, housing, and public support. And most states have occupational licensing schemes that freeze out felons from many jobs, including becoming lawyers. Felons can also be denied the right to vote and the right to serve as a coach or mentor at their kids' school.

Made in the USA
Lexington, KY
22 January 2019